SONIC VIRTUALITY

SONIC VIRTUALITY

Sound as Emergent Perception

Mark Grimshaw and Tom Garner

OXFORD
UNIVERSITY PRESS

OXFORD
UNIVERSITY PRESS

Oxford University Press is a department of the University of
Oxford. It furthers the University's objective of excellence in research,
scholarship, and education by publishing worldwide.

Oxford   New York
Auckland   Cape Town   Dar es Salaam   Hong Kong   Karachi
Kuala Lumpur   Madrid   Melbourne   Mexico City   Nairobi
New Delhi   Shanghai   Taipei   Toronto

With offices in
Argentina   Austria   Brazil   Chile   Czech Republic   France   Greece
Guatemala   Hungary   Italy   Japan   Poland   Portugal   Singapore
South Korea   Switzerland   Thailand   Turkey   Ukraine   Vietnam

Oxford is a registered trademark of Oxford University Press
in the UK and certain other countries.

Published in the United States of America by
Oxford University Press
198 Madison Avenue, New York, NY 10016

© Oxford University Press 2015

Library of Congress Cataloging-in-Publication Data
Grimshaw, Mark, 1963–
Sonic virtuality : sound as emergent perception / Mark Grimshaw & Tom Garner.
   pages cm
Includes bibliographical references and index.
ISBN 978–0–19–939283–4 (hardcover : alk. paper)   1. Psychoacoustics.
2. Sound—Psychological aspects.   3. Sound (Philosophy)   4. Mixed reality.
I. Garner, Tom (Tom Alexander)   II. Title.
BF378.S7G75 2015
006.8—dc23
2014042815

9 8 7 6 5 4 3 2 1
Printed in the United States of America
on acid-free paper

CONTENTS

ACKNOWLEDGMENTS

This book has grown out of a five-year collaboration (so far) between the two of us that has produced a number of publications primarily in the area of computer game sound but also, more recently, in the area of sound perception. Among these works have been many conference presentations, and so our first thanks are due to those conference attendees who took it upon themselves to poke and prod at our ideas both during our presentations and afterward. Such critical probing has allowed us to refine not only our concepts but also the arguments and evidence we use to defend them. Thanks are also due to various colleagues and collaborators who looked through and commented on early drafts or generously, and at length, responded to questions relating to their field of expertise or experience; these include Jonathan Weinel, Simon Harris (who was also generous enough to allow us to use as cover art just the smallest detail of his stunning painting), Hayley Garner (whose illustrations helped us to bring our fictional, concept-exemplifying scamps Claire and Alexander to life), and members of the Music and Sound Knowledge Group of the Institute of Communication and Psychology at Aalborg University. As always, thanks are due to our editor at Oxford University Press, Norm Hirschy, who has the patience and analytical insight to find nuggets of gold hidden deep within initial proposals and early, rough chapters. That the book has grown and developed from those early ramblings in the way it has is in no small measure due to the suggestions of our anonymous reviewers who in some cases, despite strongly disagreeing with our theses, were honest enough to disregard such contrariness and to deal instead with the marshaling and presentation of our arguments.

SONIC VIRTUALITY

INTRODUCTION

Sound is an emergent perception arising primarily in the auditory
cortex and that is formed through spatio-temporal processes in an
embodied system.

This book has a dual purpose. First, it discusses our perception of,
relationship to, and use of sound within a framework of virtuality,
and second, it proposes a new definition of sound that is founded
on that conception of sonic virtuality.

There are a number of motivations, personal and otherwise,
for writing this book. Both of us have a background in music and
music technology that has developed into a shared research interest
in the sounds of computer games and similar virtual environments.
Such environments are interesting for a number of reasons, not
least because of the simulation of reality that some games attempt,
giving rise to such questions as *what is real?* and *what is virtual?*
But these environments also hold interest because of the possibilities that new technologies bring, technologies that, to a large
extent, are motivated by gaming culture. For example, much of our
recent work has revolved around the technology of biofeedback and
a study of the relationship between the emotion of fear and sound
in the context of computer game environments. If the game engine
can continuously monitor the player's emotional state, can the data
obtained be used to create in real time new sound waves that can
direct the intensity of or change the emotion felt by the player? It is
such possibilities offered by current technologies and those yet to
be developed that, in part, drive the thinking presented here.

This book, though, is not about sound and computer games.
However, the study of that area, which the two of us have been con-
ducting for several years, has raised fundamental questions about
sound, and our attempts to answer them have led us to the ideas

contained in this book. It should be noted, then, that this book uses (but not exclusively) research on sound in computer games and virtual environments not only to formulate and set down our thinking on such sound, but also to theorize about sound in other environments such as those we experience in our everyday lives. The sound design of many computer games may well attempt to simulate the processes of hearing and our response to sounds, but in studying and pushing the envelope of such design, we also learn about sound in our everyday lived experiences. An interest in the design and function of sound in virtual environments leads to insights about the role of sound in other scenarios. Ultimately, it leads us to question the nature of sound as it is currently defined.

It should be noted too that this is not a book that arises from the new field of Sound Studies. Sound Studies tends to deal with aspects of culture, society, and audio technology and thus is firmly anthropocentric in its object of study. While we do take a view of culture and society in some chapters of the book and do deal with audio technology to a certain extent in the final chapter—and even occasionally make use of Sound Studies texts—we view our book mainly as a theoretical, perhaps even philosophical, discussion of the perception of sound; philosophy and the perception of sound are not topics Sound Studies typically concerns itself with. If we might be forgiven a gross generalization, where Sound Studies investigates the role of sound in society and culture, we are, in part, interested in the roles that society and culture have to play in the formation and emergence of sound.

While the evidence for our definition of sound, and various assertions arising from it, is presented in the following chapters and our definition of sound is fully presented and its utility demonstrated in chapters 7 and 8, we think it useful here to introduce some of the definition's key concepts as the means to cue and prepare the reader for both that exposition and the supporting ideas that follow. These main components comprise the definition:

1. *Sound is an emergent perception.* . . . The two key words here are *emergent* and *perception* and the last is probably the most contentious. With *perception*, we locate sound as a creative act within our mind, as something that is dependent wholly or in part on cognition and emotion and this perception does not necessarily require sensation. Thus, a sound does not require a sound wave (a material and sensuous sonic phenomenon) for it to be perceived as a sound. *Emergent* relates to the present and

ongoing act of sound perception in the here and now; the *hear and now* of sound.

2. ... *arising primarily in the auditory cortex.* ... The emergent perception of a sound is initiated in the main in a corporeal system that comprises the ear and is centered on the auditory cortex. Factors that lead to the sound perception may derive from outside the immediate body, within the wider environment and be sensed by the peripheral auditory system (the ear initially), they may arise from inside the ear itself, they may spring solely from within the brain and may involve only a part of the auditory system in the act of perception, or they may arise through the effects of cross-modality. Within the brain itself, other systems such as those involved with emotion and non-auditory cognition will contribute to the act of perception.

3. ... *and that is formed through spatio-temporal processes.* ... Sound is an emergent perception that takes place over time but, more than this, the stimuli giving rise to such perceptions are time- and space-based. Such stimuli may include sound waves that are propagated over distance and through time and that themselves can be analyzed acoustically in terms of change in relation to time either as a composite sound wave or as a number of component sound waves. There is a spatiality to such stimuli which may be mapped in the brain but which also has implications for locatedness of self. Ultimately, the potentiality inherent in particular spatio-temporal relationships of such stimuli forms part of the perception of sound.

4. ... *in an embodied system.* We take the view that our perception and senses are indivisible from the wider environment, a view that finds expression in the field of Embodied Cognition. Following on from this, perception is a body-based function and inseparable from that body rather than being a separate component of functions such as emotion. Where we refer to the mind, we intend a system comprising brain, body, and environment.

These four key elements forming our new definition of sound are explained and supported in greater detail throughout the following chapters, but when viewed through the prism of the virtual and the other theories and empirical research that we discuss, a number of propositions and assertions emerge:

• Sound emerges from spatio-temporal conjunctions of other phenomena, the sensuous/nonsensuous, material/immaterial complex that we term the *sonic aggregate*.

- This sonic aggregate comprises two sets of components: the *exosonus*, a set of material and sensuous components; and the *endosonus*, a set of immaterial and nonsensuous components. The endosonus is a requirement for the perception of sound to emerge; the exosonus is not.
- All such components—for example, sound waves and other sensations that are exosonic and cognitive processes that are endosonic—are actual in Deleuzian terms. What is virtual are the processes that lead to the actualization of sound as a perception.
- Sound is emergently perceived when the force of potential is actualized through a particular spatio-temporal relationship within the aggregate.
- The components of the aggregate are present only under the right conditions and with a perceiver to actualize it in the here and now as emergent perception, as sound. This is the *hear and now* of sound.
- Sound is the actualized singularity that "pops-out" in the virtual process of emergent perception.
- We are able to cognitively offload (to use terminology from Embodied Cognition) the location of sound onto the environment and we make use of this to locate our selves in space.
- Sound waves are inherently meaningless; sound as emergent perception is meaningful as meaning is a property of sound.
- While a sound wave may be acousmatic, sound is never acousmatic. Therefore, the concept of reduced listening is a theoretical concept that is not achievable in practice.
- Distinctions previously made between real sound and virtual sound are invalid.
- Epistemic perspective can determine the nature and quality of the emergent sound; likewise, the perception of sound can determine epistemic perspective.
- Imagined sound is sound.

Sonic Virtuality

Why *sonic virtuality*? Although much of our work to date has been carried out on the sound of virtual environments, this book has wider concerns than virtual environments and the rather narrow, popular conception of the virtual as being equated wholly with the digital. The concept of virtuality has a long pedigree despite its being intimately bound up today with computers and networks and discussions of virtual worlds, virtual reality, virtual economies, virtual learning environments, and a whole host of other virtuals that have sprung up in the wake of our modern, digital lives.

The concept of virtuality on which we base sonic virtuality is a Deleuzian one, and we take inspiration from recent writings by Brian Massumi in which he uses this concept to explain a particular instance of visual perception. We expand on this to explain the perception of sound. Here, perception is not the passive receipt of some pre-existing sound; the perception of sound is the active emergence of sound, an act of creation. From the multiple configuration possibilities of the sonic aggregate, virtual processes involving spatio-temporality and tension, conjunction and disjunction, actualize a stream of these configurations into the perception of sound. This is an ongoing, emergent perception. As with Heraclitus dipping his toes successively each time into a different river, each sound perception is not only unique to the perceiver of it, but it can never be experienced again, by that perceiver or by any other. It is only through an understanding of sound that highlights its individual emergence and subjectivity that we can begin to explain the many anomalies noted in neuroscientific studies of auditory perception and the sonic effects that remain to be satisfactorily explained by other definitions of sound. In part, this is what the concept of sonic virtuality sets out to address, but we also wish to prepare the path for the future technological exploitation of our sound perception that current definitions, while adequate for many purposes, are ill-prepared for.

The ideas expressed in this book are not directly related to either music or speech; the focus is purely on sound. One might call this *fundamental sound* were it not for the fact that this term carries with it connotations of simplicity, of primitiveness, of lesser status than music or speech, and therefore of lesser importance to our lives. It would be equally incorrect to call our topic *unorganized sound* as this means that there is no organization to the sounds and the sound systems we study here; not only has the field of acoustic ecology uncovered patterns underlying both natural and man-made soundscapes and not only has acoustics systematized structures of sound waves, but our increasingly sonically designed world is testament to our ability to meaningfully organize sounds in ways that are not musical and that do not form speech. Furthermore, as will become apparent to the reader, we maintain that, in the broadest sense, all sound is organized by the perceiver.

A few examples in this Introduction will demonstrate the types of sounds we discuss here. It includes those of the environments we live in such as natural sounds and the sounds of urban environments. It includes designed sounds such as those found on computer desktops but also those designed for films and computer games, what might be termed *sound FX*. However, it also includes the sound that is the initial auditory component of sounding music and speech before those organizing systems apply another semantic layer. While we do in this book provide examples drawn from music or speech to illustrate our thinking, and while that thinking may well have import for the study of music or speech, the focus of this book is sound that is not classifiable as music or speech. Our concern is with sound perception: how and why we hear what we think we hear.

There is a reason for being careful about the limits of our study and the terminology used. While today's academic world might have pretensions of interdisciplinarity, even transdisciplinarity, and while the ideal might be an academic utopia of adisciplinarity, where knowledge is simply knowledge whatever its provenance or methodological genesis, we must still teach and research in universities that are hindered by academic silos. Furthermore, each of these silos comes with its own terminology and methodological approaches making it difficult to conduct conversations across academic disciplines without the risk that misunderstanding will arise amid the babel of scholarly jargon. While we recognize the potential for confusion in communicating interdisciplinary research, this book *is* unapologetically and determinedly interdisciplinary at heart. It draws on ideas, theories, and research from a range of disciplines and fields including acoustics, psychoacoustics, ecological acoustics, acoustic ecology, sound design, philosophy, psychology, neuroscience, ontology, epistemology, and embodied cognition, to name but a few.

The definition with which we initially confronted the reader at the start of this Introduction is bound to be contentious for a number of reasons, not least because it proposes that sound can exist in the absence of sound waves. This in itself is not a new idea, and we detail a number of theories in chapter 1 suggesting precisely this implicitly or explicitly, but the prevailing Western scientific view of sound is that sound is a sound wave. However, as the purpose of any definition is to give us a handle on some concept that then enables us to make use of it either philosophically or practically, we believe our definition to be a particularly useful one as it helps to explain a number of phenomena not explained by the prevailing definition of sound (or, for that matter, by other definitions). It succinctly makes use of and incorporates key elements of current philosophical and scientific thinking, it places the focus and origin of sound firmly within the perceiver, and it has practical purpose as a tool to further the design of sound experiences in a variety of situations.

From Computer Game Sound to Sound as Emergent Perception

With the development of virtual reality technologies and similar technologies such as computer games, there has been a rising interest in how humans feel present in, and can be agents in, such worlds. The concept of presence is outlined in chapter 2, along with related terminology such as immersive technology and incorporation, but it should be noted that the prevailing theory of presence in a virtual world is technologically deterministic and directly related to the degree of simulation of reality provided by the technology. That is, the more immersive the technology, the more precise its simulation of reality and therefore the greater the feeling of presence a person has within the virtual world. This straightforward equation is something we argue against and we use the example of sound in fantastical computer games to suggest that what matters is a realism of form rather than a realism of content; verisimilitude within the context as opposed to authenticity in the simulation of reality.

For several years, the two of us have been involved in the study of computer game sound. In particular, we have designed and taken part in a number of experiments using technology to monitor player psychophysiology in response to the perception of sound within the particular contexts of first-person shooter and survival horror games. At first these experiments were driven by a desire to study presence in games as, we hypothesized, enabled by the immersive technology of audio. We theorized that emotion played a role in this and emotion eventually became the focus of our later experiments where we concentrated on the relationship between sound and fear.

The first experiments we were involved in investigated the role of sound in immersion.[1] These were written up in Grimshaw, Lindley, and Nacke (2008) and Nacke, Grimshaw, and Lindley (2010). They are summarized and discussed within the wider context of similar empirical research in Nacke and Grimshaw (2011). Their main aim was to investigate the role of a first-person shooter game's sound and music in the experience of immersion while a subsidiary aim was to test whether the assessment of such experience could be carried out with a correlation between subjective responses from the player and the objective measurements of psychophysiology. Therefore, the methodology made use of questionnaires and data taken from electroencephalography, electromyography, and electrodermal activity along with the use of eye-tracking software.

In investigating the role of immersion, naturally the questions were raised of what immersion actually is and, more important, how one might quantifiably measure it. In tackling this, we explained to subjects that immersion was "the feeling of being encapsulated inside the game world and not being in front of a monitor anymore" (Grimshaw, Lindley, and Nacke 2008, 3) and asked them after their sessions for their own assessment of how immersive they felt the sounds of the game to be. Following previous research connecting gameplay experience to positive emotions and immersion (reviewed in Nacke and Grimshaw 2011), we mapped psychophysiological measurements with Russell's (1980) circumplex model of emotional affect and arousal. Correlating these data to the subjective responses seemed to give the best method of assessing immersion but it is not without its issues. For example, when subjects answer a questionnaire some time after the stimulus experience. Also, while arousal (activation/ deactivation) and valence (pleasant/unpleasant) can be objectively measured to a great extent, identifying precise emotions as per the circumplex model (a model of emotions distributed within a circular space where the dimensions of arousal and valence are represented as vertical and horizontal axes respectively) and with the equipment used is fraught with more difficulty.

Nevertheless, results supported the hypothesized expectation that sound in such a game genre had a strong, positive effect on the gameplay experience, particularly in the areas of immersion, flow, challenge, and positive affect. Interestingly, a gender difference was found with female subjects registering greater electrodermal activity when both sound and music were turned off in the game, suggesting, when combined with other data, that music in this context has a calming effect on female players. This remains an avenue of enquiry yet to be pursued.

Our next experiments were designed with an objective in mind that is outlined in Nacke and Grimshaw (2011, 276–277) and they attempted to deal with some of the methodological problems discovered in the experiments described earlier. This objective is to devise a software interface between player psychophysiology and a first-person perspective game engine. This interface is intended to be a biofeedback device that essentially converts the game engine into an empathy engine through the manipulation of audio samples and, ultimately, the synthesis of sound waves in response to the player's affect state. Part of this entails foundational work on assessing parameters of sound waves that can be manipulated for emotional purposes. In effect, in a particular context such as a survival horror game, if the game engine senses that the player is not at the desired state or level of fear or calm (or related emotions), then it can produce sound waves designed to elicit that emotion.

Modern first-person perspective game engines such as Valve's *Source* engine, Crytek's *CryEngine*, and EA Digital Illusions' *Frostbite* engine are capable of processing audio samples in real time to match the expected reverberation, attenuation, and filtering characteristics of the game world's visual space. For example, the *CryEngine* uses a version of Firelight Technologies *FMOD* audio library that allows for real-time manipulation of multiple audio parameters (dependent on the relative position of in-game sound source to player character in addition to the apparent materials and sizes of the space the character is currently active within) including audio attenuation and gain, 3D positioning, and reverberation. Such systems still require the creation of audio samples distributed with the game media and this introduces a limitation on the number of samples that can be provided. The functionality of systems such as *FMOD* dramatically increases the variety of sound waves that can be produced but this variety is still limited to a set based on the included audio samples. Procedural audio (see, for example, Farnell 2011) is a form of sound wave synthesis that, if integrated with a game engine, allows for real-time sound wave creation that bypasses the storage bottleneck introduced by the use of audio samples. For example, footsteps may be synthesized not only according to game world's visual space and relative distances but also according to speed and weight of movement. We suggest that it may equally be possible to synthesize sound waves according to required emotional effect if accurate mapping between sound wave parameters, context, and psychophysiological data can be achieved.

Methodologically, we attempted to overcome some of the issues discovered in previous experiments such as the provision of subjective responses after the fact, the measurement of phasic psychophysiological data rather than tonic (that is, the use of event logging matched to psychophysiological data rather than a record of longer term data), and the complicating factors of the visual mode and context. This last is particularly problematic since it is impossible, one might think, to entirely rid experimentation on the effects of sound waves from context especially when the sound waves are presented to the subject in the framework of even a simple computer game. Our dilemma is that, in pursuing foundational research on the emotional effect of sound wave parameters, we wish to remove variables such as gaming context and graphics yet, at the same time, and given our objective, we recognize that sound waves do not, metaphorically speaking, exist in a vacuum; non-sound wave factors play an important role in the perception of the sound that emerges from the sonic aggregate that, in this case, includes not only the sound wave but components such as gameplay, graphics, expectation, and past experience.

Accordingly, the later experiments, which are ongoing, are designed either to study the more fundamental questions or to pursue the larger objective.

The first experiment (Garner, Grimshaw, and Abdel Nabi 2010) established a system of event logging whereby the subjects' subjective responses gathered during gameplay could be matched to game sound events and used to set the scene for future experimentation by concentrating on the emotion fear. The aim of this preliminary study was to identify which sound wave parameters were the best candidates for future work on their fear-inducing potential. In prior testing with participants, a number of simple sound wave parameters were assessed for degree of intensity. Correlated with a survey of the relevant literature, three parameters (3D positioning, relative loudness, and pitch) were selected for testing on five diverse sounds in a bespoke game level.

The results indicated that the three sound wave parameters selected in initial testing, in addition to the more complex parameters of amplitude envelope and timbre inherent in the audio samples used, could affect the intensity of the fear experience felt by the player and so were worthy of further study. Importantly, though, other non-audio factors identified by a questionnaire were also shown to be significant in determining the level of this experience. These were player experience and confidence; specifically, awareness of gaming conventions and the player's skills in the use of the game controls.

Of several other experiments carried out, the second we chose to present here continues the theme of the first one in this set in investigating fear and sound in a gaming context but includes the use of data gathered from electrodermal activity, electromyography, and electroencephalography (Garner 2013, 130–134). In this experiment, it was hypothesized that changes in sound wave treatments (pitch shift, sharpness, tempo, distortion, attack, localization, and signal to noise ratio) would lead to significant differences in arousal, as measured through psychophysiological data, and that the results from these data would be supported by subjective responses gathered after testing. Again, a first-person perspective game engine was used with a bespoke level design to precisely control the delivery of the audio stimuli. For phasic psychophysiological events to be more accurately matched and recorded against significant game events such as the audio stimuli, the psychophysiological data were synchronized to the game engine timeline. A video was made of the subject playing through the game level and was played back to the subject during post-test questioning to prompt more precise recall of emotional states experienced during gameplay.

While the results of the effect on emotion of direct sound wave manipulation were inconclusive, the most notable conclusion of this experiment, also noted in other experimentation, was that context is all-important to the experience of sound. Sound wave parameters, and changes in them, have an effect but this appears to be indirect. That is, changes in the parameters have the capacity to alter context and it is this that has the more direct effect on emotional states. For example, the addition of reverberation to a sound wave affects the subject's ability to localize the sound wave source; within a first-person perspective survival horror computer game context, it may lead to uncertainty and, in this specific context, may induce fear or, at the very least, caution. We also noted that with the massive range of variation afforded by combining just a few quantitative features, it seems highly likely that the best way to guarantee the desired effect in the listener is to have some manner of access to his or her emergent perception. For example, a 5-second period of silence preceding a loud bang would create a moderate fear perception (*that bang was quite scary*) while a 10-second silence would create a high fear perception.

Allied to the importance of context, what was shown through the latter two experiments described was the effect of individual disposition to the perception of sound. This is particularly salient for us as we speculate on the sonic possibilities offered by developments in technology. Context, for us, includes not just the wider environment or the specific situation the perceiver is in, but also the personal experience, memory, and psychological makeup of the individual, factors of which comprise the sonic aggregate in our conception of sound and thus, in part, effect the emergent perception that is sound. We detail this more in chapter 8 where we provide a model for working with the concept of the sonic aggregate in the analysis and design of sound experiences.

New Technology, New Insights, New Possibilities

The capacity of technology to peer under the hood of human consciousness and directly access information from the mind is certainly something that has been explored significantly within science fiction. The so-called mind-probe has permeated popular culture to the extent that it has become an established trope, regularly appearing in television series, computer games, cinema, and literature. Although the methods employed within the mind-probe do vary between incarnations, the overarching principle remains the same: to extract information (namely, knowledge, thoughts, and emotions) from the subject, usually against the person's wishes.

Fortunately, for those who find themselves as test subjects within the real-world equivalent of the mind-probe, researchers are bound to a slightly tighter code of ethics but, nevertheless, the ultimate aim remains the same.

The contemporary field of study that investigates approaches to accessing the inner workings of the human brain is that of functional neuroimaging—the process of extracting quantifiable physiological data from the brain and inferring psychological activity from those data. Neuroimaging studies have supported various endeavors, which include: identification of borderline personality disorders (Schmahl and Bremner 2006); multiple sclerosis (see Rocca et al. 2002); and Alzheimer's disease (see Jack et al. 2008). The functional aspect of neuroimaging is itself a sub-classification that also incorporates structural assessment primarily serving identification of brain lesions and other physical abnormalities on a more macro level. In contrast, functional neuroimaging examines the micro-processes, specifically the patterns generated across time by the 86 billion neurons (according to the recent "brain-soup" study; see Herculano-Houzel and Lent 2005) from which our brains are composed. Speculation enters when we consider the step, or perhaps leap, from these current applications and potential future functions. As the resolution of these techniques, both spatial and temporal, is continually increasing, researchers are moving closer toward the ability to fully map the entirety of human brain activity. With sufficient spatial resolution it would be possible to observe the activity of individual neurons and, with the required temporal accuracy, each single electrical impulse could be detected. Provided that this is coupled with computers possessing the necessary processing capabilities to enable analysis of every neuron simultaneously, the potential is there for the precise neural activity network to be revealed. The exciting possibility that relates to sound is that such technology could enable an observer to witness the emergent perception of another person, providing the observer with a precise neural account of the auditory experience; not the acoustic wave, not the inherently flawed subjective description, but the actual sound. Moving further forward, the opportunity may then arise to begin building connections between the material environment and the auditory experience, potentially enabling sound designers to construct auditory stimuli with a precise awareness of the sound that will emerge.

Behavioral scientists of the past insisted that mental imagery was entirely inaccessible until reliable results were obtained that connected observable action to internal mental processes (see Zatorre and Halpern 2005). Such experiments still relied on theoretical and abstract connections between overt behavior and covert thought until emerging technologies enabled scientists to finally observe the living brain directly. Dating historically back to the 19th century, the majority of noteworthy milestones concerning neuroimaging took place through the latter half of the 20th century and research continues.

Starting with ventriculography (radiographic observation of injected air pockets traveling across the lateral ventricles of the brain), direct observation of the brain moved to cerebral angiography (the measurement of an injected medical contrast agent, again via radiography). More recently, X-ray computed tomography (a computer-assisted technique that compiles sequences of X-ray images to reproduce the three-dimensional geometry of the brain) has given way to the most contemporary of neuroimaging techniques: functional magnetic resonance imaging; magnetoencephalography; and positron emission tomography.

Researchers developing artificial intelligence systems at the Massachusetts Institute of Technology have asserted that the cognitive mind models our existence not as an external, physical, and shared space, but as an internal, personalized, virtual reality. For them, "the only difference between interaction with the actual world and the imagined one is the set of sensors and actuators providing the lowest-level interface" (Stein 1994, 1). This notion relates to the appropriateness of presenting imagined and perceived sound as discrete entities, one of the primary discussion points that we address within the book's closing section. A second central issue of functional neuroimaging relates to how we infer qualitative psychological information from quantitative neurological data and the way we establish a connection between the observable neural phenomenon and the hidden subjective information.

Other researchers have explored the capabilities and potential of neuroscience technologies to provide quantifiable evidence and to generate new theories regarding the nature of the imagination. Beyond mining this store of knowledge to support and formulate our conception of sound, one of our main interests is in what such evidence and theories can tell us about aural imagery and the imagining of sound. Consequently, a large proportion of this book is devoted to exploring these phenomena and in arguing that the imagination of sound is, in fact, the perception of sound and that such sound should be treated as different only in its sonic aggregate composition to the perception of sound that emerges in the presence of sound waves. In the closing chapter of the book, we combine this conception with the possibilities afforded by neuroscientific technologies in order to speculate on future applications and experiences of sound.

The Chapters

Each of the following seven chapters draws on a number of the key concepts, propositions, and assertions listed earlier to build up the case for our new definition of sound. These chapters examine a number of philosophical and practical areas that aid in supporting our argument and identifying the perception of sound, and the conditions required for it to be perceived, before an eighth and final chapter demonstrates the use of our definition and concepts for the analysis and design of sound.

Chapter 1 opens our thesis by reviewing some current and, to our minds, relevant definitions and conceptions of sound. Not least of these is the prevailing Western definition of sound—that sound is a sound wave—but we also investigate the ideas that sound is the property of an object, that sound is an event, and other theories that shift the locus of sound as the object of our hearing from the material and sensuous arena to the immaterial and nonsensuous arena. In seeking a definition of sound that takes into consideration individual perception, that accounts for our everyday listening experience, that takes note of the knowledge gained from recent neuroscientific studies, and that explains so-called auditory illusions, we raise objections and present counterarguments to these definitions. Supporting these objections and counterarguments, we introduce concepts and assertions that are expanded on and argued for in subsequent chapters: the sonic aggregate, and related terminology, is introduced; sound waves are neither meaningful nor are they necessary to the perception of sound; sound is located within the mind, an enactive mind comprising brain, body, and environment; and sound can be consciously or automatically cognitively offloaded onto or placed within the wider environment (this is what we mean by the locating of sound).

Chapter 2 provides the reader with a breadth of classical and contemporary thought regarding both the positioning of sound and also of the self, asking *where is sound?* and *where am I?* The localization of sound is considered from various perspectives that include acoustics, audiology, phenomenology, and neurology, and we discuss the appropriateness of positioning sound at its source, at the sound wave, at the listener, within the world, and within the mind. Competing theories of distal, medial, and proximal locations of sound are appraised and we examine the concepts of duplex sound theory, interaural level/time difference, and neuroplasticity with relevance to the ways in which our brains process acoustic stimuli to generate a perception of place. Chapter 2 questions the embodiment effects of the unique physiologies of the head, pinna, and ear canal, in addition to the dynamic effects of the aging process on our generation of perpetual space by way of sound. Central to supporting our thesis within chapter 2 are the concepts of acoustic ecology and acousmatic sounds. Ecological perspectives relevant to sound (including Truax's *acoustic communities* and Schafer's *schizophonia* and *audioanalgesia*) are considered within the context of sound and self-localization. The impact of technology on our natural acoustic ecologies is addressed and we consider how sound has the capacity to position us not just within relative space and time, but also within social, geographical, situational, and historical space. Acoustic ecology references emotion as an integral component and we discuss the affective potential of music and sound. Connections are revealed between acoustic ecologies and contemporary computer games as we explore the concepts of immersion, presence, incorporation, interpretation, and agency in terms of their potential to localize us via sound. Acousmatic sound addresses the notion that sounds can be separated from their sources and viewed as discrete entities. Within this area, chapter 2 considers the realms of cinema and computer games in order to explore concepts of synchresis and de-acousmatized sound, discussing the impact of multimodal effects and other perceptual factors on our experience of sound. This chapter concludes that previous conceptions of sound localization have been dependent on the overarching definition of sound and that much terminological confusion exists even within disciplines. It seems that sound does indeed have a location, but the location of that location is under dispute. We argue against the notions of acousmatic sound and reduced listening and of concepts such as sound wave and sound event/object being referred to as sound; instead, such elements are individual but related components of the sonic aggregate.

Chapter 3 broadly examines matters of embodied cognition, construal-level theory, and psychological distance as a means to develop the grander concepts of acoustic ecology with relevance to our thesis of sound. The primary argument presented within this chapter is that sound is not only inexorably connected to space and time but also that space is, in fact, the singular result of the entirety of time. Taking influence from classical philosophies that include Cartesian dualism, von Uexkull's *Umwelt*, and Heidegger's *Geworfenheit*, chapter 3 examines matters of neuroplasticity, states of consciousness, and artificial intelligence systems to support the primary argument. The mind and the ecology are positioned as comparable overarching systems that incorporate the environment, the brain, and the body while emotion is presented as a device that is central to the overall process. Sound is situated within the here and now, but this does not limit influences to a specific point in time as the present is itself inclusive of remnants of the past and projections of the future. This chapter intends to support our concept of the sonic aggregate and also demonstrate its considerable size and complexity. Chapter 3 also incorporates a review of listening models and existing ecologies (that includes our previous *virtual acoustic ecology of the first-person shooter* model), synthesizing the information alongside embodiment and construal-level theories to create the *perceptual acoustic ecology*, a new model of listening that attempts to reconcile the various concepts and models into a single framework.

Chapter 4 explores concepts pertaining to knowledge, certainty, and truth with a discussion regarding epistemic perspectives and belief. Again taking classical philosophical constructs that include Freud's *Verleugnung* and Kant's writings on analytic and synthetic knowledge forms as a launching pad, this chapter also incorporates relatively contemporary thinking with regard to *justified true belief*, the problems of Edmund Gettier, and Gendler's theory of *alief*. The chapter questions the traditional description of virtuality as being akin to that which is false or unreal, a counterpart to reality. This assertion is argued against by accounting the various ways in which such lines of distinction are, in fact, significantly blurred. The interactivity of computer games that bridges that experience of real and fictional worlds, concepts of suspension of belief and disbelief that occur seemingly in the space between real and unreal, and alief, in which an individual appears to have the capacity to simultaneously think one way and act in another, all come together to enable us to question the nature of the unreal and suggest instead that what is typically understood as unreal is better described as virtual which, alongside the actual, is a mode of reality. Emotion is again positioned as a central component with regard to how our epistemic perspective is formed. All of this is brought back to sound by way of our thesis, which positions sound as the emergent response to a sonic aggregate that is itself characterized, in part, by the listener's personal concepts of knowledge and truth. Sound is argued to be subject to the influence of our belief structures and, furthermore, within our ecological framework, belief structures are equally subject to the influence of sound.

Chapter 5 presents a review of auditory hallucinations as part of a larger discussion regarding imagining sound that continues in chapter 6. The central premise of chapter 5 takes inspiration from Bertrand Russell, in his assertion that hallucinations are not errors but facts. From this, we review various arguments across the fields of medicine, psychology, and neuroscience (with even a brief nod to quantum physics for color) to formulate and support our assertion that sounds with origins primarily based within the endosonus of the sonic aggregate (a set of components originating within the brain) are as real as those formed from external sensory stimuli. We examine the phenomenological nature of hallucination, including a brief examination of the phenomenon across various modalities, but with a focus on sonic forms. We consider various established theories with regard to psychosis assessment scales, rationalization systems, and degrees of plausibility within auditory hallucination to reveal the presence of "everyday hallucinations," concluding that many forms of hallucinatory experience exist that otherwise healthy individuals are susceptible to. Auditory hallucinations are revealed to be embodied experiences that are highly immersive and intense; essentially, they may often feel equally real to equivalent sensory experience. It is our conclusion that they *are* equally as real. Chapter 5 also questions established assumptions that any experience can be truly shared and examines forms of psychotic disorders that support the notion that auditory hallucinations can be shared experiences, blurring the lines even further between that which originates from the external environment and that which occurs within.

Chapter 6 continues from the previous chapter to consider circumstances in which the human capacity for imaginative thought elucidates the noteworthy benefit of aural imagery. Seminal theories from Descartes, Locke, Hume, and Casey are reviewed as we explore the concept that imagination is neither an external nor an internal phenomenon, but rather one that exists in the space between. The nature of creation and creative processes is questioned as we ask if true creativity is impossible and that ideas are like energy in that they can only be transformed, never created and never destroyed. With regard to sound, chapter 6 explores the concepts of inner speech, subvocalization, and verbal transformation effects within the context of a broader embodied ecology of sound (in which we observe that chewing popcorn in a cinema may actually enable us to resist the on-screen advertising). Aural imagery is presented as an entity with dimensional characteristics in which we can morph and shape sound in our mind. The ecology of sound design as a practical profession is also discussed as we examine the creative processes that lead to the production of some of the highly iconic sounds of contemporary cinema, including discovering how the Tyrannosaurus got his roar. Concepts such as corollary discharge that appeared in previous chapters resurface within the context of creative imagination. The last sections of this chapter address the neurological positions relevant to imagining sound in more detail than in previous chapters. Research incorporating functional magnetic resonance imaging, positron emission tomography, and magnetoencephalography within the context of sound perception is reviewed, primarily to assess the commonalities and differences in terms of neural activation patterns that exist between "imagined" and "sensed" sound. The inconsistencies and ultimate inconclusiveness of these studies is shown to reinforce rather than oppose our conception of sound.

Chapter 7 consolidates various perspectives and concepts presented previously throughout the book alongside a discussion of virtuality from which a model of sonic virtuality is formed. Virtuality is revealed to be a significantly widespread term but one that is subject to notable variation in its interpretation. Taking influence from the works of Massumi, Deleuze, Guattari, and Bergson, chapter 7 presents a number of contemporary concepts surrounding virtuality (including the virtual cloud and disjunctive plurality) and applies them to explain our conception of sound as perception. The common or everyday assumptions surrounding virtuality are challenged and we stress that the virtual is not in opposition to the real but, alongside actuality, a mode of the real. Within our discussion, sound is positioned as a singularity occurring within the mind, an emergent perception of a plurality, the sonic aggregate—itself a vast, interrelating arrangement of endosonic and exosonic components. Chapter 7 elucidates the finer details of this system by way of examining the pathway between, and including, source and receiver. We address the effects of the source characteristics, the propagating space that separates the source from the listener, and the physiology of the listener (from pinna shape to head-related transfer function and more) as exosonic components of the sonic aggregate. Similarly, the nonsensuous components of the endosonus are considered and we examine the impact of cognition, cross-modality, and memory among various other factors. We then describe the process by which one potential configuration of these components is actualized to form the emergent perception of sound. We conclude that the content of experience is fundamentally virtual. Sound is not an objective entity, the experience of which can be shared, but rather is subjective and subject to individual shaping.

The concluding chapter starts by summing up the concept of the sonic aggregate and the numerous assertions we have made throughout the book. The sonic aggregate and the notion of sonic virtuality are then used to practical purpose in two case studies. The first is an analysis of a typical acoustic ecology demonstrating how it may be described and understood in terms of the components of the sonic aggregate and the processes of sonic virtuality. The second is a demonstration of these concepts in the service of sound design in computer games; making use of new technologies, this process of sound design as per sonic virtuality is contrasted to the current archetype of audio design. The book closes with a short speculative look at how sonic virtuality can be used to conceive of future sonic possibilities.

Concluding Remarks

Finally, we would like to alert the reader to some things that should be borne in mind during the reading of the book. As a book that draws on ideas, theories, and the empirical findings of many disciplines and fields, we wish to chart the path through the many hidden reefs of conflicting terminology (often within the same discipline) that provides the greatest opportunity for plain sailing for the reader and the least risk of foundering. Given the need to quote and provide examples from the literature, this, at times, has seemed to us a sisyphean labor. Where jargon, conflicting terminology, or discipline-specific synonyms are unavoidable, either we provide a short explanation immediately or we make it clear which meaning of the term we are using at that point in the book. We also refer the reader to the glossary of frequently used terms to be found at the back of the book.

It almost goes without saying that a discussion of sound without the aid of diagrams is a very difficult task to undertake in the visual medium of print. Yet, at the same time, to write a book on the topic of sound perception and then to cram it full of diagrams and other visual crutches appears to us to be throwing in the towel and accepting the ascendency of the visual mode. Naturally, we cannot have that! Accordingly, we have kept such visual interlopers to a minimum and instead trust to our abilities to use text to explain and exemplify. In this attempt, we delight in the use of a combination of visualization and sonification throughout the book, entrusting to the reader's imagination the task of bringing numerous stories and sonic scenarios to life. We use a cast of characters although we return time and again to the adventures of little Claire and Alexander. Such narratives function as devices to illustrate complex concepts through fictitious but plausible scenarios that are not too far removed from the personal experience of many and it is our hope that throughout the reading of this book the reader will experience many opportunities to perceive sound.

1 DEFINING SOUND

"Contrariwise," continued Tweedledee, "if it was so, it might be, and if it were so, it would be; but as it isn't, it ain't. That's logic."

—LEWIS CARROLL

Introduction

In the Western tradition, while there may be one dominant scientific definition of sound, there are several philosophical definitions (see Figure 1.1). We intend neither to provide an exhaustive list nor to comprehensively describe those philosophical definitions we do include (a number of works already do this including Nudds and O'Callaghan [2009] and Casati and Dokic [2010]). Rather, we present some of the more persistent and, to our minds, interesting and useful definitions as a means to distinguish our thinking in this book and to argue the case for a new definition.

We are particularly interested in the usefulness and practical value of our definition while acknowledging that the use-value of any definition can be lesser or greater in particular contexts. For example, the acoustic definition of sound that we discuss below we reject as being too limited in its use-value, particularly within the context of virtuality/actuality we are interested in and its use-value in terms of analysis and design of sound. However, its use-value lies in its being the most objective of the definitions we investigate below; it is the product of scientific rationality and the antithesis of the self (in Merleau-Ponty terms, it is anti-individualistic [1945/2013]) and it arose from those markers of Western scientific thought—the desire to measure, to categorize, to control, to standardize—that trailed the Industrial Revolution. Thus, it forms one of the building blocks of industrialization, mass production, and mechanical, later digital, reproduction. There is no doubt that the acoustic definition, and its latter-day flexibility in

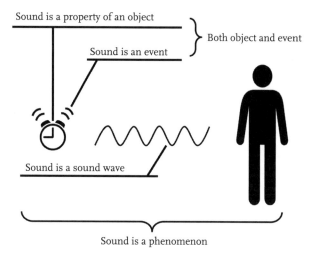

Sound is a property of an object

Sound is an event

Both object and event

Sound is a sound wave

Sound is a phenomenon

FIGURE 1.1 What is sound?

adapting to digitization, reducing the messy, infinite, and indiscrete actuality of physical phenomena to tidy, finite, discrete, and portable digital artifacts, has its uses with regard to the recording of sound waves and the production, processing, and reproduction of audio data as sound waves. Whole industries and their contingent educations and professions have been founded on this definition and the technology that owes its genesis and function to that definition has, in its enabling the portability and reproducibility of audio, changed cultural and political society for ever. However, the definition in other contexts does not satisfy us and thus loses its use-value here as we shall see.

Sound definitions have previously defined sound in relation to, yet distinct from, the human self. Thus, these definitions of sound in part define the self in relation to external events, objects, or spaces and their contingent qualities and properties. The definition we develop through this book, in contrast, is wholly founded on the self, a conception of the self that includes the environment, and owes a debt to the phenomenologist branch of philosophy, particularly that of Merleau-Ponty and the sound theorist Ihde (e.g., 2007), in that it emphasizes the primacy of perception rather than sensation. While there is much in common between our view of sound and the phenomenologist approach, we take a different direction by defining sound perception mainly in terms of virtuality (see chapter 7).

In all the definitions presented here, no less than in ours, the question they attempt to answer is *what is sound?* Each, and particularly the more philosophical definitions, attempts to justify the arguments given in support of their answer by dealing with other questions such as whether sound is itself a sound wave and, regardless of the answer to that, whether sound is an event or the property of an object. One question that is common to many is that of the location of sound. The question *where is sound?* is important enough, we feel, to devote the next chapter to it because it not only marks a significant difference between our definition and those of others, but the location, and thus the potentialities inherent in that location, has a direct bearing on the interrelationship between our perception of self and our perception of sound.

Current Definitions of Sound

The Acoustic Definition

Although it has many forms, the simplest statement of the acoustic definition of sound is this: *sound is a sound wave.* Such a definition, it would be fair to say, matches the popular and standard definition of sound in the West; the primary definition of *sound* in the 10th edition of the *Concise Oxford English Dictionary* is "vibrations which travel through the air or another medium and are sensed by the ear" (sound waves are those traveling vibrations). More fully stated, sound may be defined as a pressure wave moving through a medium and whose properties of position, frequency, and amplitude lie within the sensory ranges of the ear.

On a prima facie reading of the acoustic definition, in its objective purging of the phenomenology of experience, the definition attempts to answer the question *is it possible for two people to hear the same sound?* with a resounding *yes!* At least theoretically. It is a definition designed to root out all trace of subjective individuality in order to pave the way for standardization and mass production, for the multiple reproducibility of sound that is only possible with such a definition. One might object that the reproduction of a recorded sound in different acoustic spaces, or on different audio technology, for example, means that the sound heard will be different each time. But the audio industry, with its claims of faithful and true sound reproduction (high fidelity), is built on the belief of being able hear precisely the same sound ad infinitum. Thus, under the acoustic definition, *to hear* is reduced to a process of technological recording, production, and reproduction of sound waves and so, under the same technological and environmental conditions, the same audio data should result in consistently the same sound.

Such a definition leaves aside the question of precisely what it is to experience sound—and pushes that question into the realm of psychoacoustics.

Yet psychoacoustics itself pays little attention to experiential matters and, as it uses the same definition of sound as that used in acoustics, concerns itself almost solely with the characteristics of sound waves; this, according to Asutay and colleagues (2012) leads to an oversimplification of auditory perception that is detrimental to good sound design. Where psychoacoustics does pay attention to experiential matters, in the interests of objectivity and standardization, it averages experiential measures and levels out individual differences in order to arrive at a one-size-fits-all explanation that can then be used by industry (hence the attempts in psychoacoustics to objectify perception and experience through the use of statistics). The definition concerns itself solely with the material, the physical, the actual; the sound wave that is sound and the structure that sound takes rather than concerns of experience and the content of sound. Thus, it is theoretically possible for two or more instances of the same sound to exist because it is technologically possible for two sound waves to have the same frequency and amplitude at point of propagation. Indeed, one might even say that this is a definition of sound that even necessitates the possibility. And such a necessity is given added support through the quantization of sound waves in digital audio technology where the ambiguity and imprecision of the actual and messily physical world is replaced with the unambiguous precision of the 0s and 1s of perfect and endlessly reproducible digital artifacts.

Its reductionist approach is unable to say anything about the sound source, the event that set the pressure wave in motion, or the direction of movement of that wave. These can be deduced experientially from the particular characteristics of the sound wave, particularly in complex waves and the combinations of, and mathematical relationships between, their frequency and amplitude components, but such matters are not part of the definition because to include it would be to introduce ambiguity into the definition, an ambiguity that arises from including individuals and their mental makeups in the equation.

It is the exclusion of ambiguity in the acoustic definition of sound and the standardized necessity and expectation of being able to hear the same sound multiple times that most concerns us. While we recognize its use-value in the technological context (although, as we discuss later, we think even this is limited), it eschews the ambiguity that arises through individual cognition and perception, the personalization of sound that is part of our hearing experience. One might well sense the same sound wave (and even this is open to question given the effect of environment and the location of the listener relative to the sound source), but where two people can react not only very differently to it depending on external and internal context but can also label it with different sound sources or events, it becomes very difficult and practically useless to talk of the same sound. We seek to provide a definition of sound that accounts for perception and the individual; memory, environment, reasoning, imagination, and anything that better helps to define our highly personal experience of sound so that we may then make better analytical and design use of it.

Everyday Listening

In our objection to the non-experiential, physicalist reductionism of the acoustic definition of sound, we follow other writers. Arguing against this definition, Gibson (1966) states: "It treats physical sound as a phenomenon *sui generis*, instead of as a phenomenon that specifies the course of an ecological event; sound as pure physics, instead of sound as potential stimulus information" (86). While not developing a definition of sound (thus, for him, sound is still a sound wave), Gaver develops Gibson's perceptual view of sound in a pair of influential articles. Directed toward the design of sound objects, particularly what he describes as auditory icons for use in combination with the point-and-click functionality of computer desktops and other graphical user interfaces, Gaver also takes inspiration from Schafer's ([1977] 1994) writings on soundscapes and acoustic ecologies and focuses on how we extract meaning from sound waves. This meaning is encoded in sound waves as information, Gaver (1993b) states. If we can understand how meaning, particularly knowledge about the sound wave source and that source and the listener's environment, then, Gaver reasons, we can mathematically synthesize audio that, generally speaking at least, delivers that same information when played as a sound wave.

Driving this proposition is Gaver's (1993a) statement that the ecological approach to sound combines "the acoustics describing the propagation of sound through our environment, and the properties of the auditory system that enables us to pick up such information [which] will often take the form of complex, constrained patterns of frequency and amplitude which change over time" (8). He also distinguishes between everyday listening, which is perception of sound-producing events (these events, rather than the sounds themselves, being what he focuses on), and the musical listening that is "the experience of the sounds themselves" (1993b, 286). The distinction must be made, Gaver declares, because, hitherto, acoustics and psychoacoustics have concentrated on only those sounds that might be classed as musical in that they are harmonic and possessing pitch as opposed to being inharmonic and thus noisy. More than 20 years later, it would be a fair generalization to state that this is still the case; unnatural sound waves are used (as are, more recently, equally unnatural mathematical concoctions of various forms of broadband noise) to test and investigate hearing perception. In those cases where everyday sounds are used, methodological bias distorts the interpretation of perception and any results arising. Gaver neatly explains the problem through an imagined hearing perception experiment: in the context of an everyday sound being played to an experimental subject and that subject being required to describe what he hears, the experimenter becomes increasingly frustrated by the subject's insistence that he hears a propeller plane flying by; the experimenter requires a response formulated in the language of acoustics rather than an answer derived from matching sound to memory, an interpretation of sound that, the experimenter thinks, is properly a job for cognitive science, not for acoustics (1993b, 285–286).

If we have one criticism of Gaver's work it is that he does not properly account for the effects, if any, of schizophonia, a term coined by Schafer (1994) to describe the separation of sound from the original source object or event made possible by audio recording and reproduction technology. While Gaver states that the information encoded in a sound wave can be decoded by the listener in order to provide knowledge about the source object's dimensions or materiality or the source event's properties (although he clearly states that we hear sound-producing events, a reading of the work also suggests that we hear sound wave source objects), there is no statement by Gaver on what we listen to when we hear reproduced audio and, especially, how we deduce meaning from audio that is reproduced as sound waves. What is the source object or event when the sound wave is generated by an earphone reproducing the trumpet of an elephant as a sound wave and, given the dimensions, materiality, and properties of the earphone diaphragm (the current sound source) and its electronically induced vibrations, how do we still perceive the elephant's trumpeting?

We deal with such schizophonic conundrums in later chapters. Although not a definition of sound and thus, strictly speaking, not a part of our roll call of such definitions, Gaver's concentration on the analysis of everyday listening is important here because, along with other writers such as Gibson and Schafer, it marks an objection to the acoustic definition of sound; sound is more than frequency and amplitude, more than a pressure wave moving through a medium.

Sound as a Property of an Object

There are numerous philosophical definitions of sound that stand opposed to the acoustic definition described earlier but that, nevertheless, in the main still rely on the concept of a sound wave as a fundamental component of hearing or the perception of sound. The view that sound exists in the medium that vibrates when an object makes sound is an old conception with, for example, Aquinas in the thirteenth century stating: "In a body making a sound, that sound is only potential; the sound is made actual in the medium" (translated by Pasnau 1999, 310). In this case, the medium is air, sound thus being vibration in air, and Aquinas's thinking follows that of Aristotle and Boethius and finds later support among scientists and philosophers such as Galileo, Descartes, and Locke before becoming crystallized in the acoustic definition of sound as we know it today.

However, as Pasnau points out, there is an incoherence in the view that sound is a vibration in the medium. In particular, such a view conflicts strongly with the locatedness of our perception of sound. That is, we tend to hear and, in part, describe a sound as being located at the body that produced it rather than in the volume of air shared by that body and the ears of the listener. Birds are located outside my window because their twitters and squawks are outside my window; their sounds are outside my window. This locatedness in perception of sound, our hearing, is the reason Pasnau claims that the standard view of sound, "sounds come from an object, through the air, into our ears" (311), is wrong. Certainly, it is better, Pasnau suggests, to concede the falsity of such a view than accept that our ears are deceived in their perception of sound.

Because he maintains that our hearing is a locational sense, Pasnau states that we should view sounds as residing "within the object that 'makes' them. . . . [S]ounds either are the vibrations of such objects, or supervene on those vibrations" (316). Thus, sound is a property of the object that makes it, a property like color, size, or shape, and, as with those properties, the environment can affect our perception of sound. Pasnau, though, is less clear on what a sound wave is or what its function is. Nevertheless, it is apparent that in Pasnau's definition of sound, a sound wave is required to hear the sound (that is, the location of the source object or even the object itself) and this marks a significant difference to the definition that we argue for throughout this book.

Sound as an Event

The definition of sound presented by O'Callaghan is that of sound as an event. O'Callaghan derives this view from an interpretation of Aristotle that differs from the interpretation others give to support the acoustic definition of sound. This standard interpretation arises from Aristotle's statement that "sound is a particular movement in air" (quoted in O'Callaghan 2009, 27). But O'Callaghan derives his inspiration from two other passages from *De Anima* that state that "everything which makes a sound does so because something strikes something else in something else again, and this last is air" and that "sound is the movement of that which can be moved" (quoted in O'Callaghan 2009, 27).

Thus sounds, for O'Callaghan, are events involving change and taking place over time; sound waves and auditory perception are mere effects of sounds. The sound event is the event of something that sets a "medium into periodic motion" (37) and this event itself is generated by another event or a sound-generating object. O'Callaghan provides the example of a glass breaking: "the breaking of the glass causes the medium-affecting event that is the sound event" (37). Describing sound as generated by the periodic motion of a medium (thus, the sound wave itself is periodic) is an oversight or a misunderstanding of the terminology and physics of sound waves unless O'Callaghan is implying that inharmonic pressure waves through air—caused by, for example, unpitched musical instruments such as a cymbal or a drum, or even the example of the breaking glass he uses—are not the result of a sound event, because an inharmonic sound wave is an *aperiodic* motion. As Gaver (1993a) points out, nonmusical sounds, what he describes as everyday sounds, are typically inharmonic but the majority of studies of sound up to the time he was writing had dealt with musical sounds that are typically harmonic (3); thus, it appears that O'Callaghan, in his definition of sound, unwittingly betrays the musical bias toward the study of sound that Gaver laments.

Sound as Both Object and Event

Scruton (2009) defines sound as both object and event, specifically, secondary objects and pure events in that they neither undergo change like a physical object nor do they happen to anything (50). In this, Scruton is arguing for a phenomenologist or experiential and perceptual view as opposed to what he terms the physicalist approach adopted by those like O'Callaghan and Pasnau who argue that sounds are either "physical disturbances in physical things" or that sound is the property of an object (50–51).

Scruton proffers a number of reasons for his perceptual view. He suggests that such a view recognizes, for example, "those features of sound that make sound so important to us... socially, morally, and aesthetically" (62). Additionally, Scruton argues that his definition accounts for acousmatic sound, such as the music found on radio or audio recordings, in which the sound can be removed from its physical source without a loss in coherence and without a loss in what "is essential to the sound as an object of attention" (58). Much of his reasoning is based on a study of music perception, in particular the phenomenon of the grouping and streaming of sound and musical notes according to timbre and pitch similarity or temporal proximity and that gives rise "to a virtual causality that has nothing to do with the process whereby the sounds are produced" (64).

Scruton states, in common with past scientific thinking, that while animals have an intrinsically auditory experience when hearing music, humans alone possess music perception capabilities because they alone can perceive order in sound and this depends on their ability to acousmatize sound, to detach sound from cause (66). Do animals (or some of them) respond to certain sounds in ways that can be described as musical, and therefore, do animals other than humans have a sense of music? This is certainly a contentious question (not least because music has long been viewed as one of the prime assets of that divine spark of humanity that, we like to think, makes us unique and separate from the rest of the animal kingdom). There are, though, an increasing number of studies raising the possibility that humans are not as unique in this respect as we have previously supposed (see Patel, Iversen, Bregman, and Schulz 2009 for a review of some studies and the questions they raise). Our point, then, is that defining a theory of sounds "to make sense not of ordinary hearing, but also of those special acts of attention of which sounds are the object [i.e., music]" (Scruton 2009, 66) and using musical structures to explain this, as Scruton does, is approaching the problem from the wrong direction if music is taken to be the exclusive experience of humans. If music supervenes (at least auditorily) on sound, then we must reject such a definition as being modeled on the wrong object of attention.

Non-Cochlear Sound and Auditory Streams

Riddoch (2012), following work by Kim-Cohen (2009) and others, also argues for his definition of sound on the basis of phenomenology: sounds are "first and foremost meaningful, worldly phenomena" (14). This is an argument against scientific empiricism—in this case, the acoustic definition of sound—because such empiricism does not account for the subjectivity of hearing or the link between the auditory mechanism and the processes of sound perception. Riddoch makes a distinction between cochlear or actual sounds (i.e., those sounds sensed by the cochlea and the attendant auditory mechanisms of the ear) and non-cochlear sounds. Of non-cochlear sounds, he proposes three types: synaesthetic (the perception of sound through the stimulation of another sense); infrasonic (sound waves below 20hz that can be detected by the skin or by the chest cavity, which range from 80hz and below);[1] and auditory imagination (memory, hallucination, dreaming and so on, all of which, according to Riddoch, excite the auditory cortex) (12–13).

Riddoch further proposes that in fact all sound, including that involving sound waves (cochlear sound), is actually non-cochlear and therefore a non-physical phenomenon because the empirical sciences have failed in "demonstrating a causal mechanism linking our neurological processes with the supposed subjective effect—the world of our perception" (14). Thus, Riddoch suggests that sound is something more than the acoustic definition that sound is a sound wave; sounds "are always in the first instance meaningful sounds" (13). In this, Riddoch echoes Gaver's description of everyday listening that we discussed earlier and enlists Heidegger: "What we first hear is never noises or complexes of sounds, but the creaking waggon, the motorcycle. We hear the column on the march, the north wind, the woodpecker tapping, the fire crackling" (1962, 207).

This is a conception of sound that is similar in many respects to our own, and despite reading Riddoch's paper after the initial formulation of the ideas at the root of this book, we must acknowledge a debt to that paper's subsequent shaping of many of those ideas. Our one criticism of his work is that intriguing questions are raised with little attempt to answer them. For example, the proposition that imagined sound is sound is never taken further nor is the question of where sound is other than the statement that "sounds occur in the world" (14). These and other questions are what we deal with in the definition of sound that we begin to present in the next section.

Before we close this brief survey of other definitions of sound, we must make a short reference to auditory streaming, particularly as espoused by Bregman (1990). Bregman does not present a definition of sound per se and, although never explicitly stating that sound is a sound wave, is content to assume this. Thus, "sound enters the ear" (7) and, in introducing the word *stream*, Bregman reserves "the phrase 'acoustic event' or the word 'sound' for the physical cause [as opposed to a perceptual representation of sound]" (10). Despite concentrating on the perception of speech and music, Bregman's work is important in that it is an early statement of the necessity of analyzing the perception of sound rather than the properties of sound waves.[2] An auditory stream clusters related qualities of an auditory event; streams are perceptual units that are staging posts to a fuller description of auditory events and it is this clustering of qualities, such as low and far, high and near, that allows us to separate sounds within the auditory stream (10–11).

Sound as Emergent Perception

Many philosophical arguments supporting definitions of sound depend on the underlying assumption that sounds are sound waves (whether they be events or properties of objects that either have the sound or make the sound) or that hearing requires the presence of a sound wave—Riddoch's identification of non-cochlear sound is an exception as is Scruton's view of sound as secondary objects and events. Thus, these definitions must grapple with the conundrum of the nature of the relationship between the physicality of the wave as described by acoustics and the phenomenology of our everyday listening. Here there is some confusion and it is our view that all such definitions are crippled either by a reliance on the standard acoustic definition of sound as a sound wave or by the necessity for there to be a sound wave in order for a sound to be perceived. This standard definition is not at all clear with regard to several questions about sound, not least the question of where sound is (see, for example, Pasnau 1999, 317 [expanded on in the next chapter]). Equally, commonly voiced variations of statements such as *the sound is over there* or *the sound is coming from there* point to two different perceptual views not only concerning the location of sound but also its static or mobile nature.

A number of objections to various definitions of sound are thoroughly presented by Casati and Dokic (2010) so we do not intend to repeat them all here other than where we have briefly referred to them earlier. Rather, our intention is to demonstrate that the problem at the root of all these definitions is that of the implication of sound waves in current sound definitions (either as sound themselves or as being required for sound). By stating that sound waves are not necessary for sound to be perceived (although they may form part of the emergence of that perception), we can arrive at a definition of sound that not only overcomes the many objections raised to other definitions while accounting for various anomalies, but that also paves the way toward a practical model of sound that can be used for the design of sound. Necessarily, our account at this point must await the fleshing out of detail in other chapters so we restrict ourselves to briefly supported assertions that are more fully argued and evidenced later in the book.

In the first instance, we take our assertion that for a sound to be perceived, sound waves are not necessary. Thus we must defend the position that the thinking of sounds, the imagining of sounds, and all forms of what are typically described as auditory illusions or hallucinations are in themselves sound.

Many objections raised to various definitions of sound, and documented by Casati and Dokic (2010)—especially those that locate sound at the hearer (the proximal definition of sound location) rather than at a distant source (the distal definition) or those that locate sound somewhere between the source and the hearer (the medial definition)—appeal to error theory. That is, such statements about sound do not match our everyday, commonsense perception and language use concerning where sound is. We do not typically conceive of sound as being anywhere else than located at or originating from the physical source of the vibrations giving rise to the sound wave, therefore all definitions that locate the sound as being elsewhere are either wrong or are referring to something other than sound.[3]

Sufferers of common forms of subjective tinnitus will often state that they hear a high-pitched ringing. A variation of this statement, made particularly in the case of temporary tinnitus immediately after the triggering event, is that the person's ears are ringing; while the ears are not literally ringing like a bell, nevertheless, a sound is still perceived.

One could argue that the proximal view of sound in one way supports the idea that such tinnitus sufferers perceive sound or, conversely, that the perception of sound in these cases supports the proximal view but O'Callaghan (2007), who supports the distal view of sound, that sound as event is located at or near the sound source (which, in the case of tinnitus would be located in the auditory system), argues that tinnitus is merely an auditory hallucination. Following Strawson (1964, 65–86), O'Callaghan argues that there can be no sound here as "sounds are public objects of auditory perception" (13) and there is no sound wave to be sensed; without sensation, there can be no perception and thus tinnitus sufferers experience an auditory hallucination rather than perceiving a sound. The problem with this statement is that it not only ignores, in its sweeping generalization of tinnitus as a monolithic condition, some forms of objective tinnitus where a sound wave *is* produced within the ear, but it also ignores the brain activity that results from subjective forms of tinnitus. Such activity takes place in the temperoparietal cortex and auditory cortex, areas of the brain involved in processing auditory information and regarded within neuroscience as being a part of the perceptual system (see, for example, Plewnia, Bartels, and Gerloff 2003; Kleinjung et al. 2005; Zhang 2013).

Similarly, with aural imagery, the imagining of a sound in the absence of sound waves, activity in the centers of auditory perception of the brain can be observed that bears similarity to that activity observed in the presence of sound waves. A number of studies observe brain activity where subjects are required to imagine sound either when prompted to do so in the context of gaps in audio stimuli (e.g., Hughes et al. 2001; Voisin, Bidet-Caulet, Bertrand, and Fonlupt 2006) or in the context of silent movies (e.g., Hoshiyama, Gunji, and Kakigi 2001; Bunzeck et al. 2005). All these studies show activity in the auditory cortex that is similar in many respects to activity shown in the presence of sound waves and sensation (something we return to in chapter 6 as we review relevant studies of neural tomography that present limited distinctions between imagined and sensed sound). Some studies show activity only in the secondary auditory cortex under conditions of aural imagery (Bunzeck et al. 2005). This difference, Bunzeck and colleagues note, arises from the different processes of stimulation of the auditory cortex. In the case of the perception of sound arising from sound waves, this is a bottom-up process from lower-end processing of input stimulus to higher-order mechanisms including cognitive processes and involving activity in both primary and secondary auditory cortices. In aural imagery, this works in reverse as a top-down process but only the secondary auditory cortex shows activity (see also Zatorre 2007 and Thompson and Varela 2001 for more wide-ranging descriptions of top-down processes).

Our point here, though, is that activity in the auditory cortex, a locus of perception, is evidence that the result of aural imagery is the perception of sound much the same as that experienced in the presence of sound waves. The auditory cortex is, primarily, where both forms of auditory experience converge, bottom-up and top-down. As the auditory cortex and its associated peripheral systems are where the perception that is sound, resulting from sound wave stimulus, occurs, similar perceptual activity in that brain area resulting from aural imagery suggests that it too emerges as sound. Thus, both cases are sound and both are perception. Sound, therefore, is located solely or precisely neither distally, medially, nor proximally but within the mind. Equally, as both are sound, sound waves are therefore not necessary to the perception of sound.

Returning to the differences in auditory cortex activity noted earlier (primary and secondary auditory cortex activity with sound waves, only secondary auditory cortex activity when imagining sound), such differences are not surprising and pose no threat to our assertions and definition. In chapter 8, we expand on the concept of the sonic aggregate as a means to model sound. Within this aggregate, we identify two groups of components that we label the *exosonus* and the *endosonus*, referring respectively to components either outside the brain or inside it. Thus, the exosonus includes sound waves as well as other aspects of the material world having the potential to exert cross-modal or contextual influence on the emergent perception of sound. The endosonus comprises a range of components across memory, expectation, belief, and emotion. The endosonic components are idiosyncratic to the individual (although there is some shared experience) and it is this personalized driver that accounts for the possibility of different sounds being perceived despite the same exosonic components being available to other listeners. Thus, if only the one listener has prior knowledge of what a sound is, drawn typically from experience, the same sound wave is likely to result in the perception of two different sounds by two different listeners.

Zatorre (2007) points to the interrelationship between motor, sensory, perceptual, and cognitive systems, that is also typically a cross-modal relationship, when discussing the different perceptual activity in the auditory cortex noted by those like Bunzeck and colleagues. Although Zatorre admits the neurological basis for this cross-modal and cross-system matrix is still to be thoroughly investigated, it provides a explanation for the differences in perceptual activity across subjects with the use of the same sound wave stimulus. We not only sense sound waves but we also cognize, and the individuality inherent in such a process leads to differing perceptions between listeners.

As regards aural imagery and the differences in perceptual activity noted in the auditory cortex when compared to the activity noted in the presence of sound waves, we assert that while the perception of sound will arise in the presence of both exosonic and endosonic components (indeed, the exosonus requires the endosonus for sound to be perceived), it will also arise in the presence of endosonic components only and where material sensation is lacking. Thus, when we imagine sound, cognitive engagement leads to perceptual processes that can be observed. Because this is essentially a top-down process that converges on perception, this accounts for differences in perceptual activity to that observed in the bottom-up processing context of the sensation of external stimuli. Although a mere hypothesis at this stage, the observation that the common locus of activity in both cases is the secondary auditory cortex leads us to suggest that locus as the origin of the perception of sound.

Implicated in our definition of sound is the assertion that the location of sound is within the mind. Although we discuss the location of sound fully in

the next chapter, we need to deal here briefly with this issue because our commonsense view of the location of sound is that sound is external to us being
either a sound wave or carried to us through sound waves. In distal theories of
sound, sound is located at or near the vibrating source of the sound wave and
this view is supportive of our everyday listening model. It does not, however,
explain the widely observed phenomenon of in-head localization whereby
sound, in some cases, is perceived inside the head when listening through
headphones or earphones (see Wenzel 1992).

In order to explain how we can assert that sound is within the mind and
yet we perceive, through our everyday language, that sound is external to the
body, we turn to theories of ecological perception and, in particular, to theories
of embodied cognition. (In chapter 3, we deal more fully with how embodied cognition relates to our definition of sound.) In asserting that sound is
within the mind, our view of the mind is an enactive one that is based on the
work of authors such as Gibson (1979) and Thompson and Varela (2001). In
this conception, "the enactive approach views neural activity as one important
and indeed central element in a system involving the brain, the body, and the
world" (Noë 2004, 226). Thus, for us, the emergent perception of sound at the
site of the neural activity that is observed in the secondary auditory cortex is
at the center of a system that comprises not only the brain but also the body
and the environment; conceptually, we view the mind as the enactive domain
of brain, body, and environment. This accounts for the variety of contradictory
locations suggested for sound. Nevertheless, we assert that sound is not in a
place whose location is there to be discovered but that the locating of sound
somewhere within the mind is a process of conscious or automatic active
placement and part of the act of perception.

One of the central tenets of embodied cognition is that we offload cognition onto the environment (see Wilson 2002). Our assertion here is that
the everyday locating of sound as being over there or as coming from over
there (or even as coming from within our heads) is an example of this
cognitive offloading onto the environment. Dror and Harnad (2008) discuss
the offloading of cognition onto cognitive technologies and pinpoint language
as the first cognitive technology, one that "allowed cognizers to "offload" a lot
of brainwork onto other brains that could do it all for you, and deliver you the
results" (18). Language as speech is a specialized form of sound and anyone
who has participated in debate and discussion will recognize the description
of cognitive offloading that takes place in the ebb and flow of argument and
persuasion that occurs in such circumstances. It is a reasonably easy task to
understand how speech can be co-opted to explain the process of cognitive

offloading. The offloading of sound onto the wider environment by locating it as a symbol within that environment, rather than the nearby environment of someone else's brain, is a more difficult proposition as it develops into a more unconscious process than the conscious act of speech. It requires that we modify our traditional understanding of "to locate sound" to be one that is pro-active and similar in conception to the cognitive act of placing sound in the environment. With material sound waves, we can discover and locate their source; sound as perception is located by being placed.

The ability to do this comes from learning and experience; the necessity of doing this comes from the requirement to be and to act within an ecology. One can see the evidence for this sonic offloading by observing the behavior of newborn babies reacting to various sonic stimuli. When first faced with such initially mysterious stimuli, they start by looking around, peering into the environment around them before fixing their eye-gaze on the source of the sound waves (if visible) as a possible location on which to park the stimulus. Movement and proximity of the potential source play a role in this fixation in the early stages and, later, the knowledge gained through experience and expanding perceptual and cognitive networks lead to an almost immediate fixation on the source. This behavior can be observed in adults too where we frequently cast around to locate the source of a mysterious sound wave. The ability to localize sound wave sources is learned (and can be unlearned and relearned as will be clear in the next chapter) through combinations of motor and cognitive experimentation; readjusting the position of the ears relative to potential sources and assessing the likelihood or not that the squeak of a mouse issued from the elephant before us. We often get sound wave localization wrong too, or at least perceptually shift the location of the sound wave source elsewhere as in ventriloquism or locating sound on the cinema screen or computer monitor as we watch a film with loudspeakers or play a computer game with headphones. In these cases, it is not wrong to locate sound (as opposed to sound waves) on the ventriloquist's dummy or the screen.

Wilson (2002) has this to say of cognitive offloading: "we exploit the environment to reduce the cognitive workload. We make the environment hold or even manipulate information for us, and we harvest that information only on a need-to-know basis" (626). Consider the environment of a typical multi-player first-person shooter computer game. As a player present in the game world, I am part of an acoustic ecology rich in sounds, surrounded by multiple sound wave sources. Assuming I have experience of the game and the conventions of multi-player first-person shooters, I can make the game world work for me by cognitively offloading onto it. Engaged in a particularly vicious fire-fight, I can hear tanks moving up behind me. As I am otherwise engaged, I ascribe a location to that sound (it is behind me and getting louder), and this is an automatic process with experience, and associate meaning to it (probably enemy tanks moving in for the kill but too far away right now to bother about). Only when ready and pressed by the imminent arrival of the tanks as presaged by the increasing intensity of the sound wave do I turn to face the enemy.

Assuming I am wearing headphones or am using stereo loudspeakers, despite the fact there are only two actual sound wave sources and both out-side the game world, I make use of the visual depth of the game world and my ability to navigate through the three-dimensional spaces of that environ-ment to locate sounds in various parts of the world. This is "to locate" in the pro-active, placing sense. That is, I cognitively place sounds in the game world in which I am present despite knowing that the actual location of the sound wave sources is at the headphones or loudspeakers. In this case, the cognitive offloading is what Wilson terms symbolic offloading (629). I am not physi-cally present in the game world, merely sitting in front of a small, flat com-puter screen, but I know that there is an entire section of the game world that I cannot currently see but in which, nevertheless, activity is taking place. The sound functions as a symbol imbued with semantic significance, part of which includes the location of the sound within the game world and the meaning of the sound in the diegesis of the game, stored at that location and to be used as required.

This location of sound also operates in the actual world too. Walking down a street in a familiar city, I hear distant music off to my right. It is a warm, sunny day, a weekend, and knowing the city and assessing the quality of the sound, after some reasoning I decide that a band is playing in a nearby park. Needing to shop, I put this out of my immediate thoughts and complete my business. Returning to the street, I hear the music again. As I have previously offloaded cognitive information and reasoning onto the environment, in this case, the sound waves as symbols are the repository, I can immediately unload that cognition from the environment and proceed with a decision of whether to visit the park or not.

It is useful to provide a few more subtly different and brief examples. For example, offloading sound can be performed with aural imagery. At a crowded party, I notice entering the room a man whom I do not like and who is dressed in a loud red shirt. On seeing him, I remember and aurally imagine the laugh like a braying ass that is the reason for my dislike; I locate that sound out into the environment and on the man who is now standing near the toilet, drink in hand. Circulating through the party, I hear that laugh several times and each time exploit that sound's location to ensure I stay well away. As another example, and one where we actively place a sound with sound wave component out into the environment in order to reason about that environment, one of us, before delivering a conference paper always asks questions of the previous presenters. This is not only a confidence-boosting technique but a means also to test the quality of the author's voice in the conference space. Musicians and live sound engineers employ similar strategies when in an unfamiliar acoustic environment.

To suggest that sound functions as a symbol imbued with meaning and that we can retrieve this meaning through retrieving the sound from the location in which it has been placed in the environment is not to suggest that we agree with Gaver (1993b) when he states that meaning is encoded in sound waves as information and that it is therefore possible to synthesize sound to deliver that information and its encoded meaning at a later time and place. Sound waves are not sound; sound has meaning and sound waves are inherently meaningless. Meaning comes through the combination of that sound wave with endosonic components of the sonic aggregate and the potential of that endosonus to effect meaning comes with learning and the experience and memories we assemble as we make our way in the world.

This leads logically to the assertion that infants, in utero and within their initial stages of auditory processing system development, do not perceive sounds. Hepper and Shahidullah (1994) tested prenatal infants and discovered that they reacted differently to alternate frequencies of sine wave stimuli, with differences observable between increasing numbers of individual frequencies as they developed in the womb. However, they also noted that across all the infants tested, earlier than 19 weeks gestational age, reaction to auditory stimuli was observed but there was no difference in reaction between frequencies. This suggests that prior to 19 weeks, the auditory system can receive auditory stimuli but the infants do not perceive sound; they merely sense sound waves and begin to perceive sounds as they gain in experience, expanding their endosonus potential to ascribe meaning to the sound waves they sense. Some of this endosonus develops in an idiosyncratic manner, capable of investing highly personal meanings in sound whereas other development contributing to endosonic potential derives from shared learning and experience. Thus are we capable of perceiving sound that has unique and personal meanings while at the same time we can share sound experiences that provide similar meanings to others.

Concluding Remarks

In this chapter, we have briefly dealt with some definitions of sound chosen either because they are current and very much used or because they represent the main debates on sound. Their presentation here also served the purpose of allowing us to frame our definition of sound in terms of some similarities to those definitions and some key differences. The acoustic definition of sound and the definitions of sound as an event and sound as property of an object all require the presence of a sound wave for the sensation and perception of sound; the acoustic definition is that the sound wave is itself sound. That a sound wave is not only inherently meaningless but is also not necessary to perceive sound is an assertion that we have introduced in this chapter and that we provide evidence for in later chapters. These three definitions also have in common that they treat sound (as per their definitions) as being located outside the brain and the body of the perceiver; sound, instead, is located in the environment. According to these definitions, sound is distal, medial, or proximal and, in the acoustic definition, is either traveling or located at its source (there is some terminological fuzziness here that is explored further in the next chapter). The location of sound as expressed in these definitions is also a claim that we disagree with and we suggest instead that sound as a perception has its genesis in the secondary auditory cortex of the brain. Furthermore, we assert, using embodied cognition terminology, that we cognitively offload sounds onto the environment, which, with body and brain, forms the mind and thus the act of locating sound is a conscious or automatic act of placing sound in the environment in relation to our self. This is dealt with in greater detail in chapters 2 and 3.

We have presented two perceptual views of sound that bear similarity to our definition. The proposal that sound is both perceptual object and event is primarily driven by the need to account for acousmatics and schizophonia; that is, a sound (wave) can be detached from its source in a number of ways that are primarily technological. However, the ability to listen acousmatically leads to this theory of sound being based on the evidence from speech and music studies. We cast doubt on the assertion that only humans are able to perceive music as something more than sound (although the evidence is yet sketchy) but also feel that a definition of sound should start with sound rather than higher-level sonic systems such as music and speech. While non-cochlear sound is perhaps the closest in approach to our definition and while the concept exists and is used especially in the field of sonic arts, the evidentiary basis for it is, we suggest, only briefly presented in the literature. In presenting the evidence for sound as perception, however, we do acknowledge our debt to these earlier conceptions whose lineage may be traced back to the fields of ecological perception and the notion of everyday listening.

Finally, we have also introduced the concept of the sonic aggregate and its exosonic and endosonic components. This is developed fully in chapters 7 and 8. First, though, in the following chapter we present a more complete exploration of the question of the location of sound in particular looking at the evidence from neuroscience.

2 WHERE IS SOUND? WHERE AM I?

I opened my eyes, looked around, and asked the inevitable, the
traditional, the lamentably hackneyed postoperative question: "Where
am I?" The nurse smiled down at me. . . . She handed me a mirror. Sure
enough, there were the tiny antennae poling up through their titanium
ports cemented into my skull. "I gather the operation was a success,"
I said. "I want to go see my brain."

—DANIEL C. DENNETT, *Where Am I?*

Introduction

As we asserted in the previous chapter, the answer to the question
where is sound? is that sound is in the mind of the perceiver, where
that mind comprises brain, body, and environment. There are several exosonic components that might be part of the sonic aggregate,
including a sound wave, the primary qualities of the sound wave
source object, materiality, dimensions, and so on, and also other
elements such as the visual qualities of the source, its position relative to other sound wave sources and to our ears, and the properties
of the space the sound wave is propagated within, not to mention
endosonic components (memory, expectation, belief, and emotion).

The subject of this chapter is location of sound related to self
and of self related to sound. In particular, we focus on how the factors listed earlier inform our understanding of sound location and
locatedness of self within a variety of spaces. We begin, though, by
assessing the theories and philosophical definitions of sound we
presented in chapter 1 for what they have to say about the location
of sound.

You will notice that, other than dealing with the location of
sound wave sources, we do not discuss any acoustics answers to
the question *where is sound?* There are two reasons for this. First,

acoustics has little concern with the experience of the listener and this feeds through into a lack of concern about the relationship between listener and sound (that is, the sound wave as per the acoustics definition). This is not to say that the listener does not figure in acoustic calculations—for example, for the design of concert halls[1]—but that the focus is on the structure and content of the sound rather than the experience of it, with all its implications of messy, idiosyncratic individuals. Second, acousticians are inconsistent and imprecise as to where sound is located; very often the same text and author will give incoherent and mutually exclusive accounts. This is something Pasnau (1999) points out; thus, for acousticians, sounds are "within the brain... within the object making the sound... propagated through a medium... an auditory sensation in the ear... the disturbance in a medium, which can cause this sensation" (317). Such quite unscientific vagueness and contradiction stem from the first reason given previously.

Where Is Sound?

The View from Philosophy

As Casati and Dokic (2009) state, "a principle of classification of metaphysical theories of sounds can be based on the alleged location each theory assigns to sounds" (97). Thus, such spatial theories may be classified as distal (sound is where the source is), proximal (sound is where the listener is), or medial (sound is between source and listener) (see Figure 2.1). Similarly, accounts of the location of sound either fall into the materialist, or physicalist, view or the phenomenological, or experiential, view yet, the authors say, even accounts based on the former have to wrestle with our everyday auditory experience of location—where do we experience the sound to be regardless of where it

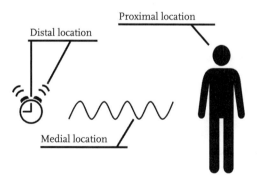

FIGURE 2.1 Where is sound?

physically is if it is indeed anywhere? That is, if I can say that the banging sound is "underneath the hood" or if I can state that the squeaking is "coming from" that rocking chair, either of which is a perfectly normal everyday statement of experience to make (but both of which say something different about sound location), should we not use those experiences as the basis of our determination of the location of sound?

In a definition that is akin to the acoustic view of sound as a sound wave (likewise a medial, and mobile, theory of sound location), O'Shaughnessy (2009) argues that sound moves through space because it is the transferal of physical force; there is an "essential spatio-temporal dynamism of sound" (118). Sounds, therefore, are not perceived at a distance, or solely at a distance, in the same way that, for example, the color of an object is. Sounds may well begin at an origin in space, a key striking strings in a piano, for example, but they are always mobile and traveling through space as they also move through time. As to whether one is able to hear the location of a sound source through the location of sound, O'Shaughnessy points to a distinction between suggesting that the sound is heard at the source and (the normal experiential state of affairs according to O'Shaughnessy) that sound is heard coming from the source (125).

Casati and Dokic refer also to aspatial theories of sound, whereby a sound has no location in space, and aspatial theories of auditory perception but they dismiss both based on the evidence of our everyday auditory perception. According to the latter theory, while we perceive sounds to be located at source, what we actually are perceiving is not the sound but the source and thus we cannot use our experience of sound as located at source to be an argument against proximal and medial sound theories (97–98).[2] Casati and Dokic, concerned with the location of sound rather than theories of auditory perception, prefer a form of distal theory of sound location, part of what they term the located event theory: "sounds are located at their sources, and are identical with, or at least supervene on, the relevant physical processes in them" (98). In this theory, sound waves are not sound but sounds are revealed through such phenomena when the sound wave's vibrating source is immersed in a medium (99).

O'Callaghan's (2007) conception of sound location expressed in his event view of sound falls also into the distal theory of sound location. In his argument that sounds are events and not sound waves, he opts for perception of sound at a distance in contrast to O'Shaughnessy. "Sounds are stationary relative to their sources" (46), he argues, claiming that in order to experience the sound sources themselves as located, as our everyday auditory experience assures us they are, sounds too must be located (32–33). Sounds, according to O'Callaghan, are events and such events are located at or near the objects making them and therefore sound is located at those source objects.

Similarly, Pasnau (1999) also points to our auditory experience of location to argue that sound is located and is thus not the traveling sound wave (31–312). This, again, is a distal theory of sound location but, unlike O'Callaghan, Pasnau suggests that sound is a property of the source object rather than an event and thus sound is part of the source object. Pasnau's view is that sound is perceived at a distance, differing from O'Shaughnessy in claiming that sound is like color in being the property of an object; what sight and hearing have in common is that both are locational modalities (313).

Scruton (2009) makes no specific mention of the location of sound in his argument for a phenomenological definition of sound. But, in his use of acousmatic sound as a supporting argument for this view (the removal of sound from its physical source as found in recordings and broadcasts—"sounds can be detached completely from their source" [58])—it appears to be an argument that sound is first located in or at its physical source before, as an "object of attention" (58), its relocation. Presumably, sound has a static location, at least initially if it is then acousmatically treated, and so this view is a distal theory of sound location but one that depends on "the experience of hearing things" (51) as opposed to the physicalist view espoused, among others, by Casati and Dokic and O'Callaghan.

In suggesting "that sounds are patterns or structures of frequency components instantiated by sound waves" (2009, 77), Nudds determines the location of a sound by focusing on the location of that instantiation. In this, Nudds appears to veer between proximal and medial theories of sound location (while denying the distal theory) because sounds are very definitely instantiated where we hear them but they may also be instantiated elsewhere: "[sound] is wholly instantiated wherever it is instantiated, including where we are" (97). He acknowledges that this theory does not prima facie account for our everyday experience of sound as being located at its source and defends his view by arguing that sounds, not being qualities of their sources, only share spatial properties with those sources—sounds can change or be changed while their source objects remain constant in their materiality or processes (94). Thus, for Nudds, sounds are not located at their sources, as in our experience of them, but appear to come from them.

Riddoch (2012), in his definition of non-cochlear sound—which, as cochlear sound is, is also "worldly sound"—is frustratingly elusive on the subject of the location of such sound. Suggesting that a commonsense view of non-cochlear sound would assume the sound to be in the brain or in the mind, Riddoch dismisses both conjectures; the brain is simply a biological network of neurons contained within a skull while the mind is not a thing or a container but a perceptual process. In the end, Riddoch opts for the rather vague statement that "sounds are heard in the world we already live in and understand in one sense or another—sounds occur in the world" (14). This unwillingness to directly answer the question appears to arise from Riddoch's desire, but failure, to find empirical evidence as to how neuronal activity becomes sound. In the end, Riddoch contents himself with this: "There is no empirically verifiable causal relation [between electrochemical patterns in the brain and sound] but rather a strictly associative relation between physical processes such as neuronal activity and the perceptions associated with those processes" (14).

Philosophical views of the location of sound vary widely between distal, medial, proximal theories, and aspatial theories, and many such views (particularly those that are distal or medial) are often based on the conception of an everyday form of listening and the idea that this phenomenological approach is what should form the basis of our view of the location of sound. Yet, even here, there is disagreement over what such everyday listening entails; do we hear sound as located at source, as coming from the source, or do we in fact hear the source rather than the sound? The evidence from audiology suggests that we are capable of relocating sound or, at the very least, our perception of where the sound wave source is.

The Evidence from Audiology

Audiology is an empirically based study of hearing that either studies human hearing processes directly or studies the hearing processes of other creatures, such as other mammals or birds, in order to infer knowledge about hearing in humans. The evidence gleaned from such studies is applied in a wide range of areas, including auditory prostheses and hearing aids, and audio reproduction devices and practices, such as loudspeakers, earphones, sonification, sound design, audio hardware design, and sound therapy; it is also used to make general assumptions or to theorize about our psychoacoustic mechanisms. These mechanisms include auditory cognition and cross-modal effects on hearing, such as those found in connection with synesthesia. As a point of departure, most researchers in the field start from the definition of sound as a sound wave; that is, an implicit acceptance of the acoustic view pervades such work. Thus, certainly as regards sound location, audiologists and those researching psychoacoustics are concerned not so much with the location of sound as with the location of the sound (wave) source. For the audiologist researching sound localization, while sound might be the object of hearing for philosophers stretching back to Aristotle, the sound source is the proper object of our hearing, and the sound itself (that is, the sound wave) is merely a means to divine the properties of that source, including its location.

A number of audiology studies have investigated the ability of the auditory system to localize sound. *To localize sound* or *sound localization* are the phrases most often used in these studies, and this betrays a paradigmatic confusion in many such studies between sound and sound source. What generally seems to be assumed is that the process of sound localization means the localizing of sound on the sound source, that is, the source of a sound is a vibrating object and that is where the sound is; so these studies assess the ability to directionally, if not distally, locate the position of a sound source in three-dimensional space. As sound is a sound wave in this field and (despite the confusing terminology noted earlier that, in some writings about localization, confuse sound, sound wave, and sound source) the localization of sound is not the actual object of study because sound, in this definition, moves, the localization of sound refers to the spatial position of a sound wave source rather than to the tracking of a moving pressure wave. Nevertheless, despite our intention in this book to primarily investigate and newly define sound, as opposed to investigating and defining the sound source, what audiologists have to say has some import as we begin to formulate our conception of the whereabouts of sound. What is of interest to us as we build up our thesis is that group of studies that investigates the localization of sound with impaired hearing, specifically where one ear is blocked or otherwise altered in its functionality so that what was previously binaural hearing becomes monaural hearing or where binaural hearing is otherwise changed from the norm.

Theories of sound localization suggest three ways in which a binaural hearing system can assess the direction of a sound source relative to the listener and these seem to be interchangeably used or combined. The two forming part of the duplex theory of sound localization are interaural level difference (sometimes called interaural intensity difference) and interaural time difference and these normally depend entirely on a fully functioning binaural system. This theory does not pertain to all species but does attempt to explain human sound localization. For sound waves arriving at the ears laterally, the head acts as a baffle, particularly at higher frequencies with shorter wavelengths, and thus the intensity of the sound wave at one ear is greater than at the other (interaural level difference); this sound level imbalance is then used by the auditory system to make a judgment on the sound source location. For sound waves of lower frequencies, and therefore longer wavelengths, the head is less efficient in its blocking and the duplex theory states that the brain makes use of the difference in arrival time of the sound wave at each ear (interaural time difference) in order to assess location.

The third method of sound localization is theorized to be dependent on the size and shape of the outer ear, the pinna and ear canal, which change the frequency spectrum of the sound wave, thus providing spectral cues and allowing, for example, the brain to acquire pinna transfer functions to aid in localization of sound (particularly in the vertical dimension).[3] Certainly in humans, head and pinnae size and shape differ from individual to individual and, in the case of the pinnae, change through the aging process.[4] How then can we continue to be able to localize sound under such changing conditions? The answer that auditory theory gives us is that our auditory system learns through experience; not only does this continue to take place as we develop from birth to adulthood, but this learning, and the acquisition of new auditory experience, can be artificially induced in remarkably rapid and flexible ways—so much so that humans and other animals even with artificially created monaural hearing can be trained to localize sound with almost the same degree of accuracy as those with binaural hearing. This is what we concentrate on in our brief overview of some relevant studies from audiology because the findings in them, and the conclusions drawn, allow us to edge closer to an answer to the question *where is sound?* that contests many of the metaphysical and philosophical answers given previously.

In many of these studies, the monaural conditions necessary to the validity of the study are claimed to be achieved through the blocking or plugging of one ear. There has been some criticism of this, notably that a monaural condition is not fully achieved and that this complicates the results reported and calls into question the strength or accuracy of conclusions reached. For example, there are claims that earplugs do not achieve complete sound wave attenuation, that earplugs do not attenuate the frequency spectrum evenly (bear in mind that the frequency range of the test signal has import for the duplex theory of sound localization), that bone conductivity of sound waves to the auditory system still occurs despite the plugging of the ear, and that perceptual bias, possibly attributable to experimental conditions and test signals as opposed to real world conditions and sounds, may affect results (see, for example, Wightman and Kistler 1997). However, such criticism typically focuses on the interpretation of the resulting sound localization impairment—for example, to what extent the information from spectral cues can be said to be prioritized over interaural level difference or interaural time difference or to what extent the latter two localization cues can be said to be removed completely, rather than suggesting that sound localization is not changed from the norm under such experimental conditions. There is no suggestion, though, that change does not occur in some manner, and it is this change that interests us.

A study by Slattery and Middlebrooks (1994) showed that plugging one ear in human subjects displaced sound localization in the horizontal plane by an average of 30.9 degrees toward the unplugged ear. Similarly, in a study on adult ferrets, Kacelnik and colleagues (2006) demonstrated, as might be expected given the role of both interaural level difference and interaural time difference, that blocking one ear led to an impairment and shift of sound localization in the horizontal plane. However, with specific task training, accurate sound localization was regained in a matter of days; and neither the lack of visual stimuli, in the case of some subjects, nor the lack of error feedback stopped this reacquisition. Without the training, the localization of sound in the ferrets remained impaired. The authors conclude that the richer and more behaviorally relevant (to ferrets, that is) the sonic training environment, and the more frequent the task training, the greater and more rapid is the reacquisition of accurate sound localization. Their suggestion is that such findings can be extended to humans to help the hearing impaired acclimatize to hearing aids.

Such neuroplasticity in the ferrets (the ability of the brain to adapt its neural pathways and synapses to changed conditions such as new auditory environments) has been shown to occur in humans too. An earlier study by Hofman, Van Riswick, and Van Opstal (1998) changed the shape of the adult subjects' pinnae (both pinnae for each subject) through the use of molds, thus disrupting the spectral localization cues and the development of pinna transfer functions thought to be utilized mainly for elevation localization. Unlike the Kacelnik and colleagues study, the role of visual cues was not assessed and neither was there any specific task training. The pinnae molds were in place for up to six weeks. During this period, the study participants' ability to vertically localize sound was initially impaired by about 20 degrees, but after several days it gradually improved. Around six weeks, their elevation discrimination was as it had been before the study started, demonstrating that the subjects had adapted to the new conditions. Interestingly, immediately on removal of the molds, the subjects' ability to vertically localize sound did not degrade, leading the authors to suggest that the brain can acquire and store a new set of pinna transfer functions from new spectral localization cues independent of, and without losing, the pre-existing set. While the experiential

shaping of our auditory system is most noticeable at earlier ages, mature auditory systems maintain "considerable adaptive plasticity" (Schnupp, Nelkin,
and King 2011, 287).

There are cases where such neuroplasticity, if it occurs at all, has little
purpose or effect on the localization of sound. One of us has a friend whose
right ear is what is known colloquially as a "dead ear." This is a complete lack
of hearing in that ear because, due to lack of nerve development during the
fetal stage, it is unable to communicate with the brain. In this case, all sounds
are localized on the left but with variation of location within that hemisphere.
Although this person has not been specifically tested, we can assume that the
brain has developed left-side localization strategies that do not involve either
of the methods forming the basis for the duplex theory (both of which require
two functioning ears), in addition to the more explicit strategy he reports of
rotating 360 degrees when he wants to locate a sound source—for example, a
voice in a crowded room.

If we take at face value that what is being studied here is the location of
sound, then there is a clear conception that sound as a sound wave is independent of the sound's source. From one view, this makes sense; in a parallel to O'Shaughnessy's use of the acoustic view of sound, the pressure wave
that is sound moves through space, radiating outward from its source. Thus,
the location of sound is a movable feast; it can be manipulated through artificial means[5] or it depends on binaural ability. Yet what is really being studied is sound (wave) source localization. This is demonstrated not only by the
design of the studies but also by neuroplasticity effects that gradually, yet dog-
gedly, locate the perception of source position to where it actually is or visually appears to be. Thus, audiology deals with sound waves and sound wave
sources and not, as we would define it, sound. It cannot, therefore, help us
determine the location of sound especially when we start to consider other factors such as the conjunctions between sound and image and our propensity in
certain situations to locate sound away from the sound wave source.

Acousmatic Sound

Scruton refers to "the 'acousmatic' experience of sound [where sounds are]
emancipated from their causes" (58) and uses this concept to support his
argument that sounds, because they can be separated from their sources, are
experiential rather than physical. The term acousmatic is used in a variety of
fields from electroacoustic music to film sound theory and, as we have discussed, to help define what sound is, but the term often has subtle differences

in meaning in each field. Fundamentally, it concerns physical space and thus the location of sound in that space, the location of the sound source in that space, and the conjunction, or lack thereof, between the two. Equally, it is a given among those using the term that because sound can be separated from its source, sound is a separate object to its source and so cannot be a part, a property, or a quality of that source. My radio is blue, yet while I can listen to it from another room where I cannot see the radio (a form of acousmatic listening), I cannot separate the color blue from it, I cannot see that color from the other room, and therefore blue is a property of the radio but the sound I listen to is not. One could argue that strong sunlight reflecting off the radio might cast a blue reflection onto the wall in front of me and that this is therefore a separation of the color, as property, from the radio. Yet the main philosophical thrust remains that color is a property of an object and cannot be separated from it—the radio has the property blue even in the dark (for a dissenting view and the opinion that color is an event, see Pasnau 2007).

In this section, we investigate acousmatic sound and listening in its several domains of usage in order to explore further the question *where is sound?* The views expressed here serve as preparation for the assertion arising from our definition of sound that no sound can be acousmatic, something that we discuss in the conclusion. According to the theories and opinions discussed here, sound and music can be designed or composed to be acousmatic and thus the concept has a particular and practical use-value within the fields of music composition and sound design (especially for films and computer games). But if empirical researchers in acoustics may be unfamiliar with the term, the concept in its broad sense is not; terms such as the ventriloquism effect or the audiovisual proximity effect cover some of the same ground as does acousmatic. Thus, in addition to discussions on the understanding and use of acousmatic in the theory and practice of electroacoustic music and film and computer game sound design, we also return to the field of audiology.

Dhomont (1995) provides a good overview of the (changing) use of the concept in electroacoustic music pointing out that the term itself has a long pedigree, being attributed to Pythagoras who apparently delivered his classes from behind a screen "in order to force his students to focus all their attention on his message." This directed attention to the message rather than to any medium, such as the speaker or musical performers in a concert hall, is a theme that Dhomont stresses for the acousmatic principle in electroacoustic music. In pointing out that acousmatic could be used to describe many aspects of our modern listening—that, in listening to the radio or when speaking on the telephone, "we are all unsuspecting acousmatic artists"—Dhomont points out that, in these cases, "it is not the message that is acousmatic but rather the listening conditions for the communication of that message." In accepting that such a listening condition, the medium, is acousmatic, he emphasizes instead the potential in electroacoustic music for the acousmatization of the message. Referring to François Bayler's 1974 definition of acousmatic music as "a music of images," Dhomont refines this definition to that of "works that have been composed for loudspeakers, to be heard in the home—on radio or on CD/tape—or in concert, through the use of equipment (digital or analog) that allows the projection of sound in 3-dimensional space."

Acousmatic sound, in connection with visual images, has also been identified and discussed by film and computer game theorists. Chion (1994), discussing sound and film, creates a binary opposition of acousmatic sound and visualized sound—that is, where the sound source is not seen and where the sound source is seen on screen (71–73). Thus, for Chion, acousmatic sound is offscreen sound (85) and "intensifies causal listening in taking away the aid of sight" (32). Here, the cause, the source of the sound, is a character or event not shown on the screen and, unlike electroacoustic music presented devoid of visual images, acousmatic sounds can be de-acousmatized by revealing the character or event on the screen.

This process of de-acousmatization (and, for that matter, the identification of non-acousmatic, or onscreen, sounds) in its matching of sound to onscreen character or event, invokes a process that Chion calls synchresis. (Anderson 1996, in stating that "If the auditory and visual events [in cinema] occur at the same time, the sound and image are perceived as one event" (83), is describing the same process but terms it synchrony instead.) This is the process of melding synchronous aural and visual objects such that we believe them to be one and is a product of meaning, context, volume, and rhythm (Chion 1994, 63–64). It is a perceptual process that marries the sound with the source onscreen. Thus, we once more have the notion of sound being independent of source (until synchretized). One might think that there is a double acousmatization taking place: the first in the act of recording, for example, an actor's voice or the recording of a car engine that is then stored in a sound FX library for later use, and, second, the acousmatic designation of the sound, whereby that actor's character or the car passing by is not depicted on the screen.

But there is, in fact, a third acousmatic process taking place, in the sense that Dhomont uses to describe the acousmatic sound brought about by the medium (the listening conditions), and that is the synchresis process. For us, what has been described as the sound source on screen is merely a product of belief; the actual sound source, or, rather, in our conception, the sound wave source, is the loudspeaker in the cinema auditorium. The loud-speaker, as sound source, can disrupt synchresis by shifting the location of sound from the onscreen or offscreen characters or events and this can occur in cases of poor synchronization of auditory and visual elements or in the over-enthusiastic use of surround sound systems. One of us authors unfailingly looks around and up at the cinema's loudspeakers in the presence of certain moving sounds[6] such as the roar of the jet engines of an airplane flying out of the screen and over the heads of the audience or the sound of film characters chatting unexpectedly and mysteriously to the rear of the cinema.

The role of acousmatic sound and synchresis has also been noted in discussions of computer game sound. In particular, the use of acousmatic sound in this context derives much from Chion's conception in terminology such as onscreen/offscreen sound and the fear-provoking potential of acousmatic sound in computer games (e.g., Garner and Grimshaw 2013) that develops Chion's observation that such sound "creates a mystery of the nature of its source, its properties and its powers" (72). In three-dimensional, immersive, and first-person perspective games, it is not entirely correct in all situations to use the synonym offscreen sound for acousmatic sound. Such usage implies that the power of de-acousmatization lies in the control of the director in the case of film whereas in these games, the de-acousmatization of sound is often a choice and within the power of the active and interacting player who can turn (as a character within the game) toward the game world sound source. Nevertheless, the same triple acousmatic process occurs in computer games as for film. The recording of sound, the synchresis of sound and image, and the use of sound reproduction hardware such as loudspeakers or headphones all demonstrate the facility and ease of the separation of sound from source, whatever that source is taken to be.

If synchresis in films and computer games depends on a prior acousmatic condition, that is, sound must first have been detached from its sound source to allow the potential for synchresis to be actualized, then a similar effect has been noted in the field of audiology. This is known as the ventriloquism effect and has been described by a number of audiologists and acousticians including Warren, Welch, and McCarthy (1981) who define it as a perceptual effect. Discussing a number of experiments in which they investigate the relative strength (or bias toward) visual and auditory modalities in tasks involving sound localization in the context of more or less synchrony between visual and auditory stimuli, Warren, Welch, and McCarthy draw the conclusion that, under conditions of high synchrony, such stimuli are perceived as "a single event" (564). Intriguingly, the human subjects' sound localization perceptions could be adjusted towards either the visual or the auditory stimulus sources by changing the degree of "compellingness" of the stimulus (for example, a speaker's face occupying the entirety of a video monitor, rather than a part, was assumed to compel attention to be drawn toward the visual modality) or by giving suggestions to the subjects that the locations of visual and auditory stimuli were one and the same (despite adjustments between the two stimuli that might have been supposed to mitigate this perception).

The suggestion that visual and auditory source stimuli locations were the same, and the resultant concordant response of the subjects, in the Warren, Welch, and McCarthy experiment described, may be interpreted as an instance of pareidolia—the urge to form order from chaos. This has been suggested by others as the reason for what is termed the phantom signal effect. For example, Lunn and Hunt (2013) have described subjects reporting the existence of sounds in the context of a lack of specific sound stimuli, such as appropriate sound waves, but against a background of white noise, particularly when the experimental conditions are such that the subjects might reasonably expect the presence of relevant stimuli.

As we move onto the next section, dealing with how sound helps locate our self, we need to ask if and how external auditory topography is mapped within the brain and then used to orient oneself toward the sound source. That such auditory topographies are realized in the brain is the prevailing thought, but what form this takes and the functioning of it is less certain. Our purpose here is not to provide an exhaustive discussion of auditory spatial mapping (of sound source location) in the brain[7] but to bring to attention the role of perception and other sensory modalities in the positioning of self vis-á-vis sound sources in the external world. In particular, our awareness of space appears to be formed from a neurological relationship between the mapping of auditory space and visual space. However, it remains to be fully established how mammalian, and especially human, brains encode this auditory space.

As Schnupp, Nelkin, and King (2011) report, "a topographic representation of auditory space" has been discovered in barn owls; auditory and visual stimuli from the same location, or very similar spatial locations, both lead to single neurons in the bird's brain and this is used to orient the head with respect to the stimuli location(s) (207). However, the duplex model of sound localization we discussed earlier does not apply to barn owls, which have asymmetrically positioned ears. Horizontal localization of sound relies solely on interaural time difference while vertical localization makes use of interaural level difference, and both function over the same range of frequencies.

Humans make use of interaural time difference and interaural level difference mainly for horizontal localization, and which takes precedence depends on the frequency spectrum of the stimulus sound wave; lower frequency waves, or waves with significant components of such frequencies, are assessed with the former and higher frequency signals with the latter. This, it is thought, leads to a different auditory topography or space map in humans than is found in barn owls. It is also thought that although such space maps are initially encoded with respect to the head's coordinates, they are later merged to some extent with visual space maps and therefore become eye-centered (Schnupp, Nelkin, and King 2011, 207–209); evidence that auditory topographies are encoded in visual frames of reference is also noted by Pylyshyn (2007).

There are two important points for us to note here in connection to our thesis that sound is located not at the source of the sound wave but in the mind of the listener, and that it comprises a number of components, the sonic aggregate. The first point is the one concerning the underlying thesis of the acousmatic; that sound can be divorced from source and projected into space. If not fully supporting our contention that sound is located in the mind of the listener, it does move it closer by projecting it away from its source.

The second point to be noted is that the sound of electroacoustic music is "a music of images." That is, and in this case, sound is not merely the sound wave but includes a number of perceptual elements. Let us take the sound of an old cine film projector that is presented as part of an acousmatic music score. The older of the two of us well remembers nights in the family home spent to the accompaniment of the whirring and clacking of the projector showing the uncanny silent movies of various holiday excursions. This is a sound that is almost unheard today and is thus unknown to many, particularly in the context of the silence of digital processes.[8] Thus, hearing the recording of such a sound wave will, for different generations of listeners, be a process of hearing very different sounds. The one might hear the projector while another might suppose it to be the sound of a lawnmower idling, whatever their experience can make of it. Thus, the sound is constructed in the mind of the listener from exosonic components and from endosonic components.

Where Am I?

While the previous section dealt with the location of sound (either in an abstract manner or in relation to self), there are several approaches discernible in the literature that concern the location of self with respect to sound or sound source. Most examples of such approaches deal with questions of spatial awareness but there are those that deal with temporal relationships and those that deal with societal relationships (which also begin to answer, through the agency of sound, the question *where am I?*). Location of self is not merely a matter of geographical or material spatiality, nor is it just a matter of time with respect to past, present, and future, but it also touches on self-awareness through place in society and the perception and conception of self that comes about not only through spatiality and temporality but also through psychophysiological processes. This section explores the locational relationship between self and sound from the point of view of the former.

Society and Psychophysiology

Often, conceptions of our location in acoustic space are wrapped up with notions of societal structures and forms. That is, the role of sound, our ability to localize sound, and our supposed ability to fashion auditory topographies in our brains is related to, if indeed it does not lead as a consequence to, the societal formations of our species. Thus, Blesser and Salter (2007), in suggesting an evolutionary basis for our auditory spatial awareness, state

> that the aural experience of space contributed, at least indirectly, to the reproductive success of our species. From a narrow perspective, our brain evolved specialized auditory substrates that could incorporate spatial attributes into awareness. But, from a broader perspective, auditory spatial awareness also contributes to our ability to thrive in socially complex groups (317)

but admit that this is a premise from which to initiate debate. They remind us that evolution, as a post hoc theory, specializes in observations that cannot be disproved without going back in time to test them; in this case, if indeed it is true that our auditory spatial awareness gave rise in part to our complex social structures or that our complex social structures led to an awareness of auditory space—we are unlikely to know if the one contributed to the other let alone which came first. In Popperian terms, the hypotheses behind evolution are not falsifiable.

Nevertheless, such speculation is of interest because it fuels further thought about conditions that might be testable at the present time. Thus, Blesser and Salter also note Humphrey's 2000 statement "that evolution progressively shifted sensory awareness of external stimuli from publicly observable reactions to private experiences" (323). Here, while we are unable to test the gradual change, we are able to test the personalization of experience and, as regards our thesis, this is of interest to us. At first sight, the suggestion appears to be that through the interiorization of experience, the individual becomes somewhat isolated from others of the same species and thus it seems to stand in opposition to the premise that auditory spatial awareness led to increasing social complexity. Yet, as Blesser and Salter state, where words fail to express emotions, our bodies, sometimes unwittingly, often betray our personal and present experience through gesture, facial expression, blushing, and so on (324). Therefore, an awareness of auditory space through sound localization not only might contribute to social formations but it might also contribute to awareness of self through both the personal experience of emotion and the public display of it (and its effects).

Sound's ability to make us aware of ourselves, our bodies, our feelings, and our relationship to society through the engendering of emotion (shared or individual, public or private) has long been recognized, particularly in the realm of music. The musical modes of Ancient Greece were believed to have an emotional effect or other influence on mood or feeling and this belief continued in the West through the medieval period, where, for Guido D'Arezzo in the 10th century, the dorian mode was for serious moods while the phrygian was mystical, to the 17th century with, for example, Juan de Espinosa, following the prevailing Baroque Doctrine of the Affections, claiming that the dorian mode tames the passions but the phrygian incites anger. Vestiges of this affective compositional approach to Western music remain in suggestions that major scales are happy while minor ones are sad, and other musical cultures continue to pursue a strong link between emotion or mood and music composition and performance (e.g., Indian ragas).

There are numerous studies of the effects of musical performance and musical listening on emotions (see, for example, Juslin and Sloboda 2002 for a general overview or Cohen et al. 2013 for an overview of the subject within the field of multimedia) but far fewer on the emotional effects of sound. Our personal interest in this field has been in the study of the emotion fear in the context of sound in computer games, particularly those of the survival horror genre. Our research here has several foci: attempts to differentiate emotions in brainwave data; codifying potentially affective parameters of sound waves; assessing the impact of context (personal and cultural, current and past) on sonic affect; and the design of an empathic feedback system between game engine and player whereby audio samples are processed for specific affective purposes according to a real-time assessment of player psychophysiology (see, for instance, Garner and Grimshaw 2011; 2013, and Garner 2011). We discuss this further in chapter 8.

Acoustic Ecology

Although we deal with acoustic ecology and its theories in more detail in the next chapter, we need to discuss those theories here for what they can tell us about the location of self in an acoustic environment. Gibson (1966), an early proponent of the ecological approach to perception, raises three points that are germane to our thesis. First, Gibson separates stimulus (by which he means light, heat, sound, and so on, rather than experimental stimulus presented to a test subject) from stimulus source; thus, there is a stimulus object that is the source and a "field of potential stimulation emanating from the source" (28). Second, he seeks to distinguish sensation from perception, stating that "the pickup of stimulus information... does not entail having sensations. Sensation is not a prerequisite of perception, and sense impressions are not the "raw data" of perception" (47–48). These two points are supportive of our thesis generally in that they point to the separation of stimulus (that is, sound wave) from source and the independence of perception from sensation such that sound perception can take place in the absence of sound waves, the stimulus that arises from the potentiality of the sound wave radiating from the source. Note, however, that in the first case, while we recognize the acousmatic possibility of separating sound wave from original sound wave source, a source, and all it connotes and denotes, is always a part of sound.

The third point that is of interest to us is Gibson's statement that "The modern world of earphones, telephones, or loudspeakers does some violence to the natural orienting tendency of the auditory system toward sources" (86). According to Gibson, this is a natural consequence of the auditory system's ability to act both as a proprioceptor (our voice, our breathing, etc., are heard inside the head) and as an exteroceptor (response to sound outside the body). Although Gibson was writing in the 1960s well before the advent of personal stereo and MP3 players, the social normalization of earphones, and the widespread availability and increasing use of noise-canceling headphones, it is tempting to think of Humphrey's statement about evolution being, in part, about the progressive shift to private experience of the sensory awareness of external stimuli where once such awareness had been publicly observable.

The violence Gibson refers to brings us to the acoustic ecologist Schafer (1994) who in addition to coining the term *soundscape* also coined the term *schizophonia* to refer to the separation of sound from its original context through the use of recording or broadcast technology (88–91). (This is similar in concept to the use of acousmatic by the likes of Scruton, as discussed earlier, but bears little similarity to its use by film theorists such as Chion.) As with Gibson, Schafer wants to draw attention to the aberration and violence done to the natural order through schizophonic technologies. With his wide study of the soundscape framed within ecological acoustics, Schafer points to the social and locational implications of this relatively new sound technology. Thus, for example, the loudspeaker and the radio are tied to imperialism and 20th-century fascism (91–93).

As an ecologist, Schafer's concerns are directed toward human society and the wider world: the effect of industrialization and human-produced sound on the environment but also the effect on humans of new uses of sound. Audioanalgesia, another of his neologisms, refers to the use of sound to block out other distractions, from the noise of air conditioners to the use of muzak; "walls used to exist to isolate sounds. Today sound walls exist to isolate [humans]" (96). In his study of soundscapes, sounds mark out spaces and territories, for humans as much as for animals such as birds. For instance, "the church bell is a centripetal sound; it attracts and unifies the community in a social sense" (54) whereas sirens are an example of centrifugal sounds, pushing people away from a center (178).

The notion of (and term) acoustic communities was developed by Schafer's colleague Truax (2001). An acoustic community is defined "as any soundscape in which acoustic information plays a pervasive role in the lives of the inhabitants. . . . [I]t is any system within which acoustic information is exchanged" (66) and parallels may be drawn between acoustic community and Blesser and Salter's (2007) term "acoustic arena" which is "a region where listeners are part of a community that shares an ability to hear a source event" (22).

The ecological approach to acoustic environments and soundscapes, that is, acoustic ecology as espoused by the likes of Schafer and Truax, has been criticized by Redström (1998). Redström claims that the phenomenological approach of acoustic ecology is based on personal experience and that wider ecological concerns and theories require "acoustic ecology to consider the acoustic environment for all species and not just humans." Thus, the focus on soundscapes found in the field of acoustic ecology is based on an interaction in which "the first-person perspective and personal experience are central" and this does not take into account the possible modes of interaction between other species of animals and plants and their environments. For example, Barot (1999) argues that the generation of certain artificial sounds (in this case, road traffic) can be acoustically matched to that of bird mating calls, thereby creating a sonic barrier between creatures in a way that limits their capacity to reproduce. There is a multiplicity of forms of interactions depending on the type of agent present in the environment.

Presence and Immersion

While not studying species other than humans in their environments, the concepts of agency and interaction have been the subjects of the design and study of virtual environments and, of relevance to our thesis, virtual acoustic environments and ecologies such as those found in computer games. We discuss this arena of agency and interaction more fully in the next chapter, so here we will briefly deal with the concepts of immersion and presence because they have significance for our experience of self and the locatedness of self in the context of sound.

Chion (1994) discusses point of audition in film that other critics have described in terms similar to point of view (89–92). Thus, there is the spatial sense in that there is a point in the screen space (if synchresis functions as claimed) or the offscreen film world (in the case of acousmatic sounds) from where the audience member hears the sound. And there is the subjective sense in which the audience identifies aurally with a character who hears for them within the film world. But Chion suggests that it is better to talk of a place or a zone of audition particularly in the spatial sense. This is because a sound wave, unlike light, is omnidirectional (it travels in many directions) and this, along with its reflection off the surfaces of an enclosed space, makes it difficult to determine precise points of audition in space.

As Waterworth and Waterworth (2014) state, in a view that frames presence as an embodied phenomenon, "being present in an external environment has its roots in the animal feeling of something happening outside the self rather than from within. In other words, the sense of presence distinguishes self from nonself. . . . Presence arises from active awareness of our embodiment in a present world around us" (589). Presence and immersion are terms that are often interchangeably used or utilized as near-synonyms (see, for example, Brown and Cairns 2004; Ermi and Mäyrä 2005). This is something that Slater (2003) in particular argues against by drawing a distinction between the physical properties of an object (immersion) and the perception of those properties (presence). Thus, an objective description of the physics of sensory stimuli in a virtual environment might allow for them to be described as more or less immersive depending on the preservation of "fidelity in relation to their equivalent real-world sensory modalities [while] presence is a human reaction to immersion" (1–2). In this view, immersion is what is delivered by technology whereas presence is a response to that immersive delivery.

Slater argues that one way to increase presence is to increase realism (4). It is not clear what Slater means by realism in a virtual environment but it appears to be linked to the notion of preservation of fidelity of sensory modalities that pertain in real-world equivalents. This is Slater's definition of immersion; thus, in Slater's thinking, while it may not necessarily lead to a sense of presence (there are other factors such as involvement and emotion), an enhancement of immersion will lead to an enhancement of the conditions necessary to a feeling of presence. This linking of technology effects to presence in an effort to replicate our "default" experience (our everyday life outside of immersive worlds) is something that IJsselsteijn, Freeman, and De Ridder (2001) also argue for, claiming that presence is "an illusory shift in point of view" (179) and that the illusion of "being there" in a virtual environment is enhanced by "more accurate reproductions and/or simulations of reality" (180).

Calleja (2014) takes issue with the technological determinism explicit in such arguments: "while high-fidelity systems are an important part of enhancing the intensity of an experience, they do not themselves create a sense of presence" (225) and Calleja argues that interpretation and agency too play key roles in presence. (To be fair to Slater, he does not, as pointed out previously, state that level of immersion alone is responsible for level of presence.) However, Calleja's main bone of contention with concepts such as immersion and presence is that they imply that the user of a virtual environment is "merely a subjective consciousness being poured into the containing vessel of the virtual environment" (231). He prefers the almost opposite view that, he argues, is closer to our experience of everyday life—that external stimuli are absorbed and organized within the mind according to prior experiential gestalts. Thus, Calleja favors the term "incorporation" over immersion or presence because the latter two "are defined by their discontinuity from the real physical world [whereas] incorporation occurs [when playing a computer game, for example] when the game world is present to the player while simultaneously the player is present, via an avatar, to the virtual environment" (232). The medium, therefore, must "specifically acknowledge the player's presence and agency within the virtual world" (233).

This acknowledgment, and the game's response to presence and agency, is one that has been made much of in claims for the interactive, and therefore potentially immersive, nature of computer games compared to other media such as film. McMahan (2003), somewhat conflating immersion with presence, lists as one of the conditions for immersion in a game world that "the user's actions must have a non-trivial impact on the environment (68–69).

In a discussion on the phenomenology of sound, Ihde (2007) states that that which is present is our central focus on self and that this is always inside, contained with horizons. This is a temporal presence; the auditory horizon is discernible only temporally and, in Heideggerian terms, the auditory horizon is the point at which sound is given over to the present—sound is a giving and listening is what "lets come into presence the unbidden giving of sound" (108–109). Auditorily for Ihde, presence is delimited by sound as opposed to silence. To hear is to be present in the world. In the realm of game sound, Grimshaw (2012) uses this to argue for the strongly immersive potential of sound (compared to computer graphics) in virtual worlds, suggesting that the game engine is a sonification engine that, in response to player agency, sonifies the player's actions and very being in the game system. Not only is the player present in the game world through (among other processes) the response to the immersive sound technologies of the game world, but the game world is present to the player in active acknowledgment of the presence of that player.

Concluding Remarks

While we are not yet at the position where we can fully justify our thesis that sound is located in the mind, we have been able to show in this chapter that there are a number of answers to the question of the location of sound (and of self in relation to sound). Many of these depend on their champion's definition of sound and form part of that definition's supporting argumentation, particularly so with philosophical approaches. Many discussions of sound and location in audiology and acoustics suffer from terminological confusion; thus sound localization should strictly be called sound source localization or, in our terms, sound wave source localization. Nevertheless, there are a number of arguments and empirical findings outlined in this chapter that we can summarize here as support for our thesis.

The overwhelming majority of arguments presented suggest that sound does have a location. However, one should be careful in what to take away from this because (1) that location is argued to be in various places and (2) the terminology used can be confusing. Are the theorists and researchers discussing materiality or phenomenological experience when they refer to sound? Is it more correct to say, based on our supposed everyday auditory perception, that a sound *is over there* or is *coming from there*—is it static or mobile? By the term "sound," do the authors really mean sound source?

There is also the majority view that sound can be separated from sound source and this can be perceptually, technologically, or both. Again, though, there is some terminological fuzziness. Precisely what is the acousmatic process that takes place, and which one is being referred to in the case of multiple layers of acousmatics, and is it sound or sound wave that is set free from the source? As noted earlier, we question whether sound can ever truly be viewed as acousmatic because in our conception of sound, where the exosonus includes a sound wave, by necessity the endosonus includes components that militate toward the assignment of source. If sound can never be acousmatic in the sense that sound can be utterly isolated from source, this also presupposes that the ideal preconditions for reduced listening, a concentration on the acoustic qualities of the sound, can never be met—in which case, reduced listening remains an unattainable goal despite the best efforts of electroacoustic composers.[9]

There appears to be general agreement that sound plays a role in locating our self. Typically, the discussion revolves around location of self in spatial terms, but there is also acknowledgment of the temporal property of sound and our responses to it that lead to feelings of presence in both the actual world and the virtual worlds of computer games and virtual reality. However, prevailing immersion and presence theories are technologically deterministic and tend to ignore other factors such as experience and embodiment.

If our discussion here has been useful in one respect, it is that we can begin to see the benefit of conceptually separating a sound wave from other sonic elements. This is useful to us because we wish to define components of the sonic aggregate that, we argue in our thesis, variously comprise sound as it is formed in our minds. In a discussion on location and sound, that is, location of sound and location of self with respect to sound, we have come across a number of arguments that, in their competing premises, support the formulation of the definition of sound that we suggest in this book.

Our overriding conclusion here is that sound is where we locate it, that is, we place sound and typically offload sound onto the environment. Within the environment, sound can be distal, medial, or proximal but it is never aspatial in its location; sound is always somewhere because sound as a perception includes the location we place it in. This placement of sound is the process of cognitive offloading that we introduced in the previous chapter. In offloading sound onto the environment, the cognition is in assessing and rationalizing the environment, its objects, and the events occurring here, and this includes the generation of sound waves. Aural imagery does not necessitate the offloading of sound onto the environment but the sound so created may be offloaded as when we associate a person in that environment with a particular laugh or a silent violin with its typical tone. Thus, sound is in the mind where mind, in the embodied view, comprises brain, body, and environment.

We are able to shift the location of sound within the environment. This is demonstrated in a number of audiological experiments and, depending on the experimental conditions, can lead to changes in the brain, neuroplasticity, and the acquiring of multiple sets of pinna transfer functions for the localization of sound wave sources, or it can be a temporary shift as when we experience the effects of ventriloquy or the cinematic effects of synchresis. In these latter cases, we may be perfectly aware that the sound wave originates from the speaker or loudspeakers rather than the dummy or characters and events on screen, but we offload and place sound where it seems most appropriate as an aid to cognizing the environment.

The offloading of sound onto the environment allows for the incorporation of other environmental factors that aid in locating our self. We deal with processes of virtuality in chapter 7 but can already begin to formulate a conception of sonic virtuality by viewing the feeling of sonically engendered presence in the world as an effect of the sonic actualization that arises from the multiple virtual possibilities of a scintillating virtual cloud. Actualization of the potential inherent in the sonic aggregate sets up a feedback loop whereby the locating of sound in the environment leads to further actualizations as we continuously re-presence ourselves in whichever world we are incorporated in and which is incorporated in us; a perceptual echo location in a self-organizing system.

This system is an acoustic ecology that is present to us but in which we are also incorporated. In the next chapter, we build up a conception of this acoustic ecology by expanding further on the role of embodied cognition in our conception of sound in the context of construal-level theory and the idea of psychological distance.

3 EMBODIED ACOUSTIC ECOLOGY

Lisa: If a tree falls in the woods and no one's around, does it make a sound?
Bart: Absolutely! Nnnneeeeeoooouuuuuuuoooowww, SMASH!
Lisa: But Bart, how can sound exist if there's no one there to hear it?
Bart: Wooooooo...

—THE SIMPSONS, 1990, *"Dead Putting Society"*

Introduction

There is no acoustic ecology without a hearer to perceive it and, equally, there is no virtual acoustic ecology without a player or user to sonify it. Virtual acoustic ecologies, such as those found in computer games and what are known as virtual environments, only exist in the presence of the active player, and every sound heard is intrinsically connected to the player's actions and presence in that world. This chapter explores the implications for our understanding of auditory processing and our sensation of audition. Keeping our perceptual view of sound at the forefront of our discussion, the process of listening is explored alongside theoretical constructs that support an integrated perspective of how we attune to the world. The primary focus of this chapter is that the human mind is not a centralized hub of information processing that can function with independence. Instead, we align our perspectives with more decentralized concepts in which the mind is formed from the internal physiology of the brain and body and the surrounding environment, and it is affected by the external state of the body and overt behavior, affective/emotional state, and past experience. Having introduced the offloading aspect of embodied cognition theory in the previous chapter, we begin chapter 3 by assessing other aspects of that concept and associative ontological theory; we do this to reinforce the plausibility of an integrated perceptual system before mining construal-level theory and psychological distance with a view to constructing an integrated perceptual model of embodied acoustic ecology. Our realization of such a model is presented toward the end of the chapter alongside relevant acoustic ecology models to elucidate the relevant theory and increase the accessibility of the final model to the reader.

Within this chapter, concepts of umwelt, embodied cognition, construal-level theory/psychological distance, and thrownness are discussed. These ideas and theories were originally presented as broad models, accounting for greater breadth and depth of interaction with our environment as opposed to restricting our freedom and capacity for objectivity. It is our intention to depict our definition of sound with the same positive outlook and, in positioning an embodied/perceptual description as the best account for what sound actually is, to offer an understanding that supports appreciation for the uniqueness of the individual, for adaptive and bespoke systems, and for the profound connection we have to our world. In the first of several appearances throughout this book, we divulge the not-so peculiar misadventures of siblings Claire and Alexander. Initially presented within our introduction chapter, these two fictitious but nevertheless rather mischievous little scamps are here employed to better illustrate a number of the concepts we discuss.

Embodied Cognition and Sound

The mind-body problem, a concept characteristically associated with Cartesian dualism, examines the relationship between the conscious, self-aware *mind* and the physical, material *matter*. Both Cartesian dualism and monist theories, which include physicalism/material monism (matter takes precedence over mind), idealism (mind takes precedence over matter), and neutral monism (both mind and matter can be reduced to a single, as of yet, undisclosed form), acknowledge, to varying degrees, that mind and matter are distinct and should be distinguished from one another. The following discussion presents some of the evidence that argues against a centralized system but it is important to note that, for our thesis, we *do* agree that mind and matter are different. As we stated at the start of this chapter, for us the mind refers to the overarching system while matter refers to the actual (material) components. Essentially, the mind *is* the ecology and, within the medium of sound, the mind is relative to the emergent perception while the components within the ecology are relative to the sonic aggregate. The mind is not within us, but rather both within us and all around us. Consequently, we acknowledge previous arguments about the difference between the mind and the body but our discussion argues against a centralized model, and we start from the premise that the mind and the body (alongside the environment, the material brain, and central nervous system) are fundamentally integrated and cannot operate independently.

The essential principle of embodied cognition questions the proposition that the mind and body are separate entities in favor of an integrated model. Within this, particularly in its view of perception, it bears similarity to a number of theories such as the ecological perception of Gibson and related externalist and phenomenologist theories. Research from a range of disciplines supports the concept of such a unified system and identifies problems with the alternative, centralized framework. Stepper and Strack (1993) revealed that the posture of an individual has a notable effect on emotional response. Duckworth and colleagues (2002) produced an experiment in which participants displayed faster reaction times to positive stimuli when responding by moving a lever toward the body, matching results to negative stimuli when moving the lever away from the body, thus revealing an association between emotional valence and physical movement. Core cognitive tasks such as reading and comprehension have also been associated to bodily states. Havas and colleagues (2007) induced smile and frown states in subjects during emotion comprehension tests and discovered that smile induction facilitated understanding of positive events and inhibited the comprehension of negative events, while frown induction facilitated negative understanding and inhibited positive understanding. Such empirical findings and assertions, among many others, justify the existence of an inherent connection between our conscious minds and our physical forms by way of documenting ways in which our thoughts are shaped, at least in part, by our bodies and the physical environment.

How the human brain processes information, conducts analysis and appraisal, makes judgments, and necessitates action is of key interest to researchers within the fields of robotics, intelligent systems, virtual agents, and artificial intelligence (AI). Within the field of robotics, some of the more conventional or earlier intelligence frameworks operated on a sense-model-plan-act (SMPA) system, a framework based on traditional cognitive theory that, much like the early models of AI, attempts to replicate human information processing via sequential reasoning and conscious deductive reasoning. Due to the truly immense consumption of computer memory required to manage information received from the physical environment in real time, this step-by-step approach has yet to meet the immediate, dynamic requirements of a system that effectively simulates organic intelligence. Anderson (2003) criticizes the central SMPA system, suggesting that in attempting to react to the dynamics of the physical world, a central system would need to store an individual response plan for every potential future outcome. The number of outcomes would be dependent on the number of variables compounded by variance of each variable and accommodating every possible interaction between two or more variables; as such, the likely number of stored action strategies would be unmanageable and unachievable. The fundamental lack of immediate responsiveness is arguably the essential problem associated with the centralized cognition concept. Clarke's (1997, 21) concept of the representational bottleneck highlights the efficiency limitations of a central processing design. This notion is related to the "assets as water" metaphor, in which the process of data representation (for example, a single static image of a bottle may, via representation, generate container, glass, green, small, light, translucent, etc.) places a restrictive clamp on the routine, increasing dramatically the time required to deal with the exponential swelling of the data.

These enclosed systems, such as several of those found within early AI and robotics, not only clearly distinguish between mind and matter but also present the former as something that can be entirely detached from its environment. They also present a framework that could be described as relatively rigid in that, structurally, the core systems of both the environment and the brain are permanent, fixed, and distinct from each other. The input and output information may be in continuous fluctuation but neither system has the capacity to alter the fundamental nature of the systems themselves. The primary limitation here, relevant to our discussion, is that this model cannot account for neuroplasticity, a circumstance in which the human brain has been shown to rewire itself in response to environmental, behavioral, and biological/physical changes (Chaney 2007) that we discussed in the previous chapter and which we introduced in that chapter in the context of the location of sound wave source. Provide specific input data to a fixed and enclosed system and you will receive a fixed output each time that information is input, so goes the early AI/robotics mantra. But this is a process that does not reflect the complexity and dynamism of the human brain.

Von Uexkull's (1909) concept of *umwelt* refers to the notion that it is the nature of our biology and physical form that largely determines both our adherence to the external environment and much of our cognition (particularly our emblematic processing). Von Uexkull's original example originates from the ecology of the common tick, in which the arachnid's "understanding" of its surroundings is restricted to essential observations and representations. Although the application of this concept to human behavior is more of a leap, and has been contested by various critics, it is not altogether ridiculous. Studies into neural development suggest that biological specialization in humans is not limited to before birth, revealing phenomena that include neurons shifting position within the brain (neuronal migration) and synapses being shut down (synaptic pruning), both of which contribute to specialization of the brain as particular pathways are reinforced and others are closed during the maturing of the human mind to adulthood. As stated earlier in chapter 2, it has been shown that the brain continues to adapt in structure well into adult life and that this neuroplasticity is notably prevalent in the auditory system (Schnupp, Nelkin, and King 2011, 287). It is well established that much of the way this process occurs is dictated by the external environment and, as a culturally acknowledged phenomenon, can be observed in the many parents who manipulate the environment of their very young children in the hope that they may foster specific talents and abilities (see Hota 1998; Vinkhuyzen et al. 2009).

Umwelt can be observed with reference to our auditory system when considering some of the biological limitations of audition. Just as the location of our ears prioritizes sound waves with closer proximity to our heads, so do the population density of cilia along the cochlea and the firing rate of auditory neurons prioritize certain frequency bandwidths and exclude extreme frequencies from our audible range. Here, the physiological constitution of the body has a functional impact on incoming sound wave data and consequently also on the emergent perception of sound itself. Umwelt theory would posit that these biological impairments are better appreciated as positive restrictions that enable us to filter information that is irrelevant to our biological imperatives without placing demand on cognitive load. Likewise, the positioning of the auditory cortex and the additional structures that support sound processing (for example, the posteromedial prefrontal cortex that assists in tonality representation [Janata et al. 2002]) are significant determiners of how the listener attends to sound waves and, consequently, modifications to these structures or to the nature of their interrelations would fundamentally alter the very nature of sound as it is perceived by the listener.

Although there is less certainty regarding the precise determiners of these neural development processes (be they biological, environmental, or a combination of both), the distinct variation between individuals in terms of neural structure supports the assertion that the brain (and indeed also the associated neural *matter* of the central and peripheral nervous systems) is susceptible to physical change in response to the physiology of the body and the nature of the external environment—an assertion that, as we shall observe later, relates very closely to embodied cognition theory. To clarify, for us these elements and their basic relationship can be elucidated by way of the Matryoshka (Russian nesting) dolls—wooden figures of varying sizes that fit within each other to form a complete set. The relation between the individual dolls reflects the associations between each individual component. For example, the brain fits within the body, which fits within the environment, and the collective of these units is the mind, specifically (with relevance to sound), the acoustic ecology.

In the seminal but arguably interpretatively challenging work *Sein und Zeit* (Being and Time 1927), Martin Heidegger presents the concept of *Geworfenheit* (best translated to mean *thrownness*). Heidegger's notion of thrownness has been recapitulated in various critiques and interpretations. One the most accessible of these is Simon Critchley's article in the *Guardian* (2009) in which he states that thrownness refers to the sensation that "we are always caught up in our everyday life in the world, in the throw of various moods." This resonates strongly with another particular view of embodied cognition theory, namely, that the mind cannot be separated from existence. Our thoughts, no matter how rational, contemplative, or retrospective, are infinitely intertwined into the fabric of existence, alongside our emotions, biological makeup, physical presence, external environment, and our past, present, and future. Delving deeper into Heidegger's ontological perspectives, Fox (1997) asserts that we cannot hope to truly understand the nature of our existence. Such a task is described by Fox as "like trying to carry water in our hands. It is not a thing to grasp or keep." Fox references Heidegger's concept of *Befindlichkeit* as "the way our thrownness is disclosed to us" and suggests that how we interpret, attend to, or *be with* our thrownness is our only genuine freedom. Although disagreement exists surrounding the exact nature of this concept, Dreyfus (1991) concludes that it is our emotional state that defines our individual *Befindlichkeit*, proposing a parallel between affect, thrownness, and embodied cognition in that an individual cannot be separated from his or her emotions; as Dreyfus states, "we cannot get behind our moods; we cannot get clear about them, and we cannot get clear *of* them" (173).

Rapid eye movement (REM) dream states provide a possible example of partial disembodied cognition, in which fractional nullification of primary sensory cortices reduces connectivity between the brain and the environment; the sensation of presence and experience is consequently internalized (Laureys and Tononi 2009, 100). Dreams originate from the forebrain regions that also govern much of cognitive processing during conscious states (Solms 1997; Bischof and Bassetti 2004). During REM sleep, the limbic regions of the brain, such as the amygdala, have been shown to measure greater activity than in wakefulness. Areas of the prefrontal cortex that receive input from limbic structures measure significant activation during REM sleep, including the areas of the forebrain that process mental imagery, spatial awareness, and symbolic representation (Laureys and Tononi 2009, 94). Research posits that higher-level thought processes can occur during dream states, including conscious perceptual representation (LaBerge and DeGracia 1999); speech production (Salzarulo and Cipolli 1974); and metacognition (Kahan and LaBerge 1994). This suggests that cognitive interpretation of internally generated data is plausible when we consider our ability to make sense of our surroundings during a dream. This raises two points that are significant to our thesis; first, that our perceptual experiences do not require the immediate presence of directly relevant material stimuli (to hear the call of an elephant within a dream does not necessitate the presence of one in your bedroom), and second, while dream states highlight that the brain and the environment are discrete entities, they can never become more than partially separated from one another and some form of connectivity is always maintained.

A lucid dream (in which dreamers are aware that they are dreaming) has significant potential for facilitating higher-level internalized thought. LaBerge and DeGracia (1999) review a number of texts that claim individuals are capable of situating themselves within a dream world, in which their simulated senses can influence their actions and react to temporal influence due to an awareness of precedents and antecedents within the dream. Sensory stimulation across all modalities, while acknowledged not to be the result of externalized physical stimuli, is nonetheless felt by the dreamer as a vivid sensation that is close to that experienced in the external reality. LaBerge and Levitan (1998) conducted studies on lucid dreamers, evaluating the differences in subjective sensation of somatosensory experiences. The results indicated that the brain is capable of modeling particular *touch* sensations; specifically light touch and pressure were vividly experienced (however pain was not) during lucid dreaming. LaBerge and DeGracia (1999, 299) go on to posit that the experiences that occur during a lucid dream are likely to be remembered after the individual wakes and, ultimately, have the potential to transcend from the dream world to the physical world and alter the course of a dreamer's waking life. Such dream-states provide a strong exemplification of sound without sound waves within an everyday context that many of us will be able to relate to in terms of prior experience.

Throughout the course of a dream, it is not uncommon (according to some) to be presented with various sounds that can be (and frequently are) attended to in a manner comparable to that during waking life. As little Alexander sleeps soundly (following passage through the gauntlet of bedtime distractions that confound and exasperate his parents) he perceives a sound—for example, the thunderous footsteps of an approaching, but rather friendly, elephant. Little Alexander may conjure representational information to identify the source (*that sounds like one BIG elephant*) or function (*the sound's getting louder, the elephant is approaching me*) of the sound, or he could localize the source of the sound wave within the three-dimensional landscape of his dream-space (*the elephant is approaching from the left*). During his dream, Alexander may respond to the sound with behavioral activity within the dream-world through engaging in actions by way of his non-corporeal form. He will also be likely, to some extent, to transcend the dream as his physical form responds to the sound (raised heartbeat in response to excitement, minute motor reflexes that relate to overt actions within the dream, etc.). In this scenario, we assert that sound is present without any physical waveform. Little Alexander is attuning to the sound in a manner that cannot be clearly distinguished from an equivalent circumstance in which a sound wave is present. He has no conscious awareness that the sound he perceives is, in fact, the internal product of his own mind because he does not identify himself as dreaming. Within that moment, that sound is entirely indistinguishable from something he might experience from physical stimuli in waking life. The sound is immediate, sensuous, vivid, and something that he would describe as very "real" indeed. This resonates with notions of auditory imagination (discussed in chapter 6), specifically that sounds experienced primarily by way of the endosonus of the sonic aggregate (i.e., originating and formulating components such as memory and imaginative processing) carry much potential for evoking emotional responses and while they may be described as internal, can be *felt* with the same intensity and tangibility as a sensory experience.

To address the concern that a dream scenario might contest embodied cognition theory (because it appears to be primarily brain-based) we must consider the question of the origin from which these sounds manifest. In *The Nature of Creativity*, Robert Sternberg (1998) states that creativity (relating to generation of ideas and insights) does "not come from nowhere, but rather from the presence and integration of the knowledge representation that is usable... in a given task" (3). In a similar vein, Roland Barthes (1977) relates the question of true originality within human creation to written text, arguing: "We know now that a text is not a line of words releasing a single... meaning... but a multi-dimensional space in which a variety of writing[s], none of them original, blend and clash" (146). Redirecting back toward the mighty stomp of Alexander's dream elephant, we would apply this argument to assert that such a sound could not be summoned from the ether but instead must have origins ultimately connected to both the physical form and the external environment.

This relates to our model of sonic virtuality (chapter 7) in which endosonic components are a requisite of the sonic aggregate that precedes the emergent sound, while exosonic components are not. For Alexander, however, this is only true within the local/immediate space-time (his dream) and while the sound of the elephant's stomp did not require any exosonic element within the dream, analysis of the wider ecology would incorporate some exosonic content. This could be directly related (Alexander was watching documentaries on elephants the previous evening) or indirectly related (Alexander has never heard an elephant stomp, but the event has been described to him as "thunderous," causing him to attribute a thunderclap to the elephant stomp). Many of our readers, no doubt, will have experienced waking from a dream in which a sound they have been experiencing in their dream is transformed into another sound—that of the alarm clock on their bedside table.

Cognitive thought during wakefulness is arguably influenced by immediate sensory input to the degree that the environment must be integrated into all frameworks of human thought processing; therefore, in considering the nature of the mind, we do so within an ecological framework. However, during unconscious states associated with dreaming, the brain appears capable of interpreting internally generated data, evoking emotional sensations via the limbic regions of the brain and also stimulating autonomic physiological activity and virtual motor responses. Furthermore, the research into lucid dreams supports the notion that the mind is able to reflect on internalized scenarios and respond with voluntary actions. Internally generated stimuli during a dream experience support the notion of *sensory simulation* (a central aspect of embodied cognition theory, discussed later), suggesting that this phenomenon can occur in both consciousness and dream states. This could suggest that during a dream state, information regarding sensory input (collected during wakefulness and stored in the long-term memory) is recalled and reconstituted as a simulated experience, essentially creating a dream-state environment within which the cognitive processes can remain embodied, situated, and sensitive to time pressures, interrelating to an environment (see cognitive offloading), and for the purpose of action/response. To close this discussion, we would make one further assertion, that the managing of internally generated data is not restricted to states of unconsciousness but rather is a permanent, ongoing sub-process that is continuously engaged within the larger ecology. With reference to sound, and as we shall demonstrate and discuss in further detail within chapter 7, this internal sub-process we denote as part of the endosonus, itself a component (alongside the exosonus) of the sonic aggregate. The degree to which the sound as experienced by the individual emerges from a primarily endosonic or exosonic aggregate depends on the complex interrelating elements of the acoustic ecology. To a certain extent, the division between exosonus and endosonus is a conceptual one, especially when we maintain that the mind is an interrelated system of brain, body, and environment, so, while we state (as we do in chapter 7) that the emergent perception of sound may be formed from endosonic components only (as in dreaming and aural imagery), the potential role of the sensory stimulation of memory, imagination, and other cognitive functions should always be borne in mind.

Embodied Cognition and the Construal-Level Theory of Psychological Distance

Considered in a rather crude but concise manner, embodied cognition theory can be understood as conscious thought processing within the here and now. To elaborate on this definition, Margaret Wilson's *Six Views of Embodied Cognition* (2002) provides an accessible and theoretically relevant dissection of embodied cognition. Wilson identifies and evaluates (based on a review of various other embodied cognition papers) these six attributes of embodied cognition as (1) cognition is situated; (2) cognition is time-pressured; (3) we offload cognitive work onto the environment; (4) the environment is part of the cognitive system; (5) cognition is for action; (6) offline cognition is body-based. Of these perspectives, the first two relate most nearly and clearly to our definition of the here and now. We discuss them both further below and also expand on the concept of offloading cognitive work onto the environment, a concept we introduced in chapters 1 and 2.

The construal-level theory of psychological distance relates closely to the situated and time-pressured views of embodied cognition. Best delineated by Trope and Liberman (2010), construal-level theory refers to the relationship between psychological distance and abstraction level of thought (high-level construals). Specifically, the concept posits that increased psychological distance encourages more abstract levels of thought (high-level construals) while decreased psychological distance promotes concrete focus (low-level construals). Trope and Liberman identify four measures of psychological distance, the first two of which connect construal-level theory to embodied cognition: physical/geographical distance (space/the *here*); temporal distance (time/the *now*); hypotheticality (likelihood of futurity being realized); and social distance (relation to the self). For example, if asked to provide an outline of idyllic lifestyle in ten years' time, an individual is likely to present a comparatively general account of his or her desires, with a more comprehensive focus on the overall scenario. If instead, the individual were asked the same question but in ten days' time, it is anticipated that the response would include more detailed and specific information.

While Trope and Liberman apply the construal-level theory and psychological distance concepts to more generalized scenarios such as the example just presented, we see a significant potential in applying them to the auditory system; specifically, that alternate psychological distance values will determine, in part, the abstraction level of representational information that is attached to sound wave stimuli to generate the emergent sound. For example, our listener is asked to describe the sonic landscape of an environment within which he has been present. According to our application of construal-level theory/psychological distance, low temporal distance (a recollection from a couple of days ago) would increase the probability that the listener's answer would include low-level, specific details (*Two birds were singing in a tree just overhead and a sheep bleated behind me. Then from my left, a soft, low rumble of engine noise gradually grew into a cacophonous roar followed by a sudden screech that lasted for a few seconds before a deafening crash of metallic and stone impacts*), whereas increased temporal distance would more likely generate a less detailed account (*I could hear animals and the typical sounds of the countryside before what must have been a very serious car crash*). Within an acoustic ecology framework, abstraction level (as the primary response to psychological distance) is replaced with affective level, the degree to which a stimulus is attuned to by way of reflective cognition and affect-led instinct. In this model, the focus is on elucidating the similarities between embodied cognition, construal-level theory, and psychological distance to strengthen both our arguments, for their rightful place within a contemporary model of acoustic ecology, and for our definition of sound as a perceptual and embodied entity, clearly distinguishable from the sound wave that we present as merely one possible component of the sonic aggregate. This model is visualized and discussed in greater detail within chapters 7 and 8.

Situated Cognition

Returning now to the six views of embodied cognition theory, we begin with an examination of the first: situated cognition. The central notion of situated cognition (the *here*) is that all informational processing takes place inexorably within the external environment and "inherently involves perception and action" (Wilson 2002, 626). This definition is later refined to "cognition that takes place in the context of task-relevant inputs and outputs" (626). Wilson critiques this explanation, suggesting that it cannot be universally applied to all cognition because phenomena such as daydreaming and remembering do not necessitate the presence of a task. For our understanding of this, as indeed with all of the embodied cognition views, we prefer to present embodied cognition as a continuous and inescapable component of cognition. We do not distinguish cognition from situated cognition, but rather state that *all* cognition is situated and therefore is always susceptible to the continuous stream of incoming data that constitutes the now. Any sensory information that is stored in long-term memory (alongside any relationship between the sensory input and associated objects, events, physiology, behavior, etc.) has the potential to influence future thoughts regardless of construal level (relating to psychological distance, discussed earlier) or context.

Wilson suggests that thought processing gradually builds a framework of automated subcortical routines. Regularities in comparable circumstances encourage an automated response generated by sensorimotor simulation— essentially a behavioral response, preceding cognitive appraisal and contextualized by conditioned representational links. Garbarini and Adenzato (2004) concur with this theory, documenting the concept of *virtual activation*, a representational system that evokes simulations/approximations of autonomic and somatic processes to embody input stimuli. The key characteristic of this process is that it engages autonomic processes in which representative information is retrieved by way of behaviorally prioritized pathways that do not require cortical processing and are therefore more efficient and able to attach representational information to a stimulus within a more immediate timeframe. This action is not quite reducing us to the sense-model-plan-act drones associated with traditional AI (as the outcome behavior is not predetermined), but does appear to be presenting our actions and our thoughts as highly susceptible to embodiment factors. We maintain our assertion that there is a difference between the internal and the external with regard to positioning the mind, body, brain, and environment. However, we acknowledge situated cognition with regard to the emergent perception of sound in that, irrespective of the endosonic/exosonic constitution of the sonic aggregate, all sound exists within the acoustic ecology of the mind, of which the environment is a component. Therefore all sound exists within the environment in the sense that it is *always* responsive it.

To elucidate the cognitive-shortcutting aspect of listening, illustrated in Figure 3.1, Alexander and Claire are upstairs, attempting to improve the

FIGURE 3.1 As far as Claire was concerned, Alexander had better hope that there really was a malevolent abomination from the netherworld lurking in his closet. Because if there wasn't, he'd have to deal with her...

overall aesthetic of their bedroom walls with permanent marker. Both are aware that their parents are downstairs (and therefore deserve to be punished for their woeful absence) and that if the adults were to catch the budding artistry in progress there would be rather unpleasant consequences. Both Alexander and Claire have cunningly utilized the sound of approaching footsteps ascending the stairs as an early warning system that will enable them to hide their creative genius should their oppressors disapprove. Although both have experience of this system, Claire has employed it far more frequently. Just as Alexander is adding the final wart to the Father-toad and Claire is completing the flames emanating from the snout of the Mother-dragon, the alarm of creaking floorboards and stomps of increasing proximity begin to sound. Little Claire responds immediately, by way of behavioral conditioning through repeated experience, because the sound waves are instinctively associated with contextually relevant physiological changes (increased heart-rate, adrenaline secretion, etc.) and overt (evasive maneuvers) movement (*I hear a sound—QUICK, HIDE!*). Conversely, little Alexander has only recently begun to implement this strategy and is therefore unable to react with such immediacy. Upon receipt of the stimuli, Alexander must make consecutive deductions to arrive at the final conclusion and appropriate response action (*I hear a sound—it's a creaking sound—it must be someone walking on the floorboards—it's getting louder and is coming from the stairs—someone is coming up the stairs—it must be Mum or Dad—QUICK, HIDE!*). The notion of representational association between sonic stimuli and physical movement and/or sensuous experience, is a perspective that will be returned to in this book. Here, cognitive processing, physiological state, and sensory experience form a trinity of interrelating components that fashion a single unified system. This example brings us back to our concept of emergent perception, in that each of the individual components of the sonic aggregate are inexorably connected to one another, and therefore a sound cannot emerge from a single component. The sound wave emanating from Alexander's creaking floorboard cannot form a perceptual experience of sound without influence from his current mental state, his physical state, or the contextual surroundings within which he is positioned. This is because these components of the emergent perception are constant and ever-present.

The notion of implicit memory, relating to perceptual fluency and procedural skill (Johnston, Dark, and Jacoby 1985) supports the developmental nature of embodied cognition. Wilson (2002) argues that implicit memory is automated action acquired through practice whereby repetition instills conditioned movements and reduces the need for full cognition. She argues that these processes of perception and action have the potential to become "co-opted and run 'off-line,' decoupled from the physical inputs and outputs that were their original purpose, to assist in thinking and knowing" (633). A potential consequence of this theory is that any prior thought process that generated representations and relations between objects has the potential to impact any future thoughts regardless of construal level.

Time-Pressured Cognition

The fundamental notion behind time-pressured cognition (the *now*) is that all human thought is subject to temporal factors and is influenced by the sensation of passing time as perceived by the individual and relating to objects or events. This concept can be reinforced when one considers the acoustical perspective of sound that is fundamentally time-based (frequencies and relative changes in amplitude are both time-dependent). Bar-Anan and colleagues (2007) illustrate how an individual's perception toward a future event could change in response to different relative temporal distances. Personal evaluation has also been described as susceptible to psychological distance influence; as research by Freitas, Salovey, and Liberman (2001) reveals, individuals are likely to employ a negative, diagnostic assessment when an event is expected in the more distant future but are more likely to prefer a positive, non-diagnostic assessment when the event is perceived as imminent. As discussed earlier in our introduction to psychological distance, greater temporal distance encourages more generalized thought (one cannot see the trees for the forest) whereas immediacy evokes increased specificity (one cannot see the forest for the trees). Time, therefore, manipulates attention and becomes a significant factor in appraisal and decision making (Liberman and Trope 2008). Temporal distances are interrelated quantifiable values that, alongside hypotheticality and spatial and social distance, establish psychological distance and influence higher-level cognitive processes such as evaluation and prediction (Bar-Anan et al. 2007; Liberman and Trope 2008).

As discussed in greater detail in the next section of this chapter, we assert that time-pressured cognition, much like its "situated" counterpart, forms a part of the sonic aggregate by way of its potential influence on the emergent perception via emotions. For example, two individuals are situated within a shared sonic environment and asked to describe their experience. One of the individuals is currently under time pressure; this could be task-related (they are told they have 30 seconds to describe the soundscape) or task-unrelated (they have a subsequent engagement and are in a hurry to finish quickly). The time-pressured cognition concept would assert that not only would their individual descriptions of the soundscape vary, but their actual experiences would be distinct. Without time pressure, the listener would likely notice a greater number of discrete auditory sources alongside a more reflective and comprehensive account of the acoustic, relational, and contextual information that formed the sonic aggregate (*I could hear birds in the tree behind me. There were probably around 10 in the tree. They sounded cheerful*). With time pressure, the temporal influence on the emergent perception could dramatically reduce such detail even being perceived because the mind, accounting for the pressure, engages a more generalized audition.

Based on reflection of the various perspectives and concepts detailed here, an auditory processing framework can be shown to be a two-level model of processing: cognitive associative functions that bypass conscious appraisal to directly connect sensory data to both the autonomic nervous system and motor responses; and full cognition where reflective thought and representational information are clearly defined and the entire situation is rationalized and comprehended. In addition, we suggest that such a model should not present these two levels as a dichotomy but rather as a continuum, acknowledging the potential for scenarios in which cognition may be simultaneously engaging both full and partial cognition for individual processes within a single task. An example is a concert pianist who engages a fuller cognition to focus on a specific and particularly demanding passage of notes in the treble clef, while his left hand manages the bass clef automatically (via muscle memory). Within such a system, the brain remains a continuous and essential component but one forever connected to the internal physiology and the external environment. This model also suggests that an interconnected system is not only probable but preferable, as the integration allows more efficient communication between the brain, body, and environment than what would be possible with a detached, centralized system that requires full representational processing of stimuli to generate an understanding and response.

Cognitive Offloading

According to Wilson (2002), we offload cognitive work onto the environment "[because] of the limits on our information-processing abilities" (626). Wilson believes we use the environment to hold and manipulate information and, referencing Kirsh and Maglio (1994), describes *epistemic actions* as environmental manipulations to work around the representational bottleneck of cognition during execution of novel tasks. Just as a police detective might arrange the photographs of a crime scene in the hope that a pattern will emerge, there are various everyday activities for which people across the world offload their cognition, enabling them to work more efficiently. Cognitive offloading is exemplified by Kirsh and Maglio in their study of the game *Tetris*, in which they argue that players utilize their control over the blocks not just to execute a strategy but to formulate it prior to action. As we discuss in greater detail in chapter 6 (creative use of aural imagery), an established approach to commercial sound design entails the arrangement of placeholder sonic ideas as a means of formulating a soundscape design. Cognitive offloading, therefore, supports the value of an ecological perspective of sound in its revealing of commonplace connection between the exosonus and the endosonus.

Acoustic Ecology

The capacity to perceive sound positions and immerses us within our existence and provides significant opportunities to understand and relate to the world. It has the capacity to convey significant emotional content in various contexts that include film and computer games (Parker and Heerema 2008). Research suggests that human recognition of emotion peaks during exposure to sound wave stimuli, suggesting that audition has a greater association to affective response than any other mode of sensory input (De Silva,

Miyasato, and Nakats 1988). Sounds have the potential not only to influence an audience's perception of a visual scene (Tinwell 2009) but also to generate immersion, depth, and emotional color. This section integrates the theoretical notions, discussed in the previous section, into an embodied model of acoustic ecology. Beginning with a review of seminal acoustic ecology frameworks and research concerning the nature of listening, this section progresses to examine the virtual acoustic ecology and the affective acoustic ecology before presenting and discussing an attempt at an all-encompassing model of acoustic ecology that marries virtuality, embodied cognition, psychological distance, and our new definition of sound.

Breinbjerg (2005) describes the anthropocentric nature of the listening experience and reminds us that (unlike vision) audio stimuli cannot be shut out without artificial means. He suggests that sounds facilitate the perception of physical properties attributed to objects outside our visual perspective and can also confirm and enhance the perceived details of physical properties that lie within our visual perspective. Breinbjerg also describes the function of listening as a way of realizing the *design of the set* (immersion in the nature of the environment) and the *narrative* (objects and/or actions that the listener may need to react to) of a landscape. Kromand (2008) supports this notion, proposing that sound exists as a purveyor of information and immersion. Tuuri and colleagues (2007) posit that perceptual processing is intrinsically linked to the functionality of sound, stating: "The procedural chain of events, actions and causalities in a situation can give an indicative meaning even to a meaningless beep" (15). This statement typifies our new understanding of sound as we assert that every sound wave is inherently meaningless; from a simple beep to human speech, representational information from various contextual, environmental, and physical sources is essential for the formation of a meaningful sound.

Several research studies have provided potential explanations for how we attend to sound and have developed distinctive forms of listening to that effect. Gaver (1993a) discriminates between two forms of audition: *specific* (a focus on characteristics more attributed to the sound wave); and *everyday* (a focus on the events that are revealed by way of the sound). Everyday listening is presented as a subconscious, autonomic process (comparable to the behavioral processing short-cut illustrated by the escapade of little Claire and Alexander earlier in this chapter) in which the identifiable steps within the cognitive process are relatively few. For example, as our listener is crossing the street she would not engage a comprehensive sequence of deductions before arriving at a response action (*Stimulus—low frequency rumble/*

approaching/close proximity to road—engine—car—quickly cross to avoid colli-sion) but rather make an immediate connection between stimulus and source (or even stimulus and action). Chion (1994) associates everyday listening with *causal listening* and defines the process as *ecological* and *event-oriented*. Chion also discusses Schaeffer's (1952) concept of *reduced listening*, an attuning to the sounds themselves (specifically the acoustic properties such as intensity, duration, and frequency/pitch), much like Gaver's specific listening. While we acknowledge this as a concept, in line with a prior assertion we made in chapter 2, reduced listening is theoretical and not something that is actually achievable in practice. With regard to the study of sound in computer games, Collins (2006) describes causal listening as the "preparatory function of game sound, affording the player information relating to game objects' positions and dynamics." Cusack and Carlyon (2004) posit that these discrete *modes* of listening can be organized along a continuum as there exists a hierarchical structure to the soundscape, ranging from an encompassing overview (e.g., the entire symphony) to a focus on a highly specified singular component (the volume of D sharp the lead violinist is playing in bar seven, measure three).

Ekman (2009) suggests that attention "will guide the traversal of the 'listening hierarchy' and so determine what detail the listener will and can attend to at each moment" (3). Attention is one of four influences contrib-uting to audio perception, as identified by Ekman alongside proprioceptive sounds, emotions, and multimodal processing. Proprioceptive sound refers to sound occurring inside or conducted through the human body (swallowing, heartbeat, sounds conducted through bones, for instance). Ekman suggests that extreme stress can also impact on sonic perception. Using examples of scenarios involving soldiers and law enforcement officers, Ekman describes auditory acuity (an increased sense of clarity and specificity) and auditory blunting (the loss of sound detail or inability to hear very loud sounds) as involuntary perceptual filters, and observed from a survey that auditory blunt-ing is a commonly occurring phenomenon in scenarios generating extreme stress. According to Massumi (2005), increased acuity is a potential response to the apprehensive terror phase (senses are primed and attention focuses on data associated with the threat), while blunting neatly integrates with the horror phase (innate physical response behavior is prioritized and present sensory data and cognitive appraisal are attenuated until the action reaches a stop). Emotional influence incorporates personal preferences, cultural, and social factors, and Ekman (2009) proposes that these factors "compose a frame of reference in evaluating heard sounds" (3), a function that reveals similar-ity to the notion of *semantic listening* (Chion, 1994). Multimodal perception describes the impact of data acquired from other human senses on auditory perception. Recent research has typically explored multimodal phenomena in terms of audio/visual effects but several articles address the concept as part of the acoustic ecology of a computer game experience (e.g., Ekman 2009; Grimshaw and Schott 2008).

Grimshaw and Schott (2008) support Chion's (1994) three-part construct of *semantic, reduced,* and *causal* listening but also incorporate a fourth. This mode, entitled *navigational listening,* is defined by Grimshaw and Schott as a mode of listening that guides the individual through the world via audio beacons. Grimshaw (2007) argues that central aspects of human interaction with sound (that is, sound waves) are the abilities to conceptualize the position of the object (as relative to the individual); to identify movement, speed, and direction; and to support kinaesthetic interaction with objects within the environment. Schaeffer (1952) suggests that sounds can facilitate the identification of spaces or territories without requiring visible boundaries and Breinbjerg (2005) extends the notion of auditory space by categorizing sonic spatial types. *Architectural space* describes areas with quantitative and measurable sizes/boundaries such as an indoor environment while *relational space* describes the space indicated by the distance and position of sound wave sources in relation to the listener. Breinbjerg also describes the notion of *space as place*; the phenomenon of semantic meaning attributed to the audio environment that identifies a place within a historical and geographical context. This concept can be compared to the notion of temporal functions of sound; as Grimshaw (2007) asserts, sound "also has the ability to indicate a point or period of time in the past, present or future" (204).

Before we complete our tour of the modes of listening we feel it is important to take a very brief detour to note that within our thesis, these associative information points are not contained within the sound wave but rather within the virtual cloud that incorporates both the sound wave and the listener. We cannot hear the sound of an 18th-century musket being fired without an awareness of the relevant historical context, and we cannot gain such awareness from merely auditioning the sound wave.

Tuuri and colleagues (2007) provide a comparatively more comprehensive theoretical model of listening and identify eight discrete modes. Relating the process of audition to construal-level theory, the authors position the eight modes along the construal-level theory continuum: from the low-level construals associated with pre-cognitive listening to higher-level source, context, and quality orientation. In this framework, a distinction is made between *connotative* (immediate, free associations labeled pre-cognitive) and *semantic*

listening (cognitive evaluation of symbolic/conventional meaning); a separation supporting the assertion that higher-level associative thought functions
can transcend from the conscious to the pre-cognitive by way of behavioral
conditioning. The specific modes of listening support the process of an
intense emotional experience; at the pre-conscious level, *reflexive listening* connects the sound object to the autonomic responses of the body for immediate
physiological support (e.g., a sudden noise may cause a startle, increased respiration, and perspiration), while connotative listening stimulates the perception of associated virtual stimuli (simulated multimodal sensory input that
supports the audio).

Within a more generalized cognitive appraisal, *causal listening* utilizes
the information gained to identify a potential source while *empathetic listening* uses the same data to assess affective content and propose emotional
motivation. Requiring more attuned focus on the sound, *functional listening*
describes an attempt to identify the function of the sound and, consequently,
the possible function of the source object. At the higher construal level of
audio comprehension lie semantic, *critical* (an evaluation of the associative
strength between audio and function), and *reduced listening* (an awareness of
the acoustic properties of the audio signal). Although comprehension of acoustic properties via reduced listening requires conscious higher-level cognitive
appraisal, variations in these parameters (position, movement, loudness, etc.)
have been shown to influence pre-cognitive and emotional responses (Ekman
and Kajastila 2009; Garner, Grimshaw, and Abdel Nabi 2010).

Before contextual information is attributed, a sound wave is effectively
little more than a bare scaffold, a skeletal frame that, by itself, affords no
semantic significance for the listener. As Hermann and Ritter (2004) argue,
the physical sound pressure information, if presented in any other sensory
modality, would be completely indecipherable with regard to ascribing meaning. As with other already established models of acoustic ecology, we position
contextualization as a crucial component. Situational knowledge, assumption, and expectation provide a filter that removes associations perceived to be
irrelevant (Bar 2004), allowing the mind to more efficiently reach appropriate
conclusions (for example, someone who owns a dog is likely to filter associations between light impact sounds heard during the night and the concept of
an intruder as source, attributing the sounds to movements of the dog). This
returns us once again to our emergent perception of sound, itself the product
of an aggregate of sonic components. As we discuss in much greater detail
in chapter 7, these components (as individual entities) are virtual in that they
cannot be perceived themselves as auditory experiences. While it is possible to

consciously describe contextualization, we cannot experience it; we can only experience the emergent perception that is generated when that context is aligned with the other components. Bar and Ullman (1996) argue that contextualization occurs in two stages: first, the sound stimulates the generation of associated sensory simulations; then, second, the collective information is correlated to more salient representations stored in the long-term memory. Contextualization has the capacity to alter completely a listener's perception of sound wave sources, and preceding sound wave signals are also capable of manipulating the perceived source of a subsequent sound wave (Ballas and Mullins 1991; see also chapter 2).

In *An Introduction to Acoustic Ecology*, Wrightson (2000) states that sound cannot be disconnected from the natural environment. The acoustic environment is determined by a culmination of all processes and physical properties of the world and consequently cannot be sustained without change to its nature during environmental changes. The soundscape is connected to both the individual and the environment through a bi-directional influence potential (Truax 1984) that incorporates both external and internal sound. Internal sound is referred to by Schafer (1977) as internalized dialogue, from which he suggests that such a phenomenon can modulate attention and attenuate sounds originating from the environment; he also believes that individuals may consciously restrict environmental sounds to support internal dialogue and may additionally amplify incoming environment sounds to attenuate internal dialogue. Sound reflects the ecology, establishing equilibrium across the sonic spectrum (incorporating frequency, tempo, rhythm, and volume), allowing individual sound waves to be distinguishable in even dense audio environments (Krause 1993). Listening becomes an embodied experience, dependent not only on the past memories of listeners but also on their present state and the countless interactions that occur between them and the ever-changing environment. Wrightson (2000) presents an example to elucidate this point, referring to the impact of industrialization on both the functions of sound within human society and the gradual deterioration of audition accuracy; human hearing, once capable of determining a range of audio subtleties, can now only describe sound in (comparably) polar extremes. Industrialization has also been charged with damaging the acoustic ecology in a way that ultimately is threatening to life. As earlier mentioned, Barot (1999) suggests that birds' capacities to reproduce can be limited by exposing them to a sonic barrier of artificial sounds similar to their mating calls and that blocks communication between the creatures. This argument supports the fusion of sound perception with ecology, suggesting an interrelationship whereby life has the capacity to influence sound and sound has the capacity to influence life; a concept succinctly outlined by Truax (1984).

The concept of an acoustic ecology within a virtual environment (specifically a first-person shooter [FPS]) closely reflects both embodied cognition theory and traditional acoustic ecology frameworks in that it illustrates an integrated system; it incorporates the listener, the soundscape, and the environment as interrelating and interdependent components of a single system. The acoustic ecology of the first-person shooter (Grimshaw 2008a—see Figure 3.2) was developed around a relatively rare scenario. However, it can arguably be extended to better illustrate the nature of sound in other computer game genres and virtual environments. It can also be translated to elucidate auditory processing in what we would all probably prefer to describe as the *real* world. Grimshaw and Schott (2008) describe FPS audio engines as *sonification systems*, in which individual sounds and collections of sounds have both intended meaning (as established by the designer) and received meaning (player interpretation). Grimshaw (2008a) elucidates the nature of this system via identification of the various functions of FPS sound: the individual relationships that exist between components of the system; the perceptual factors that influence interpretation; and the unique circumstances that contextualize the ecology within a computer game framework.

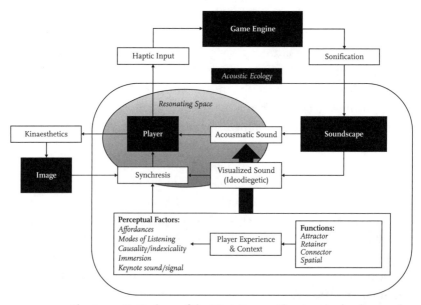

FIGURE 3.2 The Acoustic Ecology of the First-Person Shooter, single-player only.

The model shown in Figure 3.2 takes its influence primarily from computer game studies and psychoacoustics, concentrating on the connections between player, game engine, and soundscape. It is acknowledged, however, that the system illustrated here could, with minimal adaptation, operate as a more general model; changing the *image* node to incorporate all other sensory modalities and replacing *game engine* with nodes that accommodate the various phenomena of the external environment. The next steps would first be to address the nature of the player in greater detail in order to acknowledge the various embodied elements that have the potential to influence the perception of sound. Second, the terminology (specifically the use of the word *sound*) needs to be adjusted to incorporate our prioritization of sound as a perceptual entity, differentiating sound waves from fully embodied and emergently perceived sound. This more general model of sound is presented in the following section. The framework presented in Figure 3.2 is an adaptation from the Grimshaw (2008a) publication that treats sound as sound wave.

The Perceptual Acoustic Ecology

This model primarily takes its influence from the model in Figure 3.2. The perceptual acoustic ecology model (Figure 3.3) centralizes sound within the framework and attempts to consolidate the wide range of information discussed throughout this chapter. Listening modes have been placed along a continuum from high abstraction to precise detail. The various embodied concepts are accounted for and all fulfill part of the function of sound perception, adding flesh to the proverbial bones of the acoustic waveform and creating what we perceive as sound.

A concept of neural feedback is included to account for circumstances in which the outcomes of certain processes and activities are reintegrated into the perceptual processing system. These can be observed between the pre-perception node and the output neural impulses, updated physiological states and behaviors. To exemplify, we return, once more in this chapter to Claire and Alexander. Little Claire is affording her parents brief respite and is deeply engrossed in a book of grizzly children's horror stories, probably in the search for some inspiration. Despite her diligent campaign of protest, Claire is sharing her room with little Alexander who has recently been rifling through his father's stationery and has acquainted himself with the joys of both consuming ink capsules and repeated activation of click-top pens. The silence of the room is desecrated with the gradually increasing intensity and tempo of *click-click-click-click*.

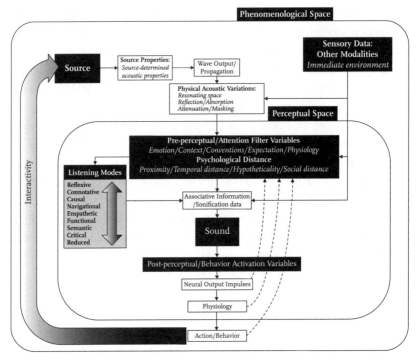

FIGURE 3.3 The Perceptual Acoustic Ecology Model.

Beginning in the physical (external) space with the source, Alexander's pen generates the sound wave that permeates the room. As the children have recently moved to this house, the room is relatively bare and the acoustic space bounces the wave off the multitude of reflective surfaces. The waves flood Claire's ear canal and hurtle toward the apex of the cochlea, transforming the waveform energy into electrical impulses. As she is at the pre-attentive stage of processing, the impulses are decoded and classified by way of the psychological distance node, which will determine the nature of the attention filter and relative emotional and cognitive activation. Temporal distance is minimal as the stimulus is happening in that instance. Proximal distance is also very low as the source is close by and the stimulus itself is in direct contact. Hypotheticality is also judged to be very low once it is established that the sound is not imaginary. Finally, social distance is classified as low because the subject of this scenario is Claire herself. Consequently, the psychological distance determines that the attention filter not only attunes to the *click* impulses but also prioritizes them over the majority of competing entities (other stimuli in the environment, thoughts, physiological sensations, etc.). Claire cannot escape the sound; she cannot focus on anything else and is consumed by it.

The impulses generated from the sound wave of Alexander's incessant *click-click-click-click* are taking prominence in Claire's mind and are appraised in relation to her expectation (*I came up here to find peace and quiet so that I could read*); to the context of the scenario (*I was really enjoying my book before that sound started*); to her changing physiological state (*My heart rate is increasing. I can feel my temperature rising also and I am literally starting to shake*); and to her sensation of emotion (*I am frustrated, irritated but above all, very, very angry!*). Her increasingly agitated state prompts more autonomic, affect-related listening modalities. Claire's priority is not to understand the sound (critical listening), nor is it to appreciate Alexander's reasoning for creating the sound (empathetic). Consequently, Claire may not even identify the sound as the clicking of a pen but, instead, listening will be connotative (sound is distraction), causal (sound is Brother), navigational (sound is to immediate right), and reflexive (respond to sound immediately). Moments later, Mum and Dad race into the bedroom. Little Alexander is in a fit of hysterics and sports a swelling bruise under his left eye. Questioning reveals that Claire has no recollection of what Alexander was doing that drove her to distraction, only that he was responsible for making a sound that interrupted her reading.

Concluding Remarks

Audition is not a truly objective process and this chapter has presented an examination of embodied cognition and psychological distance to reflect on auditory processing from a perceptual and ecological perspective. This discussion has gone so far as to suggest that embodiment factors during audition have the potential to affect the sound we perceive in a way commonly believed to only be achievable by way of direct manipulation of the sound wave and the external environment. For one listener to hear popcorn cooking in a microwave and another to hear a Geiger counter it is not necessarily a requirement that you present them with different sound waves.[1]

Referring back to our perceptual view of sound, this chapter has documented a wealth of research perspectives and theories that resonate significantly alongside our view. Sound as an *emergent perception* coincides with acoustic ecology and embodied cognition theories in that all posit that human experience is a collaborative aggregate, arising from the precise position, relation, and characteristics of each and every diverse variable (both internal and external, virtual and actual) within the ecology of existence. In addition to a notable focus on the influence of the embodied environment, the role of *spatio-temporal processes* is also acknowledged within this chapter in the time-pressured and situated views of embodied cognition.

The discussion documented in this chapter has also served to support one of our key propositions that relate to the overarching sonic virtuality concept, specifically that sound "pops out" as a singularity (developed further in chapter 7). The integrated systems of both acoustic ecology and embodied cognition theories assert that what is experienced by the individual is unceasingly connected to temporal, spatial, environmental, psychological, and physiological factors. Although not frequently and explicitly documented within existing research, this notion could logically progress to the proposition that our perception of sound is a perceptual unification of countless variables resulting in a singular experience, the singularity of sound. This is dependent on two considerations. First, that sensory stimuli cannot be separated from embodiment factors, a point repeatedly and increasingly championed by embodied cognition theory. Second, that our conscious perceptual experience is linear (we cannot consciously perceive two items simultaneously). The latter of these conditions is itself a contemporary debate, with some neuroscience research asserting that information can be processed within the brain in a non-linear fashion (van den Noort, Bosch, and Hugdahl 2005), but this refers only to pre-conscious/unconscious processing. Research specifically examining the prefrontal cortex has presented evidence that the neurons of the conscious brain regions are specialized and do not function as "multi-taskers" (Cromer, Roy, and Miller 2010, 796). Furthermore, several recent texts have been published that explicitly refute multi-tasking as myth (see Rosen 2008; Loukopoulos, Dismukes, and Barshi 2009).

Sound is therefore not the singular and independent entity of the sound wave but rather a perception of that waveform (if it exists) in conjunction with the infinitely complex and inseparable contextualizing variables of space, time, and self. The following chapter continues our exploration of the ecological model of sound with an account detailing certain elements of the endosonus, specifically our overarching representations and understandings of knowledge, certainty, belief, and truth.

4 KNOWLEDGE, CERTAINTY, TRUTH, BELIEF, AND ALIEF

Reality is that which, when you stop believing in it, doesn't go away.

—PHILIP K. DICK, 1985

Introduction

This chapter addresses our definition (*sound is an emergent perception arising primarily in the auditory cortex and that is formed through spatio-temporal processes in an embodied system*) by way of an exploration into the concepts of truth/fabrication, knowledge/belief, and certainty/uncertainty, all of which are scrutinized within the specialized framework of sound. The following are key arguments that are elaborated on and defended in this chapter: (1) distinctions made between virtual sound and real sound are invalid; (2) affective state is a key component in cognitive processing and knowledge generation and therefore must be incorporated into any model of auditory processing; (3) epistemic perspective has the potential to determine the nature of sound; (4) sound has the potential to determine epistemic perspective; and (5) sound is not a physical phenomenon but a perceptual entity, arising within the mind.

With regard to the first (and arguably most fundamental) of our arguments, and as a prelude to this discussion, we first briefly present what we entitle the "everyday" understanding of virtual sound in order that our assertion has something to position itself against. The everyday definition posits virtual sound as that which is associated with the digital world such as software, digital devices (phones, tablets, etc.), virtual reality applications, and computer video games—a form of sound that is counterpart to "real" or "natural" sound (see Bronkhorst 1995; Pulkki, Karjalainen, and Huopaniemi 1999; Nishikawa, Makino, and Rutkowski 2013; Pagliarini and Lund 2014). We use the term "everyday" to refer to this understanding because, in the majority of relevant literature, the precise nature of virtual sound is not explicitly addressed. Instead, the everyday definition of virtual sound is implied through its assumptive association with artificial/digital/ electronic systems.

We commence with various concepts characteristically associated with virtual and diegetic environments (truth, knowledge, certainty, reality, and alief) and relate them to auditory processing and information attribution to sonic stimuli. The subsequent section addresses the potential impact of epistemic perspectives on knowledge generation and classification, including an examination of *justified true belief* theory and the *Gettier problem*, before we close with two proposals. First, that the epistemic framework of the individual can dramatically alter the representational information attributed to the sonic aggregate that formulates the emergent perception of sound. Second, that sound itself has the profound capacity to influence both a person's belief structure and his or her understanding of knowledge.

Belief, Alief, and the Influence of Affect on Personal Epistemology

> Suddenly a train appeared. Women cried out with terror. Men threw themselves to one side to avoid being run over. It was panic. And triumph. (George Reyes, "Chez les Lumière" [Bottomore 1999])

In 1895, the Lumière brothers premiered *L'Arrivée d'un train en gare de La Ciotat*, in which a steam locomotive was filmed moving directly toward the camera. Although the reaction to this now infamous example of motion picture illusion has become something of an urban myth, it is generally acknowledged that both individuals and groups have, on occasion, been drawn into a work of fiction so immersive that they respond to it as if it were real. This could be explained as the result of similarities between the neural activity patterns of real and associated unreal/virtual/representational events (Blascovich and Bailenson 2011). Empirical studies within neuroscience have unfortunately produced very little evidence in relation to comparable neural networks between equivalent real activities and simulated representations (e.g., firing a pistol at a range or in a computer game). However, recent functional magnetic resonance imaging (fMRI) experiments have suggested that mental reimagining of an experience from long-term memory can produce patterns of brain activity highly correlated to those produced during the actual event (Buchsbaum et al.

2012). Although such claims are not without criticism, a pertinent question is nonetheless raised: if it is true that recall from memory and actual experience produce comparable neural activity patterns, could this not also imply similar correlation between virtual experience and physical experience? Here it should be noted that the term "virtual" is referring more to its modern, technological definition (specifically, games/simulations, imagined experience, fiction, and memory) as opposed to "virtual as potential" (see chapter 7). While we warm up the fMRI machine, this hypothesis could explain how our ability to clearly distinguish actuality from virtuality is restricted, and although we may be motivated to believe the contrary (certainty supports decision making and acceptance of circumstances and offers comfort in control), our grasp on truth, certainty, reality, and knowledge could, in fact, be rather limited.

This section of the chapter explores the nature of belief and associated concepts within the context of computer games and the modality of sound. Recent ontological perspectives and concepts are scrutinized to assess their good fit into an overarching framework of knowledge and truth for computer gameplay experience. The section concludes with a discussion about this framework and suggests that it is our affective state that resides at the helm of our perception of reality, both within games and beyond.

From an ontological perspective, computer games represent a significant stage in our understanding of reality. Years before, the fictional novel became a physical embodiment of diegetic realities, previously existing only as stories within the memory and transmitted by speech. Written works of fiction enabled the individual to read the text and enter alternate existences, connected to reality but distinct from it also. Similarly, various forms of theater and then the motion picture presented fictional realities that could be observed and shared simultaneously by many. Across time, people experiencing these entities have reported powerful sensations of immersive belief in which, on some psychological level, they experience a blurring of the distinctions between reality and fiction.

The primary contribution of computer games to this phenomenon is arguably interactivity. Introducing interactivity has given fictions and diegetic narratives great immediacy and presence, and the requirement of direct user action creates a distinct bi-directional bridge between the fiction and reality. While entities outside the computer game have enabled interaction with artificial realities, narratives, and characters, none have done so to such a dramatic extent and, if asked to name an interactive medium within which individuals can explore and interact with worlds beyond our actuality, computer games and similar virtual worlds would likely be a common response.

Originally documented in the early 19th century by Samuel Taylor Coleridge, suspension of disbelief referred to the concept that an individual may disregard fantastic elements of a narrative to enable immersion into the diegetic world (see Ferri 2007). J.R.R. Tolkien's quest of Frodo Baggins to Mordor would have been less likely to enrapture readers and audiences if they were constantly assessing the realism of the narrative by way of direct comparison to (what they considered to be) reality. One interesting component of the suspension of disbelief concept is that it must contain a degree of perceived truth, relatable to human interest. This brings to mind circumstances in which people have attempted to further the power of disbelief by integrating fictional material into factually oriented systems. If you were to visit Google Maps and ask for walking directions from *the Shire* to *Mordor*, you would be presented with the following warning (working as of June 2013): "Use caution—One does not simply walk into Mordor." Suspension of disbelief may originally have been defined within the context of literature. However the concept of accepting the fantastic on the condition that clear reference to reality and human experience are also present has been expanded on to consider computer games (e.g., Schwartz 2006; Lewis, Weber, and Bowman 2008). Here, the general proposition is that computer games present material that contains enough association with our popular conception of reality to recontextualize fantastic elements within a more plausible and *actual* framework.

Suspension of disbelief can be observed in sound design, notably, in computer games or films that require soundscapes and point sounds to sonically characterize fantastic creatures and environments. A lightsaber may not (yet. . .) exist and therefore no sound currently can be auditioned that is a lightsaber, but yet, within the same moment, it can.

While there can be no direct foundation in the physical world, the sound of the lightsaber is arguably highly believable due to indirect connections to reality. The sound is highly reminiscent of a fluorescent lightbulb, a device with several physical characteristics shared by the lightsaber. The development of the lightsaber timbre is also matched to the movement of the device onscreen, the oscillations carefully synchronized to the visible thrusts and parries. While there is no guarantee that such a device will be manufactured beyond fiction, the sound of the lightsaber is unmistakable and for the majority of listeners, undeniable. Interestingly, should such a device ever become a reality, its sound would potentially be quite different from the fictional incarnation and there is the opportunity for people to dislike the actual product because its sound is not "authentic."

In *Belief and Imagination: Explorations in Psychoanalysis* (1998), Ronald Britton deliberates on suspension of *belief*, a theorization that a fact may be known to an individual but not believed. Related to the Freudian term *Verleugnung* (disavowal), suspension of belief was presented (by Freud in 1938, documented in Britton 1998) as a scenario in which a person may acknowledge the existence of an entity but dramatically underrate its significance: "Belief is willingly suspended to avoid the emotional consequences, and the resultant state is one of *psychic unreality*" (1998, 15). Suspending one's belief is a behavior that makes recurring appearances within literature, film, television, and computer videogames as what we identify as the "this is not happening" effect. From the government agent dressed in an alien suit, himself the victim of an alien abduction, rocking back and forth in a cage, his head in his hands repeating "this is not happening" (Jose Chung's "From Outer Space," *The X-Files*, 1996), to one of a band of four zombie-apocalypse survivors, having just reached an airlift extraction point to find the last helicopter moving away to the horizon, they bend down toward the ground in exhaustion before exclaiming "this is not happening" (*Left 4 Dead 2*, Valve 2009).

In terms of auditory perception this could relate to scenarios in which sound is demoted in priority or even "tuned out completely" to avoid stress and anxiety; for example, after prolonged exposure a child may pathologically ignore the sound of her parents shouting (Cohen 2013). This concept has distinct similarities to that of *cognitive blunting* (a lack of emotional reactivity often characterized as an underestimation of threat; see Abrams and Taylor 1978) and can be exemplified, again with reference to sound, in computer game contexts in which the player refuses to acknowledge the threat associations that he or she has instinctively attributed to a particular sound. As the player moves through the bowels of a derelict spacecraft, the deep growl he hears coming from the ventilation system immediately above him is embodied with associative imagery that clearly signifies a snarling beast of some sort. Our player, however, suppresses this instinct and chooses to believe the sound is merely the air conditioning system malfunctioning; in this way he can avoid panicking.

The nature of both suspensions of belief and disbelief is such that we cannot presently observe them, only their subsequent effects. Consequently, we cannot state whether the underlying system is simply an attenuation of belief/disbelief or an active entity in its own right. Tamar Szabó Gendler (2008a) asserts the latter and presents the concept of *alief* as a discrete agent acting within psychological processing. The concept of alief "can be characterized as a mental state with associatively-linked content that is representational, affective, and behavioral, and that is activated—consciously or unconsciously—by features of the subject's internal or ambient environment" (1). According to Gendler, a key feature of alief is that it is responsible for directly activating behavioral response, a characteristic that is perhaps the most controversial aspect of this concept. Gendler describes alief as existing in one of two forms: concordant with belief, and discordant with belief. Concordant alief is purported by Gendler to be unobservable as its response effects are identical to those produced from belief. In contrast, discordant alief refers to circumstances in which the alief directly challenges and overcomes an associated belief. Gendler asserts, irrespective of whether alief and belief are in agreement, that human response (described by Gendler as "behavioral activation") is always determined by alief, without which we simply would not be able to act within the world.

The basis for Gendler's concept has been challenged, most commonly by the claim that integration of an active unit does not further our understanding of how belief, decision, and action work (Mandelbaum 2012). However, irrespective of the appropriateness of the term alief to such an explanation, the proposition that there exists an underlying state of affairs in which an individual is prompted to behave in a manner that directly contradicts his apparent belief structure or sense of knowledge or certainty is less susceptible to questioning; thus we are content to use the term as a succinct reference to this proposition. We argue that one reason for the existence of a phenomenon such as alief is the abundance of exemplifying, real-world examples one can generate in which alief is observable.

If we consider some of the original examples Gendler presents to illustrate alief, we can observe several consistencies between them that may better describe the underlying phenomenon:

> An atheist refuses to sign a pact to sell her soul to the devil, despite knowing the pact is a prop, created by another person for the purposes of an experiment (Gendler 2008a, 556).

> A participant observes wine being poured into two glasses. One glass is labeled *poison* (a label she herself affixed). She insists on drinking from the other glass (Gendler 2008b, 636).

> A tourist refuses to stand on a clear glass walkway, suspended over the Grand Canyon though he believes it to be perfectly safe (Gendler 2010, 256).

To provide a computer game sound example, consider an individual playing through an intense survival horror game, walking down a darkened corridor with visibility near zero. From within the darkness, he hears a tortured and unnatural scream echoing down the corridor; reacting, the player raises his weapon and pulls the trigger—only to hear a *click* sound. He immediately recognizes the sound as the pistol hammer hitting an empty chamber and he consequently believes the weapon is out of ammunition. As the source of the scream seems to be drawing closer to the player, however, we hear several more *click, click, clicks* as he continues to depress the trigger; the player is desperately trying to summon one more bullet from the ether. In this scenario, Gendler would describe the process that led to this belief-contradictory action as an alief. Such an event could be explained by suggesting that the player was subconsciously repeating a clichéd action he would have likely observed in film or television, in which weapons are repeatedly clicked in case of misfire. However, even if this were the case, an alief is still present. Virtual guns (typically) do not misfire and ammunition status is almost always reinforced by a heads-up display, showing the exact number of bullets remaining. We are not insisting that this example could only be acceptably explained by way of alief, but there does appear to be a phenomenon present by which established beliefs (*my weapon has no more ammunition*) are challenged by an irrational thought process (*a few more pulls of the trigger—just in case*) and despite the available evidence supporting the former (gun did not fire, ammo heads-up display reads as empty), the observable action relates to the latter (the player keeps trying to fire).

We propose that the primary factor unifying all of these examples is emotion, specifically fear. In Gendler's examples, fear is evoked by way of uncertainty. The atheist may claim to *know* the pact is false but the underlying fear of the alternative (eternity in hell) raises doubt due to its emotional weighting (*I know it's not real but why take the chance—just in case*). The participant may know that logically there cannot be poison in the glass, but fear of the alternative (the wine really is poisoned) drives her action (*what if this is a trick and somehow this wine is poisoned? I should avoid it—just in case*). The tourist can observe many others walking safely across the walkway and believes it to be safe. However, fear of the alternative (it will collapse and I will fall to my death) determines the response (*there's always the chance I could fall. Better not tempt fate—just in case*). The player knows his ammunition is depleted, but in the face of death pulls the trigger irrespectively (*I have no bullets remaining but I'll fire again—just in case*). All of these beliefs are clearly based on evidence, logic, and deductive reasoning while the opposing aliefs are emotionally motivated.

The neural dynamics of these scenarios can be related to Liberman and Trope's (2010) theory of psychological distance (see chapter 3), in which they present four variables (distances) that influence thought processing and decision making: temporal, geographical, social, and hypothetical. Relating to the previous survival horror game example, the player would assess these four variables: temporal distance (how much time would there be to escape); geographical proximity (spatial distance from danger); hypotheticality (chances of death if attacked); and social connection to potential victim. In this case, temporal and geographical distances would both be small (the screams imply that the source is close and approaching rapidly) as would hypothetical and social distance (*your* death is almost *certain*). Liberman and Trope assert that as psychological distance decreases, thought processes become less abstract and more specified. We extend this, based on neuroscience theory, to suggest that as psychological distance reaches extreme lows, an *affective threshold* is breached. In response, cognitive neural activity scatters and the affective processing assumes majority control. This could explain how, as the tourist moves closer onto the platform, temporal and geographical distance decrease causing increased fear and inability to draw comfort from the rational knowledge that the platform is secure. Suddenly, a danger that seemed extraordinarily unlikely becomes consuming. Gendler also presents examples that do not appear to relate to fearful experience:

A spectator watches a television rerun of a sports match and loudly shouts at the players (2008a, 552).

A man sets his watch 5 minutes fast to avoid being late (2010, 286).

A woman searches for her wallet to hold money she has been given to cover her expenses, despite having recently lost her wallet (2010, 257–258).

Fear is not explicitly present within these scenarios but there does appear to be an implication of anxiety, an emotional experience described as "overlapping" with fear (Öhman 2010, 710). Irrespective of the presence of fear, a comparable outcome (contradiction of belief as observable in action) occurs nevertheless. We would assert that an additional consistency is observable; this time it is attention filtering and immersion. The spectator is aware the match is a television rerun but his immersion in the game reduces his attention on that fact and, instead, focuses on evidence that would hold true if the game were live and he was actually present (the sound of the crowd cheering, the color of the playing field, etc.). Setting your watch 5 minutes fast is often effective as a short-term immersion within a false reality you have created (unless your watch was actually 5 minutes slow beforehand—in which case you have yourself a Gettier problem—explained later). You may know the watch is incorrect but brief glances during a hectic morning routine filter this information and focus attention on the immediate data (the observable time). The woman searching for her wallet is also briefly immersed within a false reality due to her attention, filtering out her knowledge that the wallet is missing and focusing on a more immediate alternative (*I need to find something to hold this money. Of course, a wallet would work perfectly!*). While fear may not be central to these examples, we would posit that emotion is steadfast at the helm. The spectator has a significant passion for his team and consequently is more susceptible to attention filtering and immersion. The man with the fast watch is under emotional stress from temporal pressure and therefore his processing of representational data is limited and stimuli are responded to at face value. The woman experiences elation in response to discovering a solution to her immediate money-holding problem; consequently, knowledge that would contradict the affect-driven task (of searching for her wallet) is restricted.

As with the previous concepts, alief in circumstances that are not immediately fear-related can also be exemplified with reference to sound:

A young motorist customizes her hatchback exhaust to create a timbre closer to that of a sports car. By way of the idea that she is driving a performance car, the resultant sound creates an alief when it causes her to drive faster.

A man is attending a karaoke party but is acutely aware that he is tone deaf and insistent that he cannot and will not perform. His friends attempt to coerce him to perform with rapturous applause, a chorus of cheers, and an almost hypnotic mantra, gradually increasing in tempo and intensity. The soundscape is emotionally overwhelming, and the man launches into an enamel-stripping rendition of *My Way*.

A woman is involved in a certain massively multi-player online role-playing game of the fantasy variety and has been playing for seven hours. She knows she has to stop playing (her eyes are beginning to strain and she is late for an appointment) but her mind is replaying, again and again, the grand sweeping sound indicative of advancing an experience level. The emotion-driven motivation the sound creates overrules her knowledge, and she continues to play despite the belief that, after seven hours of trying, she will not advance and will always fall at the last hurdle.

Referring back to our thesis, specifically the concept of the sonic aggregate, the notion that individuals may experience sound and simultaneously engage with that sound in contradictory ways across varying states of consciousness testifies to the complexity and scale of the relationship of the components of the aggregate. These vignettes are potential scenarios in which the sonic aggregate is not bound to a single understanding but rather a potentiality of multiple, context-based understandings.

If we are to accept that emotional activity has the capability to suppress cognition (Lerner, Small, and Loewenstein 2004; Phelps 2006), then we could propose that if the stakes are raised high enough, the individual's capacity to appraise data comprehensively and rationally is heavily restricted. As a result, the certainty value of anyone's beliefs can be undermined (albeit temporarily, in most cases). In their work *Emotion*, Shiota and Kalat (2011) discriminate between the constant and unyielding linear epistemology of Western culture and the interrelated, constantly evolving dialectical epistemology of the East. They identify correlations between these alternative epistemologies and a general characteristic of emotional experience, namely, ambivalence or mixed emotions. Shiota and Kalat identify a causal association between epistemology and emotion, suggesting that the discrete Aristotelian differentiation between truth and façade leads Western cultures to experience unambiguous emotional states while the more obscure Confucianist distinctions lead Eastern cultures to greater emotional ambiguity. This distinction between Eastern and Western cultures reflects the desires of Western academic and technical philosophy to reject ambiguity in favor of precision and objectivity. This may also explain the enviable ability of Eastern horror makers to create remarkably effective soundscapes that instill genuine terror in audiences across the world. We expand on this position and assert that the causal effect is bi-directional and the emotional profile (whether of the individual, group, or even culture) has equivalent potential to influence our epistemic beliefs within both ephemeral and perennial scenarios.

Returning briefly to the Grand Canyon, our intrepid tourist may consider himself an empiricist, deriving truth and certainty from observable stimuli (*I have been informed by an authority the walkway is safe. I see many people on the walkway and they are fine. I therefore know it is safe*). As he approaches the walkway, psychological distance shifts attention toward the fear-inducing alternative so that, as its power increases, the certainty of safety decreases and knowledge is downgraded to assumption (*I'm sure it's probably safe*). The tourist may then take refuge in foundationalism-based arguments (*I did that bungee jump last year and that was fine, and this is probably even safer. They wouldn't let people on it if they weren't absolutely sure it was safe*) as psychological distance decreases further. A foray into skepticism could follow; as the poor tourist takes his first tentative steps onto the walkway he begins to question every logical argument considered thus far (*how can I possibly be certain this walkway is safe, I just don't know anymore*). This process is, of course, hypothetical but does nevertheless resonate with the other concepts documented earlier and it remains possible that the nature of our relationships with knowledge, certainty, truth, and reality are heavily susceptible to the surrounding environment and our affective state.

With reference to sound, Tuuri and colleagues (2007) differentiate eight discrete modes of listening that are determined by the degree to which our mental functioning is being dictated, either by more cognitive or more subcortical influences (fully discussed in Garner 2013 and also in chapter 3). Relating this back to alief, sounds that evoke significantly intense emotional states will dictate that subsequent auditory processing will be focused in a particular way until a normative affective level is regained. This "high-intensity emotional" state will influence not only listeners' internal mental processing but also their overt external actions. For example, our theoretical game player is navigating a virtual forest environment within which he must walk over an old bridge across a substantial gorge. Prior to playing he has been shown (and is convinced) that the game will not allow the bridge to collapse. As the player begins to cross, the soundscape encourages a neutral and relaxed state, only presenting the player with the sounds of his virtual footsteps. The neutral state supports high cognition and a critical listening mode (meaning the player is evaluating the realism of the sound). This listening mode reinforces his sense of safety, and he is not thinking that the bridge could collapse as he moves quickly and smoothly onto it. When the player is halfway across, there is an abrupt creak and snap of one of the wooden footholds and he immediately halts. The unexpectedness of this sound wave creates an instantaneous rush of intense emotion that determines, in part, how the sound wave is listened to and how the sound is perceptually formed. Reflexive listening (automated peripheral processing that completely bypasses the cognitive brain regions to enable immediate aversive action) is engaged, causing the player to completely abandon in that instant his prior certainty regarding safety. After a few moments the emotion begins to subside and the player is able to evaluate the sound again more critically. However, as he continues along the bridge, although he still believes that it will not collapse, he proceeds with far less haste and much greater care.

The overarching proposition of this section is that our experience in the world has fundamental influence over how we respond to it. Chiefly due to our affective state, epistemic perspectives are not always fixed, and crucially, as they fluctuate, so does the stream of information that our attention extracts from a stimulus as do the output propositions (statements of knowledge/belief) that we generate. What we believe to be true as knowledge can be reinforced or completely undermined by the emotional nature of our embodied experience. Similarly, a particular emotionally intense scenario has the potential to drive physiological and behavioral responses that completely contradict an established cognitive belief structure. Additionally, this phenomenon is not limited to short-term effects and, with retrospect, may cause individuals to update their belief structure, perhaps through realization that, once severely tested, they have abandoned that particular belief, as evidenced by their behavior. The following section goes into greater detail in examining the potential impact of such a process on the means by which we perceive sound, questioning whether our epistemic perspectives could impact the way in which the mind realizes, characterizes, and contextualizes sound. Furthermore, through our perceptual view of sound, we assert that the reverse is also true: that the changing disposition of our knowledge and beliefs is an influencing factor on the structure and content of sound itself.

Epistemological Perspectives and Auditory Processing

This section presents a concise explanation of the most prominent approaches to knowledge and assesses their import for our view of the perception of sound. Much as we asserted earlier, here we maintain that the nature of our belief structures and attitudes to knowledge (epistemological perspectives) have a distinct bearing on how we process sound and on our cognitive and behavioral responses to sonic stimuli. Therefore we posit that epistemological perspectives (incorporating truth, certainty, meaning, existence, and knowledge) are worthy of acknowledgment within the endosonic set of our sonic aggregate framework. Bearing in mind the wide variety of epistemological perspectives, this section by no means intends to provide an encyclopedic account of epistemology but instead focuses on some of the primary schools of thought that exist within this philosophical study in relation to sound and our experience of it.

Within the pages of *Critique of Pure Reason* (1781), Immanuel Kant discusses two dichotomies of knowledge; first, the "analytic-synthetic" distinction, and second, differentiation of a priori and a posteriori. The former dichotomy relates to the structure of a judgment. Analytic knowledge is gained simply by way of understanding the meanings of the terms within the proposition, as the predicate (e.g., sound wave) is embedded within its associated subject concept (e.g., an acoustic entity is a sound wave = a sound wave is sound). Conversely, the predicate in synthetic knowledge exists outside of the subject concept (e.g., the sound of the teleport was loud). A priori and a posteriori refer to the requirement of experience to form knowledge, the former capable of generation independently of experience and the latter necessitating it. It is widely acknowledged that all analytic knowledge is also a priori (does not require experience to obtain knowledge). Less certain however is the assertion that all a priori knowledge is also analytic, with Kant championing the notion of *synthetic* a priori, questioning if it is possible to generate propositions beyond the constraints of analytic knowledge but without actual experience. The synthetic a priori became the foundation for transcendental idealism that, in turn, reconstructed contemporary metaphysics, natural science, and pure mathematics (Meibos 1998).

The distinctions between these forms are arguably quite obscure and it has been asserted by Quine (1953) that no statement can ever be truly analytic because some form of experience is always a requisite at some point. For us then, analytic statements are best understood as those that arise from judgments based primarily on prior "established knowledge" from the past, while a synthetic statement will be subject to more temporally immediate input. We should also note that this understanding would further suggest that synthetic statements can age, essentially becoming more analytic in character, should their foundation not be updated. The relevance of these distinct forms of knowledge to sound can be elucidated when we consider how multiple listeners, presented with the same material soundscape, form bespoke sonic aggregates based within their individual minds. These aggregates can be distinguished between listeners by the knowledge structure they employ during audition. For example, while attending a music concert one listener may appraise the performance from an analytic position, as she carries preconceived ideas and expectations. The immediate acoustic soundscape may also evoke intense memories of past musical experiences that add to the sonic aggregate, contextualizing the immediate stimuli to create a unique experience. Another listener may conversely experience the performance from a more synthetic position, with no prior expectations. During audition she makes little connection to past experiences or associations and instead focuses on the immediate sensory environment.

For many within the general population, knowledge is a much simpler concept and could possibly be traced back to our childhoods, in which we are told that "to think" is to have an opinion whereas "to know" is to be certain and true. What our parents seem to have failed to account for is our delightful talent for inferring additional information. In this case, we learned that if to think is merely opinion, then there is much greater strength in our arguments if we say *we know*. For example, little siblings Alexander and Claire are arguing over whose turn it is to use the Sing and Splash Fish Bath toy they both cherish so much. Neither child remembers who used it last. Dad, in his infinite wisdom, directly questions the squabbling rascals in an attempt to discover whose turn it is, first addressing Alexander, who responds *I think Claire had it last*. Dad turns to Claire, who has mastered this strategy ahead of her little brother; she responds *I know that Alexander had it last!* Dad is presented with all the evidence he needs and promptly awards the Sing and Splash Fish Bath toy to Claire, who is now feeling rather smug.[1]

Auditory perception can be related to our experience of "thinking" and "knowing" when we consider how sound is formed in response to a sound wave stimulus. While sound waves can be crafted in a way that adjusts their potential to be "known" (fully comprehended in terms of meaning, function, context, etc.), this is only a potential that (in terms of artificially manufactured sound) is based on the creator's assumptions of the listener. Such contextual content cannot physically travel within the waveform. Consequently, when the actual sound emerges it may be very different from the designer's intentions. If a sound wave is "known," then it will more likely be embodied by certainty and a specific individual context (*I know that sound is birdsong*). If we "think" we understand the sound wave, then the sonic aggregate becomes more cluttered, potentially including the correct context but also information regarding potential alternatives and, of course, any sound that emerges will also be further characterized by a sense of uncertainty and associative emotional influence (*I think that creaking is just the pipes, but it could be the kids out of bed, or the wind, or an intruder...*).

The potential to perceive sound as widely contrasting in meaning can significantly impact our responses, creating scenarios in which a single sound wave can evoke very different responses between listeners. For example, while using an early home computer operating system interface, a user is presented with two tones, one of ascending pitch, and the other descending.

The tones were designed to be sonifications of incoming and outgoing email messages, the former by being reminiscent of an approaching object and the latter reflecting an object moving away. However, when our listener contextualizes the descending tone, he visualizes a rocket ship coming into land and associates this tone with something moving toward him. Consequently, each time he sends an email, the confirmation tone makes him believe he has just received one and he immediately checks his inbox to find it empty, again.

Alternative scenarios may also present themselves where individuals have no clear justification for their beliefs nor are they actually true, yet the holder nevertheless insists that a particular proposition is something that she "knows" as a result of intense emotion-driven motivation. This relates to the suspension of belief principle discussed earlier. For example, little Alexander and Claire are once again fighting something fierce. Policed by their parents the question is proposed: *Who started it?* The inevitable eventuality occurs: *He did! No, she did!* The truth was that little Alexander started it (some hair was pulled as part of an empirical study on gender pain threshold differences) and he presents no evidence or logical argument to support his claim. However, he is terrified that if the blame is put on him, then the punishment will be severe and his aversive, fearful state is so intense that the knowledge concerning the actual instigator has been genuinely forgotten.

Intense emotional stress has been connected to our capacity to recall sensory (including auditory) experiences (see Christianson 1992). The potential for emotion to impact on our cognitive processes could be connected to our physiology, thus accommodating embodiment theory. Muchnik, Hildesheimer, and Rubinstein (1980) argue that extreme stress raises the level of blood catecholamines in the ear and overstimulates cochlear sympathetic innervation, with the effect of attenuating the sound wave and causing the listener to experience a muted soundscape (relating to Ekman's example, outlined in chapter 3, in which soldiers may experience auditory acuity or blunting as a result of extreme stress).

The purpose of this section is not to promote a particular epistemic perspective over the many alternatives but instead to elucidate the presence of these tenets and their power over the realities of the belief-holders. This assertion is then applied to auditory perception as we posit that personal epistemic perspectives are capable of manipulating the very nature of sound. A review of several of the more prominent epistemological perspectives reveals two overarching and, interestingly, contradictory observations. The first is the instability and interpretative nature of each perspective's core propositions. Several pathways have diverging sub-perspectives that have been generated in response to critiques of the original. In contemporary philosophy, such appraisals are presented rather frequently, contributing to the instability and fluctuating characteristics of the study. The second observation is that few of these perspectives are unique and, instead, share several features with neighboring attitudes. The empiricist's reliance on sensory data resonates with the externalist's association of knowledge to factors that exist outside of the mind. Both the idealist and the solipsist maintain that there is no certainty of the existence of an objective world beyond our perception. The positivist, rationalist, reliabilist, and skeptic all believe in the necessity of empirical data to the acquisition of knowledge. Conceptual discord arises most prominently in the fine details or semantic differences but, nevertheless, it appears that although the existence of many different opinions with regard to the nature of knowledge and truth is unquestionable, the differences themselves are only sometimes hugely significant.

One of the most long-standing characterizations of knowledge is that of *justified true belief*. Referred to as "the standard account of knowledge" (Dancy 1985), justified true belief is essentially a three-point requirement for a proposition to be worthy of being called *knowledge*; it must be (1) true; (2) believed to be true; and (3) justified in being believed to be true. For example, while playing a computer game, the player perceives a sound she believes to represent an approaching alien horde. If her belief is true (the sound was indeed indicative of an imminent alien threat) and she is justified in this belief (the last three times that particular sound was perceived, it immediately preceded an alien attack), then justified true belief would consider the proposition as knowledge.

With regard to epistemic theory, the state of play shifted dramatically in 1963 with the advent of scenarios that appeared to fulfill the requirements of justified true belief yet could still be argued not to qualify as knowledge. Consider this example, again relating to computer game sound: immersed in a dense virtual soundscape with computer-generated characters hustling and bustling all around her, the player hears a phone ringing and believes it to be her cellular phone. The sound she is hearing is actually from within the game, yet her belief is justified as, coincidentally, the sound has the same tone and rhythm as her phone's ringtone. However, her actual cellular phone, by chance, is also ringing at that exact moment, and when she stops the game, the ringing continues, revealing her belief to be true.

The ringtone vignette is an example of a Gettier problem, named after Edmund Gettier, who asserted that justified true belief was critically flawed and that it is possible to believe a truth, but through a false justification. In such scenarios, the outcome that the individual perceived as true (known) does, in fact, occur but was reached by way of chance and not knowledge. Within the game sound example, all three requirements of *standard knowledge* (justified true belief) are met, essentially as the result of what is commonly termed an illusion being presented simultaneously with the truth, with the sensory input from the illusion masking that from the true sound. Other Gettier problems are dissimilar in their finer details, but all appear to embody the same overarching structure: false perception precedes true conclusion. This *false premises* simplification corresponds to all alternative forms of Gettier problem. Classic examples listed by Gendler (of which the first two are the original *cases* documented by Edmund Gettier in his 1963 article) include these:

A man (Smith) presumes a rival will surpass him in a job interview (false premise) and knows that this man holds ten coins in his pocket so concludes that, *the man with ten coins in his pocket will get the job.* In actuality, Smith is awarded the job but both men are carrying ten coins, so even though the initial premise is false the final conclusion is correct. (122)

Jones believes Smith owns a Ford (false premise) and by way of *disjunction introduction logic* (a comparison of ridiculous notion against justified knowledge) finally concludes that, *Smith owns a Ford or Brown is in Barcelona.* In actuality, the ridiculous notion is true which, as the initial premise is false, results in the final conclusion being correct. (122–123)

Smith makes a connection between a set of evidence and the notion that his wife is having an affair (false premise). His final conclusion is that his wife is being unfaithful. In actuality, all of the evidence Smith gathered is indicative of a surprise birthday party his wife is planning for him. However, his wife is also having an affair and therefore his final conclusion remains correct. (Burns 2014)

We now refer back to our overarching definition of sound, presented within our opening chapter: *Sound is an emergent perception arising primarily in the auditory cortex and that is formed through spatio-temporal processes in an embodied system.* Relating to the notion of virtuality, this description incorporates two of our introductory component propositions that have particular relevance here: *the virtual component of sound is initially potential;* and it requires *a listener for it to be formed within the here and now.* Based on this, it becomes possible to characterize the concept of sonic virtuality as a Gettier problem. To better illustrate, the player is interacting with a virtual environment and attuning to its soundscape. She is considering the nature of the game she is playing and distinguishes sound waves emanating from her speakers or headphones as virtual because they have origins within the game (like previous example 3, the false premise is the logical deduction or assumption of causality that the player is making). Her final conclusion is that sounds arising from a computer game are virtual. Based on our fundamental definition of virtual, the logical deduction utilized is ultimately flawed, but the player's final conclusion remains correct. The sound waves emitted from the television set *are* virtual, not because of their origin, but because at the point of derivation they have not yet reached the auditory processing routines of the brain. It is consequently no more than an energy waveform, a collection of amplitude and frequency distributions with no meaning or semantic associations yet attributed, thus, potential, thus, virtual. Sound waves, material and sensuous, do not carry the additional information that becomes the fundamental characteristic of a sonic experience; said information is ascribed, from the mind of the receiver, to the spatial and temporal contextualization within which the sound wave occurred. Referring back to the beginning of this chapter, our theory underlying the example illustrated is in clear contradiction with the "everyday" definition of virtual sound, which would differentiate real from virtual sound based on the identified origin. For us, real and virtual are not counterpart, virtual being instead positioned as a mode of the real. All components of the sonic aggregate are actual (e.g., loudspeakers, sound wave, memory, emotion); the virtuality exists in the possibilities of the aggregate, one of which is actualized into the emergent perception of sound.

Analysis into both the nature of Gettier problems and the fundamental arguments that differentiate the various schools of epistemic thought indicates that the component of justified true belief most under scrutiny is justification. There appears to be present a relative *continuum of justification standard* that differentiates epistemic perspective by which particular attitudes demand (what could be described as) increased exhaustiveness of evidentiary analysis. This essentially separates perspectives by how much scientific rigor is required before the mantle of knowledge can be awarded to a proposition. For example, coherentism necessitates that a proposition is concordant within the system it is a part of and, therefore, to satisfy requirement for knowledge, it must contradict as few established knowledge-units as possible. Coherentist listening would therefore be expected to observe genuine knowledge in propositions with properties that are consistent within an associated set. For example, the listener auditions the sound of a zombie growl in a survival horror game that shares many properties with a sound he has heard before. The more prior experiences of this sound, consistently presented in tandem with an attacking zombie, the player has had, the greater the attributed truth-value (*This sound is typically representative of zombies in most other games I have played and films I have seen. I have just heard the sound and therefore I know that a zombie is about to attack*). In comparison, an empiricist argues that knowledge comes only, or primarily, from sensory experience and observation.

Depending on whether the nature of your empiricist perspective leans toward "knowledge comes only" or "knowledge comes primarily," empiricism can be significantly more demanding than constructivism, as the proposition must be directly derived from observation. To presume that a particular sound was inherently indicative of a specific object/action based on related scenarios would be incorrect. Instead, the meaning of the sound could only be established as knowledge once the connection was directly observed within that particular context (by which point, and in the context of a survival horror game, you'd likely be a brain buffet for the undead). Within these strict limitations, very few conclusions could be designated as knowledge because any inference or deduction causes invalidation of the proposition.

To elucidate this in greater detail and with reference to computer game sound, we return to our prior assertion that sound is *not* the physical waves of energy distributed from the source but, instead, is the emergent perception constructed by way of neural processing and existing only in the precise temporal present, originating in the brain and located in the mind. Based on this concept, sound can potentially be fundamentally altered depending on epistemic perspective. We also return to little Alexander and Claire, who are actually playing together during a brief moment of sibling cooperation. Playing a survival horror game that is undoubtedly too mature for them, the two have found themselves in a darkened derelict warehouse. Above them is a faint sound that both of them recognize as a woman crying. Neither is presented

FIGURE 4.1 As his sweat absorbed into the sleeves he was using to cover his eyes, his heart drumming in his chest—and he could swear a skeletal hand (this time not belonging to Nana) hovered menacingly just behind his neck—Alexander considered that this game might be a little too mature for him.

with any supplemental information within the precise context of the game. Alexander takes a foundationalist perspective, assessing the sound against abstract but reliable theory (*Crying indicates sadness. Someone needs my help. I hear the sound of an innocent woman crying*). Contrary to her little brother, Claire employs a coherentist analysis, appraising the sound within a less general and more contextually relevant system—that of the survival horror genre (*Crying indicates deception. Someone is trying to lure us in. I hear the sound of an enemy*). Later in the game, the duo is exploring an old manor house and both hear a scratching sound through one of the walls (see Figure 4.1). Claire takes an empiricist approach to evaluation, assessing the acoustic features of the sound (*The sound is soft, steady, and stationary. There's nothing to be scared of. I hear a mouse*). Little Alexander, however, is more the skeptic, doubting all immediately available information and considering alternative propositions (*We've never heard that sound in this place before. It could be anything. We should be scared. I hear a monster*).

Coming Full Circle: From Sound to Emotion, Then to Knowledge and to Sound

This concluding section addresses one final question for which we seek to present a potential answer: is it possible that the relationship between epistemic belief and sound is bi-directional? If we refer to our last example in the prior section, it could be questioned: would Alexander have employed a skeptical appraisal if he had not been afraid? Did fear ascend from epistemic perspective, or did epistemic perspective ascend from fear? If the sound evoked the fear that, in turn, determined the perspectives regarding knowledge, does sound not have potential? This brings the conceptual process full circle and presents scenarios in which sound determines emotion, that determines epistemic perspective (and also belief, alief, etc.), that returns to determine sound. If we are to acknowledge the existence of these various contrasting epistemic approaches to knowledge and certainty, we can also concur that, currently, there is no universally approved conceptualization of knowledge, nor is there likely to be such an agreement in the foreseeable future. The simple question raised here is, for what reason is there such a divide across humanity with regard to the nature of something that we all have a concept of? Is there a variable, within human thought processing, that causes this divergence between people of not only different cultures, but potentially between two people who have experienced the majority of their lives together within a shared environment?

Our proposed answer to this question lies within the pragmatic perspective, asserting that a proposition becomes knowledge when there exists an emotion-driven motivation for the individual. While pragmatism is traditionally less subjective and "benefit" typically refers to more altruistic ambitions, we assert that knowledge is simply an expression of certainty, an epitome of belief-security and emotional congruence that drives decisive action. The fundamental variable of belief itself is justification, a requirement that can be satisfied largely by motivation, with logical deduction and sensory evidence significantly susceptible to individual bias. Therefore, we position motivation by way of emotion as the significant determiner of knowledge perception. If this concept were true, then it could be expanded further by relating to existing theory that associates motivation with emotion (Weiner 1985) to posit that our affective states have the potential to direct our epistemic perspectives and that any phenomenon capable of influencing emotion could also manipulate our sense of certainty with regard to any current proposition. Our proposal takes one further step, connecting our research into the affective potential of sound (see Garner and Grimshaw 2011; Garner 2013) to assert that sound (by way of emotion, to motivation, then to knowledge) actually has the capacity to manipulate our epistemic perspectives and our personal understanding of knowledge. In accordance with our thesis, sound is the emergent perception, arising within the mind and formed from the sonic aggregate. For us, sound is not a sound wave but a collective of virtual components, a highly significant one of which is emotion. Within our perspective, it is not best to think of sound influencing emotion that in turn affects epistemic perspective, but rather to think that emotion is a part of the sound and consequently, the effect sound has on perspective is much more direct.

Concluding Remarks

While it would certainly be simpler and more convenient (in terms of our examination developing our understanding of the mind) if cognitive thought processing were an isolatable, independent system, the various concepts presented within this and previous chapters all point toward an integrated system within which even our personal ontologies are not set in stone. Embodiment factors are a constant influence on our adherence to the world and can, in many ways, determine our perception. The constitution of sound as a perceptual entity depends on how we attune to it. Epistemic belief and affective state significantly impact the specific contextual information we apply to a sound wave (should it be present) and it is that information that determines the perceived sound. This street is not one-way, however, and it also seems a more than plausible proposition that the affective and cognitive potential of sound to influence future perceptions forms a cycle within which sound influences belief and that that, in turn, influences sound (we return to this when we discuss biofeedback and sound in chapter 8). This chapter has reinforced the emergent perception and sonic aggregate concepts from the Introduction and chapter 1 through arguing against a fixed epistemic system. The fluctuations in our belief are another dynamic component of the perceptual system, influencing our experiences and understanding and the perception of sound that emerges.

Returning to our first assertion from the chapter opening: (1) distinctions made between virtual sound and real sound are invalid. This assertion refers to the "everyday" definition of virtual sound (i.e., sound that is perceived as originating from a digital source within a "virtual world" context) that we oppose. Our examples of auditory Gettier problems within computer gameplay scenarios illustrate how easily "virtual sounds" can be perceived as real (from the non-virtual/physical world) and how the opposite is equally possible. Our examples describing the potential of game sound to evoke emotion further support this lack of real/virtual distinction in that many sounds within the ecology of a computer game have potential to significantly alter the affective state of the listener that is equivalent to (and in some cases exceeds) the potential of "real" sounds.

Our second assertion posited that (2) affective state is a key component in cognitive processing and knowledge generation and therefore must be incorporated into any model of auditory processing. This chapter has referenced the critical importance of emotion throughout and it has been identified as a central driving force that enables the mind to determine belief/trust and alief, epistemic perspective, and sound perception. Without emotion within such perceptual cognitive systems it is extremely difficult to explain the human capacity to construct individual systems of knowledge, establish personal belief and action response structures, and (most important within the context of this book) generate the individualized emergent perception that is sound.

Our third and fourth assertions state that (3) epistemic perspective has the potential to determine the nature of sound, and (4) sound has the potential to determine epistemic perspective. As mentioned, the relationship between sound and knowledge is bi-directional. This chapter has presented several illustrative examples that demonstrate everyday scenarios in which, by way of emotions, the perceptual characteristics of a sound can determine what we establish as truth or fallacy, certainty or uncertainty, knowledge or thought. The reverse is also demonstrated via the hierarchy of listening theory, within which our epistemic perspective may determine what information/characteristics we attribute to a sound wave (or retrieved memory) to produce the fully embodied emergent sound.

Finally our fifth, and arguably most pivotal, assertion states that (5) sound is not a physical phenomenon but a perceptual entity, arising within the mind. The structure that brings together each element (acoustic space, sound wave, memory, emotion, etc.) is wholly dependent on this proposition. If sound is thought of as an objective physical entity, then we cannot account for the observable variations between listeners in response to sound wave stimuli, or indeed any of the phenomena discussed within this chapter. A physical sound wave cannot "carry" contextual or associative information to the listener. If such a thing were possible, then variation between listeners' experiences (observable at both a behavioral and neurophysiological level) could not be satisfactorily explained.

5 IMAGINING SOUND

AUDITORY HALLUCINATIONS AND OTHER PATHOLOGIES

They say when you talk to God it's prayer, but when God talks to you
it's schizophrenia.

—FOX MULDER: THE X-FILES, 1998

Introduction

In 1912, Bertrand Russell wrote that "hallucination is a fact, not an error; what is erroneous is a judgment based upon it" (Russell 1912). For Russell then, if we were to experience a sound that had no observable connection to the external world, that was not and could not be shared with others within the same space, then such a sound would qualify as both hallucinatory *and* real. Therefore, the sound that exists within the mind, while not physical, is actual. While Russell's rather poetic statement is, perhaps intentionally, slightly ambiguous and the meaning derived from it inconsistent, that hallucination should be considered fact is what is of interest here. Hallucinations (as in hallucinatory entities that are perceived) exist within reality, while the experience of hallucination also exists within the external and actual environment. The impact of such an experience is observable and most often significant, both to the individual experiencing the hallucination and to the environment within which the individual is situated and embodied.

Russell's assertions also raise a particular issue with regard to terminology that is perhaps best addressed before we continue: that of the distinction between a hallucination and a delusion. Within the field of modern medicine, a hallucinatory experience largely refers to "a false perception that is sensory in nature" while a delusion is "a false idea, sometimes originating in the misinterpretation of a situation" (Alzheimer's Association 2014, 1). The latter has associations with the previous chapter (chapter 4) concerning belief—in particular, phenomena such as Gettier problems. While hallucination and delusion are related throughout literature, it is the hallucination with which we are the most concerned. This is because we assert that sound is an emergent perception that occurs within the mind irrespective of whether the origins are endosonic (as would be the case in the event of an auditory hallucination) or exosonic (associated with immediate physical material such as a sound wave) and that both origins are "perceived sound" in that, to the listener, they are sensuous experiences that can be felt. It is worth noting that the very differentiation between hallucination and delusion, that is itself widely accepted, describes hallucination (and by association auditory hallucination and, arguably, the endosonus) as "sensory" and based in "perception."

This chapter forms the first half of a two-part exploration into imagined sound that concludes in chapter 6 with discussions into active (intentional) sonic imagination and its creative application. Together, these chapters address the bases for imaginary sound as actual sound, examining both pathological and intentional forms, to make inquiry into how we invoke imaginary sounds as part of both hallucinatory experience and for creative purpose (for example, when designing sound for fantastic, otherworldly creatures and objects). We also ask whether imagined sound can qualify as sound at all and ask *what is the nature of uncontrollable endosonic sound as experienced by those who suffer from auditory pathologies?* We examine the roles of past experience, shared culture, clichés and expectations, materiality and physicality, and remnants of our evolutionary pre-history in their associations with imagined sound and reinforce our definition of sound as perceptual by way of this chapter's principal assertion, that sound sourced from within the brain *is* sound, and has equal validity and actuality to sounds that relate to a physically present acoustic waveform.

We have already laid the groundwork to this assertion in previous chapters. In particular, we have noted the similarity in auditory cortex activity when subjects are asked or expected to imagine sound to when they receive external auditory stimulation. Differences in activity (for example, lack of observable activity in a person's primary auditory cortex when imagining sound as opposed to observable activity in both primary and secondary cortices in the presence of a sound wave) we suggest are due to differences in the exosonus and the endosonus of the social aggregate (and the consequent weighting between them) as well as to neurological differences between top-down processing and bottom-up processing.

Before braving the depths of this chapter we should start with a reiteration of our distinction between endosonic and exosonic entities. Throughout this discussion we repeatedly differentiate these terms, defining "exosonus/ exosonic" as sounds that (within the immediate spatio-temporal space—the "here and now") primarily have origins that are external to the brain of the individual. In contrast, endosonus/endosonic refers to sounds that primarily have origins that are internal to the brain. For the purposes of this chapter, these terms serve to distinguish sound that is directly connected to (the result of or originating from) an external object *and* in part results from a physical sound wave (such that occurs in the external environment) from sound that, simply, is/does not. Endosonic sound events are not to be confused with sounds generated from within the body (such as heart beat or respiration) much in the same way as self-generated sounds should not be confused with proprioceptive or motor-action-related sounds. Endosonic sound refers to a motivating origin (see, for example, the locating of sound in chapter 2 and the embodiment of sound in chapter 4) "inside the brain" or, perhaps more accurately, "within the mind."

Referring back to our perceptual definition of sound, our thesis asserts that all sound exists entirely within the mind and sound waves themselves are not sound. Within our definition, a sound wave can be a fundamental component of sound but does not itself undergo transformation into sound. This does not mean that the cause of sound is entirely internal; as part of the embodied component of our definition, all perception is, in part, determined by the external environment and we would assert that perception is, at no point, entirely internal or external. However, we do propose that, within our model, it is necessary to categorize sounds by their internal/external orientation for the purpose of explaining and discussing auditory hallucinations, sound memories, aural imagery, and creative generation of original sounds.

Finally, in its conclusion, this chapter expresses our view that a perceptual theory of sound is crucial to enabling sound theory as a discipline to accurately reflect the theoretical motivations and to utilize the technological developments that are creating an increasingly individualized society, one that demands unique media content that is of high personal relevance.

Hallucination and Sensory Psychopathology

"What is REAL?" asked the Rabbit one day, when they were lying side by side near the nursery fender, before Nana came to tidy the room. "Does it mean having things that buzz inside you and a stick-out handle?" (*The Velveteen Rabbit,* Margery Williams, 1922)

Try to consider the most fundamental and universal dimension, one that can be readily attributed to any conceivable entity or action. Our attempt at this first arrived at binary differentiation, equal and not equal (two things are either the same or they are not the same). It then occurred to us that "equal" might itself be most accurately described as an abstract concept, essentially an illusion that enables sentient organisms to better interact within their environment. Initially this sounds rather implausible but if your conditions of equality are stringent enough, every evaluation reveals difference between two entities. No two people are the same. Any mass-produced products (no matter how rigorously variations in construction are controlled) will have minute but discernible variations in dimensions and weight. If we were to examine the currently smallest known constituents of matter, the proposition that all such particles are identical remains theoretical (see Goldstein et al. 2004) and while physics has generated a principle of indistinguishability, this "merely defines what we mean by [identical] particles" (Cabello and Cunha 2013, 1). Of course, it could be argued that even if such a principle were proven to be absolute, no two particles could occupy the same position in space and time (even if they can be in two places at once).

For us then, the term "equal" is actually impossible and only "difference" is the single absolute dimension. We extend this theory to perception and assert that no two sounds can be identical and that this includes two simultaneous perceptions of a single stimulus. This relates to our perceptual acoustic ecology framework that positions sound within the mind and the mind as a virtual summation of the elements brain, body, and environment. Within this framework, the nature of any sound is characterized by all these components, their sub-elements, and the relationships and processes between everything (the virtual cloud). Therefore any change within this system will alter the final form of the emergent sound (of course, this is not to say that such an alteration would always be perceptible to us). Formalized structures such as representation and language may result in two listeners stating that the sound they perceive is a car. However, if you could acquire greater access to their experience they may both perceive the sound as a V8 muscle car engine; this would of course require that both listeners shared a significant interest in car engine sound. Let us imagine that our two listeners are actually expert engineers who are competing in a challenge to determine who has the most attuned listening skills. As the detail required from the competitors becomes more specific we become more likely to discover a differentiation in their perceptual experience. Taken even further, our competitors are required to distinguish a 1965 (or 1964½ if you're a connoisseur) Ford Mustang engine from a 1974 model. Our first competitor correctly makes the distinction as his embodied perception of the sound wave ("his sound") is that of a 1965 Ford Mustang. Our second competitor, however, cannot provide an answer, as his sound does not include any information with which he can discriminate the two models and for him, the sound that he is hearing is simultaneously both models and neither model.

Our assertion here is that if the specificity of the detail between the experiences is increased, one would inevitably and reliably arrive at an eventual difference between the two (provided that such a distinction was detectable). Inescapable differences between our perceptual selves mean that absolute shared experience cannot occur and, therefore, absolute objectivity of perception is impossible. This blurs the line distinguishing exosonic and endosonic sound in that, because human reception to stimuli is perceptual, all sonic experience is unique to the individual irrespective of its origin. While pressing a seashell to their ears, one listener perceives waves on an ocean while, to another, the shell is clearly emitting a sound like the static of a television set. The importance of this argument is that it questions the power of the physical definition of sound that positions the experience of listening as an objective experience. To subscribe to this theory, referring back to our car engine competition example, would mean that both competitors heard the same sound. This understanding cannot account for why two people listening to supposedly identical sounds cannot describe them as such. To fully explain this distinction, a theory of sound must acknowledge that sound, as a perceptual phenomenon, cannot be objective.

As part of our perceptual and embodied theory, all sound is neither internal nor external in that it exists solely as an emergent perception within the mind (that is itself an embodied system integrating the external environment and the internal brain). Therefore, the theoretical gap between auditory hallucination and perception of external sound waves is decidedly small. A hallucinatory sound can, in terms of impact and consequence, claim entitlement as *real* to a significantly greater degree than an acoustic waveform that is not heard, attuned, or responded to. The gentle whirring of the ventilation fans within our personal computers will likely produce a very actual waveform that, despite being almost continuously present throughout the day, is barely registered while the same continuity of an auditory hallucination for a schizophrenia patient, although not resultant from any external physical source, can be so perceptually dominating it can actually become debilitating (Ross and Pearlson 1996). This questions any notion that an auditory hallucination is without sensation or perception. The endosonic events do not require a material stimulus in order for them to be both perceived and to comprise substantial sensuous content.

Oliver Sacks (2012, ix) traces the term "hallucination" back to the 16th century, at which time it referred to possessing "a wandering mind" until Jean-Étienne Esquirol (1838) proposed the definition that would become the contemporary standard, that hallucinations were "a thorough conviction of a perception of a sensation when no external object, suited to excite the sensation, has impressed the senses." Sacks condenses this definition, stating that hallucinations are "percepts arising in the absence of external reality" (2012, ix). The distinction here is between internal and external, not real and unreal. For Sacks then, hallucinations are not separate from reality but are localized within a particular region of it.

Research continues to address a range of hallucination forms, including Charles Bonnet's syndrome (complex visual hallucinations experienced by otherwise psychologically healthy individuals—see O'Farrell et al. 2010), musical hallucinosis (auditory hallucinations in which music is heard without any external source—see Weerasundera 2013, and exploding head syndrome (the sensation of a loud, self-generated bang that wakes an individual from sleep—see Ganguly et al. 2013); the last two of these hallucinatory forms we will explore in detail within the next section of this chapter.

Hallucinations have been documented across all five sensory modalities. Paracusia refers to auditory hallucinations while phantosmia relates to the olfactory sense. Gustatory, visual, and tactile hallucinatory experiences have also been documented (Hausser-Hauw and Bancaud 1987; Lewandowski et al. 2009). Sacks (2012) identifies four features characteristic of hallucinations in addition to perception without confirmation from the external reality: (1) They cannot be shared or directly co-experienced with others. (2) They appear very real and convincingly emulate "normal" perception. (3) They tend to be startling and emotionally intense. (4) The subject is passive and has limited or no control over the nature or content of the hallucination. The first characteristic is arguably the one most responsible for the widespread assumption that hallucinations are of a pathological nature. Shared experience is a foundational element of our interactions within the world and is a key component of our development as children (Holdaway 1979; Liebal et al. 2009). Shared experience is often crucial to establishing a sense of objectivity and reliable existence beyond our own minds; a solipsistic perception of objects or events that cannot be perceived by others within a shared local space can undermine our everyday (particularly social) being. This reveals one of our criticisms of the traditional understanding of hallucination in relation to our earlier assertion that sensory-based experience also cannot be truly shared.

While we do not necessarily oppose the notion that hallucinations cannot be shared experiences, it would be inappropriate not to briefly touch on *the Madness of Crowds* and *folies à deux* (madness of two—also known as "shared psychotic disorder"). Research into this phenomenon may refer to both delusions and/or hallucinations. In this phenomenon, first described by Lasegue and Falret (1877), Madness of Crowds is spread much like a contagion. It affects so-called secondary patients who are typically closely associated (and share an isolated existence with) the primary patient. Case studies pertaining to shared psychotic disorder reveal that when the delusional beliefs of the primary patient are discontinued, the same is also true with secondary patients (Luther and Roy 2013). Haqqi and Ali's (2012) review of this phenomenon notes that family history and genetic connections are highly characteristic of shared psychotic disorder. They also note that schizophrenia, persecution, and grandiose delusions in the primary patient were notably consistent features in many cases.

As seems to be consistent in literature concerning delusions and hallucinations, case studies provide much of the evidence with which such conditions are described and understood. This affords us access to some specific details that directly contradict Sacks's (2012) first attribute of hallucination. Abu-Salha and Dhillon (1998) document the case history of an eight-year-old girl who believed that her neighbors were recurrently breaking into her home and violently assaulting her. According to the doctor's notes she experienced these events as vivid multisensory hallucinations. The girl was comprehensively assessed for mental and physical conditions and, with the exception of attenuated emotional response and depression, exhibited no symptoms of ill health, psychomotor problems, speech abnormality, poor cognitive functions, or memory impairment. She also had no history of psychiatric illness and her intelligence and developmental history were both within normal limits. The case study then disclosed that the girl shared a significantly close relationship with her mother and both were relatively isolated from outside contact. Evaluation of the mother resulted in a diagnosis of Psychotic Disorder Not Otherwise Specified.[1] What is of relevance to us is the similarity in how the mother and daughter related their experiences. In the descriptions of both, each was pinned down, sexually assaulted, and injected with intravenous drugs. The consistency between the specific details of their imaginary ordeals presents a good example of multiple individuals experiencing highly comparable hallucinations.

With reference specifically to their auditory experience during these events, we assert that this exemplifies the power of virtual sonic elements to construct a fully formed sensuous experience in the absence of the actual element. Much in the same way as a harmonic tone can be perceived as the pitch that relates to its fundamental frequency, even if the fundamental frequency itself is not actually present, so too can immersive auditory experiences occur in the absence of an actual sound wave. This supports the notion of experience as purely perceptual and that the neural structure with which the brain semantically processes information can potentially cause a sensory stimulus, object, and even whole narrative or event to be sensually perceived in the absence of external stimuli. Neither mother nor daughter actually experienced the ordeals they described. They did not sensorally hear the sounds of the intruders breaking in nor did they see the intruders approaching them. They did, however, share an abundance of environmental, historical, and genetic characteristics that, we would posit, in some way combined to present a mental representation so intense that it was mistakenly presumed to be actually happening.

Of course there is a distinction to be drawn between perceptions originating from external (environment-based) stimuli and those formed in their absence. What we are asserting is that the output (referring to patterns of neural activity that drive perception and action) remains similar irrespective of the different process; we make this assumption based on the intense, immersive, and sensuous character of hallucinations that are indistinguishable from reality for those who experience them as well as the neurological evidence from aural imagery presented in previous chapters.

Of the shared personality disorder case reports we reviewed, there are no claims that patients experiencing hallucinations did so simultaneously or were able to perform shared interactions with hallucinatory objects (such claims would have arguably supported our assertions further). However, the rarity of shared psychotic disorder and the difficulty in studying it with a view to answering specific questions means that shared interactions during shared psychotic disorder could be a possibility.

Returning to Sacks's (2012) second and third characteristics of hallucination ([1] they appear very real and convincingly emulate "normal" perception and [2] they tend to be startling and emotionally intense), we posit that the latter point is largely responsible for the former. Athenian philosophies argued over the nature of human emotion. For Plato, emotions were "misguided evaluations [that] should be kept under strict control" (Knuuttila 2004, 5), while Aristotle saw emotions as a functional system within a human society. Stoicism, which proposed enlightenment through logic and reason, would argue that emotions arose from false judgment. Relating to the concept that emotions have the potential to influence cognition and ultimately belief structure (discussed in detail in chapter 4), we ruminate on the possibility that in addition to emotions rising from false judgments, false judgments (in this case, hallucinations) can arise from emotion. This notion can best be exemplified with emotional contagion. Tsai and colleagues (2011) define emotional contagion as "the widely observed phenomenon of one person's emotions being influenced by surrounding people's emotions" (384). Grandey (2000) notes that emotional contagion is often exploited consciously, sometimes even malevolently, as a means to manipulate the judgments and behaviors of others. Grandey exemplifies this phenomenon with the role of debt collectors who promote anxiety to encourage customers to make payments. Within music and sound this phenomenon can be observed frequently in musical performances held in large stadia or amphitheaters, where the environment is controlled with the intention to ignite excitement that spreads through the crowd in waves and builds exponentially to create hysteria.

Emotions (particularly anxiety and stress), substance use, physiology, and (most prominently in everyday life) context have the potential to cause hallucinatory experience in individuals who are otherwise physically and psychologically healthy (see Lincoln 2007). Many of us can provide anecdotes in which we thought we heard or saw something but on closer inspection and with additional information convinced ourselves that we did not. We will also likely be able to recount events when an object we were searching for was hidden in plain sight yet we were absolutely convinced that the object was not in our immediate space (to inevitably face embarrassment when a third party condescendingly points out our ignorance). These circumstances might share characteristics with delusional behavior but would be unlikely to lead the individual experiencing them to face a medical diagnosis. In a seminal work, Roland Fischer (1971) presented the *perception-hallucination continuum* as a map of the many states of human consciousness. Within his model, perception is centralized while hallucination and meditation occupy its left and right side respectively. According to Fischer, perception occurs during moderate levels of emotional arousal while hallucination reflects hyper-aroused, ergotropic (energy-expending) states and meditation corresponds to hypo-aroused, trophotropic (energy-conserving) states. Moving in either direction away from the central perception state denotes "a gradual turning inward toward a mental dimension at the expense of the physical" (1971, 897). In more recent research, Lincoln (2007) acknowledges the existence of hallucinatory experience in healthy individuals and asserts that a circumstantial differentiation (focusing on distress and beliefs) between healthy individuals and those diagnosed with a psychological disorder is essential.

Fischer's continuum has relevance to some of our earlier work regarding the effects of emotion on modes of listening (Garner and Grimshaw 2011; see chapter 2 also), specifically that the intensity of our current emotional experience embodies auditory processing to the extent that it is largely responsible for how we attend to an exosonic auditory event. For example, two individuals are placed within a woodland environment with appropriate soundscape. With reference to Chion (1994) and Turri, Mustonen, and Pirhonen (2007), a listener in the grip of an intensely fearful experience would be more likely to respond to any sudden exosonic event with a physical reflex action (*reflexive listening*). He would also be expected to focus heavily on the identification (*causal listening*) and localization of the event source (*navigational listening*) so that he might have a greater chance to evade any potential threat. For this listener, the emergent perception is heavily shaped by particular virtual components of the sonic aggregate (in this case, intense affective state). It is our assertion that this process could have such a significant impact on the emergent sound perception that the listener's experience could be categorized by some as hallucinatory. For example, his reflexive listening might generate a sound that is significantly (perceptually) louder to him than it would be if he were in a more neutral affective state. His preoccupation with causal listening could cause him to miss-associate exosonic events with a threatening object/source, leading him to believe with certainty that an object is present within the local environment when, actually, it is not.

Two questions are raised here: *at what point does an experience cease to be perception and become hallucination,* and *is there such a thing as degree of hallucination and how could such a distinction be measured?* Research has presented the concept of "degrees of plausibility" in hallucinations (Franceschi 2004), referring to how plausible the hallucination is to the individual experiencing it. With regard to auditory hallucinations, Franceschi identifies nine factors that contribute to the plausibility of such an experience; included are structured versus unstructured (sounds with clear structure appear more plausible); external versus internal (in relation to the human body, the former reinforcing plausibility); and *locus* (the perceived object/source of the sound event—sounds that have logical connection to an object appear more plausible [e.g. voices coming from a telephone as opposed to a lamp]). While these factors coherently differentiate hallucinatory experiences from the perspective of the sufferer, Franceschi does not directly address how a third party might differentiate hallucinations in others. The Scale for the Assessment of Positive Symptoms (Andreasen 2004) presents 34 features relevant to the diagnosis of schizophrenia, seven of which directly address hallucinations, separated primarily by modality (visual, auditory, olfactory, etc.). The scale enables diagnosis by way of marking the presence of each individual factor and the severity with which it manifests in the patient. The term "severity" refers to dimensional measures, which are themselves subject to multiple approaches and methodological disagreements between researchers (Haddock et al. 1999). One particular system that relates heavily to the auditory modality and has been scrutinized for validity is the Psychotic System Rating Scales (Haddock et al. 1999). This system provides a clearer definition of severity within this context by way of quantitative measures (frequency and duration) alongside qualitative measures (loudness of symptoms, behavior controllability, negative content, perceived origin, and disruptive impact on behavior).

Relating such dimensions to auditory examples, the relevance of the exosonic event to perception is complex and qualitative and would be better measured in degrees. For example, an individual might be convinced that she has just heard her phone ring even though this event did not actually occur. Should there be no clear contextual or environmental relevance to support this (e.g., she knows her phone is switched off/she is not expecting a call/she doesn't even own a phone and there are no phones in her immediate environment, etc.) then the experience could be considered more hallucinatory. Comparatively, should she be expecting a call, knowingly have her phone nearby and be experiencing intense and relevant emotion (e.g., she is extremely anxious and is desperate to receive a call), then the hallucination can be rationalized to a greater extent than the former scenario. This one has certain resonances to the concept of justified true belief (JTB) outlined in chapter 4, and the requirements of this measure of knowledge can help differentiate these "degrees of hallucination." Referring back to the previous scenario, neither version is actually true (the phone is not actually ringing) yet both are believed to be true. The difference lies in the third requirement of knowledge, being justified in believing something to be true. Whereas in the first account, the listener had little contextual support to justify her belief, in the latter she had significantly more. For us, these contextual supporting elements are part of the virtual cloud (see chapter 7), a dynamic mass of connected elements that is not only a part of the sonic aggregate but is also the means by which the aggregate is transformed to manifest the emergent perception of sound. Staying within our example, these virtual elements could include the listener's susceptibility to hallucinatory experiences; the immediate chemical/hormonal composition of the listener's brain; the prior presence of relative actual stimuli (i.e., phone ringing); and all of the contextual elements already documented. As previously stated in chapter 4, we would also assert that knowledge systems such as JTB are themselves significant potential elements within the virtual cloud and, by way of the perceptual process, also of the emergent perception of sound. For example, should the listener's own personal knowledge-belief system be based on JTB to the extent that it was a fundamental component of her innate belief system, then it could be posited that the listener's perceptual bias toward a need for justification (provided it were extreme enough) would result in her perceiving sound in the absence of acoustic stimuli, provided a justifying context was present, while *not* perceiving sound in the presence of acoustic stimuli if the context were absent.

If a perceptual experience was clearly associated with an external and material entity but the sound was not contextually relevant, the degree to which the latter point were true would determine the hallucination severity. For example, if you were to hear a distinctly high-pitched and gentle voice tone clearly originating from a heavyset and prominently grizzled outdoorsman you could be forgiven for a double-take. However, you are not likely to consider the perception delusional because a logical, if infrequently occurring, context could be applied to the experience. In contrast, should that same gentleman start beeping electronically and whirring mechanically then, because the explanatory context is one that we would (currently) describe as fictional, hallucination suddenly becomes the most appropriate explanation.

Another form of experience that relates to hallucinations in otherwise healthy individuals is the notion of "perceptual blindness" (also known as inattentional blindness; see Most 2010) referring to circumstances in which an individual is so consumed with a particular thought, task, or stimulus that he or she forms no perception of an unrelated object or event even though it is directly in the person's line of sight. The classic example of this is the *invisible gorilla test* in which a participant observes a short video of several individuals passing basketballs to one another. The participant is asked to count the number of passes occurring during the video, during which another individual wearing a gorilla outfit steps into the central foreground of the court and begins to dance. Although the gorilla is in plain sight and is significantly more theatrical than the basketball passes, the majority of participants don't mention it, exhibiting surprise when they are then shown a repeat of the video, where the gorilla is clearly present.

Should the perception be contextually relevant, then two alternative forms of hallucination are presented. Focusing on the auditory modality for exemplification, the first form is one in which a sound is physically present and is perceived as imaginary by the listener because the contextual information surrounding the sound is contradictory (false negative). For example, the "meow" of a cat in an adjacent room might cause a listener to investigate. Finding the room seemingly absent of cat (or any feline-related evidence) and determining that the presence of a cat within this context is highly implausible, the listener is convinced that she must not have heard a cat at all (who actually *is* there, hiding under the floorboards). While this could arguably be described as delusional behavior, such events are comparatively frequent, particularly if you include circumstances in which the *sensation* is not disbelieved, but rather the *perception* (e.g., the listener acknowledges that she heard something, but concludes that her original belief that the sound was a cat's meow was incorrect).

The second hallucination form is essentially a reverse of the first and occurs when contextual information leads us to believe we have heard an exosonic event that has not actually been propagated (false positive). This would be as good a time as any to revisit our resident fictional exemplifiers, little Claire and Alexander (see Figure 5.1). Claire is in her room, studiously doing her homework, when she is abruptly interrupted by Alexander who bursts through the door screaming THERE'S A MONSTER IN MY CLOSET!! at the top of his lungs. Claire reluctantly comforts little Alexander as he explains he heard the sound of a monster in his closet. On investigation, Claire discovers that before going to sleep, Alexander had been watching a monster movie. Claire also astutely notes the heavy rain beating against Alexander's windows and the eerily intricate shadows cast across the bedroom from the deciduous trees in the rear garden. Finally, she notices that for all his terror, Alexander is still half asleep. Otherwise there is no evidence of any sound coming from the closet, nor signs that sounds were being emitted previously. Claire correctly concludes that Alexander falsely perceived the sound and tells him (in a manner befitting an elder sister to a brother with an overactive imagination) to shut up and go to bed.

FIGURE 5.1 For Claire, the advantage of recognizing Mother's approaching footsteps was a distinct one—something lost on little Alexander, whose destiny with the naughty step was now all but assured.

We suggest that these forms of hallucination could relate to shared psychotic disorder and emotional contagion in that an environment and a context that are highly consistent with the hallucination can be experienced by any persons within that space. Furthermore, the individuals within that space form part of the reinforcing environment. Had Claire also been up past her bedtime watching the same scary movie there is the possibility that she would have experienced the same (or similar) false positive and consequently exacerbated Alexander's hallucination. This could potentially have escalated with each of them supporting and intensifying the other's imagined experience. While a physical object/stimulus may be absent, the reciprocation of contextual and environmental information increases the presumed objectivity of the hallucination. Alex may have had some doubts that a monster was actually present and roaring away inside his closet, but his sister says that she can hear it too, so it must be real.

With regard to auditory hallucinations, it is the false positive form (perceptual experience of sound in the absence of an immediate, propagating sound wave) that we are most interested in. This form of hallucination distinguishes between scenarios in which a sound is falsely perceived in the presence of contextual support versus situations when a physically present sound wave is not perceptually auditioned because of the highly inconsistent contextual information. The scenarios presented, while technically forms of hallucination, are arguably commonplace enough that many would describe such occurrences as misconception rather than delusion or hallucination. Claire is not in any way concerned that her brother might be medically unwell because she is reassured by the contextual information that makes the perception entirely false, but to her mind, rational. If, however, Claire could see no contextual or environmental circumstances with which to explain Alexander's behavior, it is fair to assume that she could potentially conclude that her brother is "hearing things" and that he has mistaken an endosonic-based sound for an exosonic-based one.

Abstraction level relates to a particular Psychotic System Rating Scale measure (Haddock et al. 1999) and distinguishes highly specific delusions that incorporate entities typically considered concrete from more general delusions relating to abstract or obscure stimuli (and also judgments, opinions, and beliefs). This can be observed in differentiating the archetypal attitudes toward an individual suffering from subjective tinnitus and one experiencing an auditory verbal hallucination (AVH). Whereas the former experiences a more abstract ringing sensation, wherein diagnosis of psychiatric pathology is improbable, the symptoms of the latter condition can often be described in great detail (e.g., *a male voice, late 50s, angry tone, continuously telling me I'm worthless*) and have much greater association with mental illness. Such an attitude is admittedly supported by research that describes auditory verbal hallucinations as a commonplace symptom of schizophrenia.

The central argument here is that sound cannot be expressed as an actual element because this definition cannot accommodate hallucinatory experiences, which are themselves not solely events reserved for individuals with medical conditions. Both false-positive (hearing a sound that has no direct connection to an immediate acoustic waveform) and false-negative (not hearing a sound despite the presence of an immediate acoustic waveform) hallucinations can be everyday, albeit rare, experiences that relate to the virtual cloud, an encompassing matrix of elements that determines whether sound occurs and in what particular form.

Forms of Auditory Hallucination

Harry: Do you think I should have told them? Dumbledore and the others, I mean.

Hermione: No Harry. Even in the wizzarding world, hearing voices isn't a good sign. (*Harry Potter and the Chamber of Secrets*, 2002)

Hearing sounds, particularly voices, has long-founded negative connotations relating to mental pathologies and detachment from reality. Within fiction, voices within the mind act as narrative devices, commonly to establish associations between a character and either insanity or evil. The phenomenon has arguably become an established trope within culture that traverses literature, music, cinema, television, web-based media, and computer games. Just as Harry Potter is warned by Hermione Granger that hearing voices instills rather negative connotations and assumptions, "even in the wizzarding world," the primary understanding concerning hallucinatory experience, particularly auditory verbal hallucination, is that of a disorder. For many years researchers have sought to treat auditory hallucinations, most typically because of the associations with schizophrenia (see Hoffman et al. 2000; Sommer et al. 2008; Amad et al. 2013). Indeed, many individuals who experience such hallucinations describe them as intense, frightening, and distressing. This, however, is not unanimous and it has been observed that some individuals may find comfort or reassurance in their experiences to the degree that they may even seek them out (see Chadwick and Birchwood 1994).

Referring back to the continuum of hallucination, the varying forms in which hallucinatory experiences can occur (specifically those that do not connote mental disorders) can be related to the assertion that not all experiences along the continuum are inherently negative. We argue that there is certainly a precedent for suggesting that false perception can actually be advantageous. In 1996, Carlo Rovelli famously proposed the *relational interpretation* of the double-slit experiment, in which he proposed that it was the presence of an observer, during the experiment, that determined whether electrons behaved like particles (when observed) or waves (when not observed). However, mathematical calculations that accepted Rovelli's theory produced the most meaningful results, much to the dismay of opposing theorists.

Ultimately, Rovelli's theory may be disproven somewhere down the line, but what this does support is the position that false perception can yield significant benefit.[2] Within a survival horror computer game, this benefit is often particularly pronounced when a player is attuning to the soundscape in order to facilitate appropriate action. More often than not, it is highly advisable to treat every auditory event that does not immediately emerge as a "safe" sound (particularly those that are acousmatic) as the sound of a threat. This strategy may produce many false positives as the player attributes threat unnecessarily to safe events and objects. However, when the inevitable threat does make its appearance, the player is significantly more likely to be prepared and able to engage a successful coping strategy.

One form of common anecdotal exemplifier is in scenarios where individuals mistakenly perceive an absent stimulus and that experience encourages them to take a positive action—for example, the husband who is tentatively reclining with a beer when he perceives the sound of a knock at the door. Frantically, he scrambles to check as he fears it will be his wife and he had promised to correct the mess he had made in the kitchen the prior evening. Reaching the door he sees no one is there and realizes his perception was false. While a wide range of sonic aggregates could, within this hypothetical, have generated such an emergent perception, we would argue that there is significant potential for the aggregate to be formed primarily of endosonic elements. These could include the listener's emotional state (high alert/anxiety) and an established semantic connection between the sound of the door knock and the arrival of the man's wife, the constant worry of which is causing the sound to emerge repeatedly via the imagination. As time passes, a judgment error (possibly relating to a failure in corollary discharge—outlined later in this chapter; see also chapter 6) may cause such an imagining to accidentally be perceived as the result of an actual exosonic event. Our listener considers the event briefly, then decides to take the experience as a divine warning and makes his way into the kitchen.

Auditory hallucination, also referred to as a "paracusia" (although this term can refer to general hearing deficiencies too), describes the conscious perceptual experience of sound that occurs without a relevant acoustic stimulus. Experiences in the auditory modality are common among hallucinations in general (Weerasundera 2013) and the existence of auditory hallucination is widely accepted and is referenced within the International Statistical Classification of Diseases and Related Health Problems manual (currently ICD-10, reference R44.0, WHO). Auditory hallucinations have been linked to a range of psychiatric conditions that include dementia and delirium but also to intoxication or withdrawal from particular substances (Fricchione, Carbone, and Bennett 1995). Environmental causes of auditory hallucination can include high altitudes, low oxygen, and low atmospheric pressure levels (Taycan et al. 2013).

Phenomenology of Auditory Hallucinations

The following section documents some of the more specific forms of auditory hallucinations, including those associated with music and speech but with a focus on sound. We also consider the neurological causes of such experiences and, from these examples, support our argument that sound can exist in the complete absence of a sound wave.

Referring to a question first raised within the introduction of this chapter (*what is the nature of uncontrollable endosonic sound as experienced by those who suffer from psychopathologies?*), the following outlines some of the more prominent diagnoses relevant to auditory hallucinations.

Exploding head syndrome is an uncommon form of auditory hallucination in which individuals who suffer from the condition are wakened from sleep by a loud, internally generated (endosonic) bang that is typically presented during a transition between sleep states. Ganguly and colleagues (2013) document "the sound of an explosion, gunshot, door slamming, roar, waves crashing against rocks, loud voices, a ringing noise, a terrific bang on a tin tray, or the sound of an electrical buzzing" (14) as common descriptions of the endosonic sound as experienced by those suffering from exploding head syndrome. The phenomenon is more common among women but otherwise there are few other discernible commonalities between patients, with reported ages ranging between 10 and 50 and the pattern of attacks including singular occurrences, gradual increases/decreases, and unpredictable periods of respite (Pearce 1989). While cases of the condition are few and far between, the patients documented within case studies consistently describe their experience as indistinguishable from an external sound (see Pearce 1989; Chakravarty 2008; Ganguly et al. 2013).

Comparable in many ways with exploding head syndrome, tinnitus "is the perceived sensation of sound in the absence of a corresponding external acoustic stimulus" (Langguth et al. 2013, 920). Tinnitus typically differentiates itself from other auditory hallucinations by its lack of language characterization (as with auditory verbal hallucinations) or musical organization (as with music hallucinations). Tinnitus-related sounds are habitually buzzing, ringing, or hissing sensations that may be continuous, intermittent, or pulsing (Langguth et al. 2013). Somatosound tinnitus (also known as objective tinnitus), in which the sound has a particular bodily source and can be auditioned by people besides the sufferer, is highly irregular and it is the subjective form that is most commonly reported. Referring back to chapter 1 of this book, we address the appropriateness of presenting tinnitus as a hallucination. This is with relevance to O'Callaghan's (2007) description of the condition as "merely" hallucinatory sound. While we acknowledge that sound associated with a tinnitus condition is not primarily exosonic, it is nevertheless (like all forms of auditory hallucination) "real" sound. Langguth's (2011) review of tinnitus documents associated symptoms that include anxiety, depression, insomnia, and hyperacousis (oversensitivity to certain frequency ranges). Attempts to provide treatment by way of physiological approaches are largely ineffective but ongoing developments in understanding neural etiologies have shown promise (see Roberts et al. 2010). Tinnitus, unfortunately, remains a significantly heterogeneous condition and sufferers have no guarantee of permanent effective treatment. The key here does appear to be the brain and an increased understanding of neural pathways and activity patterns may lead us to a solution (see Norena et al. 2002; Roberts et al. 2010; Zhang 2013). Referring to a question first raised within the introduction of this chapter (*what is the nature of uncontrollable internal sound as experienced by those who suffer from psychopathologies?*), the following outlines some of the more prominent diagnoses relevant to auditory hallucinations.

Musical hallucination is an exceedingly rare form of auditory hallucination. Weerasundera (2013) conducted a case report in which a healthy elderly woman with no evidence of relevant physiological or psychological conditions expressed a sensation of hearing music (specifically the singing of hymns) intermittently for several weeks. Many historical reports of musical hallucination are of a high profile but now are, arguably, observed as apocryphal tales such as those of Joseph Haydn and Robert Schumann.[3] Weerasundera (2013) cites research associating musical hallucination to conditions and circumstances that resonate with other hallucinatory types. Such conditions include non-dominant hemispheric etiology (in which the right hemisphere activation is greater during musical perception); hearing impairment; forms of psychosis; brain lesions; and substance intoxication or withdrawal. Over-activity of the auditory association cortex has also been proposed as a potential cause (Cope and Baguley 2009) as has social isolation (Fischer, Marchie, and Norris 2004) and sensory deprivation (Sanchez et al. 2011). Musical hallucination has also been linked to obsessive-compulsive disorder (Hermesh 2004) and, like exploding head syndrome, is thought to be more prevalent in women and the elderly (Evers 2006).

With regard to more general hallucinatory experiences, sensory deprivation has been shown to be highly effective at evoking hallucinations in individuals who are not susceptible to such experiences in their daily lives. Mason and Brady (2009) revealed that sensory deprivation had effects comparable with substance abuse and described hallucinatory experiences by respondents that included a heightened olfactory response, visual or sonic perceptions of "important/significant" objects that were not present, and even a sensation that a sentient ("evil") presence was with them in the anechoic chamber.

Auditory verbal hallucination describes the sensation of hearing internal-ized voices and it has been associated with psychosis and decreases in quality of life (Falloon and Talbot 1981). Recent studies have preliminarily identified the left inferior frontal gyrus and transverse temporal gyrus as the regions within which auditory verbal hallucination originates (van Lutterveld et al. 2013). Predominantly, the voices experienced during an auditory verbal hal-lucination are disparaging and derogatory in nature, often belittling and criti-cizing of the subject (Johns et al. 2001). Tierney and Fox (2010) describe the "anorexia voice," a form of auditory verbal hallucination relating to the behav-ioral disorder anorexia nervosa, in which the internal voice explicitly threatens the subject with painful or humiliating consequences if he or she fails to con-tinue to comply with a regimented and destructive diet.

A number of research works (see Johns et al. 2001) have suggested that auditory verbal hallucination and other modalities of hallucination result from a failure of *reality discrimination*, the ability of an individual to distinguish between perceptual experiences originating from external (the environment) and internal (the mind, self-generated) sources. According to this theory, and with reference to sound, failure of reality discrimination would occur if the individual mistakenly attributed an auditory verbal hallucination to a physical source that is present within the person's local environment. This typically would manifest as the perception of a foreign physical entity, speaking from within the mind.

We return to the influential capacity of emotion described in a study by Morrison and Haddock (1997) who assert that emotionally charged scenarios or stimuli are significantly more likely to cause misattribution of self-generated experiences to external sources than neutral scenarios or stimuli. David (2004) proposes impairment in auditory feedback (spe-cifically, an atypical cognitive response to the inner voice) as a further etiological explanation. Defective or impaired self-monitoring (Hoffman 1986) is a particularly well-agreed theoretical origin of hallucinatory expe-rience (including auditory verbal hallucination) that suggests a more gen-eral cognitive disorder in which individuals cannot differentiate between those stimuli that are the direct result of their actions and those caused by forces outside of their control. For them, all stimuli occur externally to their action. When such individuals experience an imagined entity with no external source observable, they cannot associate the self-generated material to any source and consequently the stimuli manifest as phantom experi-ence. Blakemore and colleagues (2000) conducted an interesting study in which responses to a tactile stimulus variation were assessed across six groups separated by psychiatric condition (schizophrenia, bipolar affective disorder, and healthy control) and consistent presence of auditory hallucinations. Participants were presented with two comparable tactile stimuli, one self-generated and the other experimenter-generated, then asked to rate the perception (intensity/significance) of the experience. The results for the non-auditory verbal hallucination groups across all psychiatric conditions revealed significantly lower perception ratings if the tactile stimulus was self-generated while those who regularly experienced auditory hallucinations reliably rated the self-generated stimulus as equal to the stimulus engaged by the experimenter. The authors concluded that the inability to differentiate self-generated experience from external experience was the direct cause of their belief that an endosonic sound originated within the external environment.

Regular experience of auditory hallucinations has been associated, by way of empirical investigation, with poor scores in frequency tone pattern and staggered spondaic word tests (McKay, Headlam, and Copolov 2000). The latter procedure presents spondee words (disyllabic words with equal stress put on both syllables) as a test of communication problems between the hemispheres of the brain. Results suggest that deficient interhemispheric pathways within the auditory cortex could account for AVH experiences. Correlations between increased right hemispheric activation during speech perception (increased left activation is standard in healthy individuals; Gavrilescu et al. 2010) and AVH has supported researchers in the proposition that interhemispheric abnormalities are a likely cause of AVH (McKay, Headlam, and Copolov 2000).

Reviewing research concerning the neurological cause of auditory hallucinations, there is arguably a high level of commonality between the theories of reality discrimination and self-monitoring. Furthermore, the increasing quantity of empirical neurological evidence has supported the concept of self-monitoring to the extent that it is becoming an extensively accepted theory. A paper by Sommer and Wurtz (2008) documents the notion of corollary discharge, a micro-process that could potentially underlie self-monitoring and related disorders that lead to hallucinations. Corollary discharge refers to a discretely altered copy of a motor command (fixing gaze on an object, pressing against a surface, etc.) that informs the perception routines of the brain that the change within the sensory input stream is due to direct intervention of the individual and not an external force. We could extend the notion of corollary discharge and posit that this micro-process could feature in perception of *all* stimuli and not solely motor actions. This would incorporate the experience of audition and explain how listeners typically differentiate between a sound formed primarily from their environment (exosonus) and a sound formed primarily from their brain (endosonus).

Self-monitoring theory posits that a fixed neurological routine causes a sound wave to be perceived alongside a relative corollary discharge. This identifies the sound as internally generated (from within the brain) and causes the listener to perceive a sound that he or she would attune to differently if the corollary discharge were not present at the time of perceptual sound formation. Referring back to chapter 3 and the tale of Claire, Alexander, and the click-top pen incident, the action of little Alexander clicking his pen repeatedly in the presence of his elder sister might have no detrimental impact on his capacity to focus on other things while Claire, on the other hand, is being driven to distraction, and consequently some assertive action. The corollary discharge and self-monitoring theories would assert that while everyone within the local environment is receiving the sound wave, the individual who is generating the sound wave is also producing a corresponding corollary discharge routine that identifies the perceived sound as internally generated. This may limit the potential for distraction to the extent that little Alexander becomes unreceptive to the sound wave because the sensory input stimulus and the corollary discharge activation have cancelled each other out. However, as Claire is not producing the same internal activation pattern, the sound wave becomes significantly more apparent, and intrusive, to her.

Concluding Remarks

Relating the notion of impaired self-monitoring and reality discrimination to our perceptual definition of sound, for the individuals who experience auditory hallucinations, the documentation of their experiences largely describes the sounds generated within their minds to be as real as sound perception that is in response to a physical sound wave. Their sensuous experience of sound without a sound wave has the same potential as a sound with physical associations within the external environment to evoke emotion, alter judgments, affect behavior and, ultimately, even change a belief or element of a personality. We further propose that these sensuous qualities of auditory hallucinatory phenomena indicate that our connections between perceptual experience and the external environment cannot be purely objective. The neurophysiology of each individual is the determining factor in whether a sound is understood as internally or externally generated. Evolutionary neuroscience would argue that in humans as a species, our brains have evolved to distinguish between sounds that emerge primarily from the endosonus and those that arise from the exosonus in order to enable more effective interaction with our environments (again relating to corollary discharge and associated cognitive functions). The notion here relates to the established acoustic definition of sound (sound is a sound wave—see chapter 1) in suggesting that our brains are wired to enable us to cleanly differentiate the actual, objective environment of the material world from the imaginary, subjective environment of the perceptual world. However, this does not make the distinction a universal truth and one could even question to what extent such a perspective is beneficial within our contemporary and rapidly developing world.

Here, we can recapitulate a key assertion from our introduction: that the perceptual theory of sound can afford an equal (and potentially an even greater) benefit for interaction as the traditional dichotomy between the real and the unreal within the world at a crucial time in which the endeavors of the human condition, from science and technology to arts and philosophy, are resulting in a rapidly changing environment.

The prior perspectives on sound may no longer provide the comprehensive value they once did. Contemporary society is arguably one with a passion for individualization, personalization, tailored experiences, and recognition of subjectivity. As discussed in later chapters, developing technology is on the verge of delivering media that can adapt in real time to suit the immediate needs and desires of the individual user, placing the emergent perception of experience (as defined by the consumer) ahead of the generalized intentions of experience (as defined by the creator). Consequently, there is a need within this new age (in terms of technology, theory, and population attitudes) for a conceptualization of sound that reflects these new priorities. This is not to say that preceding definitions are without merit or even that, if such a thing were quantifiable, the perceptual perspective offers more bang for your buck in terms of pragmatically applicable philosophy (and we discuss the pragmatics of our theory in chapter 8). Instead, we would assert that the nature of our environment has shifted to the point that acknowledgment and integration of this perceptual perspective would move us closer to the possession of a *contemporary theoretical tool kit*, with which we can work with sound in a more optimal way and with the profound number of modern applications it has.

6 IMAGINING SOUND

ACTIVE IMAGINATION AND IMAGINATIVE APPLICATION

Reality leaves a lot to the imagination.

—JOHN LENNON

Introduction

Mary Warnock states: "Imagination is a vast subject" (1976, 9) so we acknowledge that the following discussion, through necessity, is concise. Consequently, it is not our intention here to comprehensively examine the nature of imagination but rather to summarize several relevant perspectives regarding creativity within imagination that also relate to sound and contemporary sound design. In contrast to the previous chapter, here we address sound of primarily endosonic origin that is generated by way of the conscious, intentional, and creative imagination processes. Before we begin, the term "sound design" we feel should be addressed with regard to our thesis. For us, sound design more closely refers to the emergent perception rather than the professional production of audio material. As such, sound cannot be designed in a practical manner as it exists within the mind and not an actual space. We would argue that the most appropriate term is "audio design/designer." However, matters are further complicated by the notion (discussed later in this chapter) that sounds can be imagined and transformed within the mind. Therefore, we distinguish audio design, which we consider to be a technical-creative process occurring primarily within the environment, from sound design, which we position as an imaginative-creative process. There is, however, a difficulty that arises here as it could be argued that sound design is an integral component of audio design. We later argue that this may not always be true, but we acknowledge its probable relationship and therefore the term "sound design" is utilized throughout this chapter.

Definitions of imagination vary in subtle ways. For Piaget, imagination is the process by which perceptions formulate concepts and understanding (see Mitchell 2013, 473) while for Kant (1781) "imagination is the faculty of representing an object even without its presence by intuition" (470). Murphy, Peters, and Marginson (2010) relate imagination to prediction, suggesting that imaginative thought "enables us to look around corners" (2). The consistent theme here is the function of imagination as a forerunner, be it for responsive action, long-term preparation, or comparison of theoretical outcomes; the connection here is that imagination is expected to be actualized. Klein, Damm, and Giebeler (1983) describe imagination as a process consisting of memory, impressions (meaning perceptions), and ideas, and that its power draws from its being the exclusive means of transcending the physical laws of space-time and causality. Gendler (2011), in *The Stanford Encyclopedia of Philosophy*, distinguishes imagination from perception, belief, and memory retrieval by the former being the only one *not* requiring that the subject be considered true.

In *The Child, the Family and the Outside World* (1992/1964), Donald Winnicott considers the imagination as a discrete, intermediate entity that exists between the internal and the external. Winnicott famously presents the example of the child's stuffed bear, an object that simultaneously inhabits the imagination and the physical environment. For the child (according to Winnicott) the bear actually exists in neither internal imaginative space nor external physical space but rather in a separate level of consciousness. To elucidate this, consider a scenario relatively common when young children are observed at play. The child's toy (in accordance with her perception) is an actual entity, an inanimate collection of fabric, fluff, and stitching. It is also however, simultaneously a sentient being, in possession of intentions, motivations, and personality to name a few. According to Winnicott, the child's perception and imagination can account for this duality, enabling the toy to be both alive and not alive within the same moment.

In the second book of *An Essay Concerning Human Understanding* (1722), John Locke expresses the necessities of perception on imagination and of sensory input on perception. For Locke then, imagination of an entirely original sound is impossible because we can only form imagined sound from what we have already perceived. The impossibility of pure originality in sound creation can be readily supported in historical analysis of musical composition within which there often can be observed a clear progression of compositional development as previous ideas are reconstituted by way of variation techniques (variation techniques being creative entities that themselves are also already established or evolving in the same manner). Locke's position is most certainly not without contestation; Edward Casey (2000/1939) argues that imagination is "free from undue dependence on perception or thought and free to project pure possibilities that exceed the mere probabilities that obtain when imagining is considered a mere function of the organism" (ix). While Casey does proceed to acknowledge some limitations with regard to the purity of imagination, his thesis is very distinct from that of Locke's.

Warnock (1976) traces a line of philosophical thought concerning imagination back to Descartes's writings on consciousness. Proceeding through Locke, Berkeley, and Hume, she notes a consistency of perspective in that imagination is described as tied to perception and the difference between thought and sensation is presented as indistinct. Quoting from *Treatise* (1888), Warnock presents Hume's framework of thought, in which ideas and impressions are the overarching units. For Hume, impressions incorporate direct sensory experience of external stimuli (referred to as sensations) and also emotions (referred to as passions) while ideas are described as remnants, reflections of weakened impact that evoke a more neutral response that appropriates them toward logical deduction and reasoning. Hume positions imagination, but not memory, within *ideas* and suggests that memories hold more emotional potential and therefore should largely be regarded as impressions. For Hume, imagination is a mechanism of transposition, combining impressions (which may have arisen from sensory input or memory retrieval) to form ideas and, in turn, reintegrating the ideas back into the process to be morphed and updated. Hume's terminology is inconsistent with our own, but it is nonetheless possible to draw a comparison between his framework and our own. From the concept given, Hume appears to distinguish impressions from ideas by way of their experiential impact, the former being more immediate, bright, and vivid than the latter. The terminology of Hume is problematic when we contrast it against our own. Our initial response was to mark impressions as synonymous with the exosonus and ideas with the endosonus. However, within our framework the endosonus incorporates memory while, for Hume, the term "ideas" does not (memory is part of impressions). Where we can draw a distinct opposition with Hume is in our assertion that the imagination is not merely a mechanism of transportation and is more appropriately categorized with impressions than ideas.

In an article for the *Chicago Tribune*, Davis Schneiderman (2013) posits (as stated in his title) that the "concept of original content is pure fiction." His argument largely relates to the straightforward notion of "everything comes from somewhere" and this includes anything produced from within your imagination (relating to our earlier understanding of Locke). Returning to Hume's concept of the imagination as a mechanism of transposition, here no actual creation takes place but rather processing, in which ideas, sensations, emotions, and any other entity that can exist as a form of thought collide and reconstitute much as elements form compounds.

Currie and Ravenscroft (2002) present three contrasting forms of imagination, each distinguished by way of particular characteristics. In their model, sensory imagination (perception in the absence of stimuli), re-creative imagination (conception of an experience from outside their own perspective), and creative imagination (combining existing ideas and experience to form something unique) are three discrete classifications of imaginative thought. All three of these forms most certainly resonate when we are considering the creative process of sound design. Creative imagination is arguably a prime component within sound design while sensory imagination would enable designers to develop sonic ideas without the need to have hundreds of "inspirational" sound recordings immediately to hand. Of equal importance, re-creative imagination clearly relates to the need for a designer to appreciate the reception of the sound from the perspective of the audience.

The previous chapter examined endosonus events within unintentional and sometimes pathological contexts—circumstances in which various forms of sound in the absence of a sound wave are experienced subconsciously and without the intent of the listener. In this chapter we address the opposite; endosonic instigations of sound perception that are produced deliberately and for creative purposes. This chapter presents a discussion regarding subvocalization and inner speech, within which we discuss the nature of endosonic sound that, although not consistently associated with the conscious mind, performs useful functions that support, rather than hinder, our everyday interactions. These particular inquiries are kept brief to enable our focus to remain primarily on that sound that does not fall under the categories of speech or music. Continuing with an examination of some of the many creative endeavors that incorporate imaginative processes, the final section of this chapter concludes with a consideration of how the complex and embodied environment within which sound designers operate impacts on how they imagine sound and the ways this affects the final material that they produce.

Aural Imagery, Subvocalization, and Inner Speech

One question that is central to our discussion here is, *to what extent, if at all, do we create sounds in our heads?* This is an issue that raised some contention between us as we were discussing the nature of sound within dream states, one of us insisting that sound can be experienced during a dream and the other convinced that it cannot. The argument behind the latter assertion was that we might experience imagery of visual and motor processes that, by way of representational association, embodies the central notion of a sound to the degree that the sound itself does not need to be present for us to experience it. For example, while a dreamer might be presented with a moving visual representation of an elephant crossing the plains, its sizable feet impacting the earth with apparent force, no sound would be heard. Instead, the dreamer would generate the notion of a sound based on the physical properties presented by way of the visual input. This idea can be observed to some extent in the study of music acoustics, specifically the phenomenon of "missing fundamentals" in which, if enough harmonics pertinent to a particular fundamental frequency are present, the pitch of a tone can be clearly perceived even if the fundamental is removed (for example, presenting a listener with a composite tone of 1kHz, 1.5kHz, and 2kHz will likely generate the emergent perception of a 500Hz tone, in much the same way that the "Pac-men" figures generate the emergent perception of the Kanizsa Triangle [see chapter 7]). However, while the missing fundamental phenomenon might relate to the notion that endosonus events are illusions brought about by semantic connections, it does not necessarily prove the assertion correct. If we are to agree that sound exists within the mind, is there a clear distinction to be made between sounds that have their origin also within the brain (endosonus) and those that are instigated by external entities (exosonus)? Within an embodied, ecological perspective it is difficult to identify with confidence the origin of human experience because each element is inexorably connected to the wider environment. For example, if a sound is experienced as the result of memory recall we might first suggest that its origin is endosonic (an internal sound instigation—the memory caused us to experience the sound). However, it could be asserted that because the memory is actually a stored representation of a prior auditory experience that was itself caused by an auditioned (external acoustic) event, then the true origin is in the exosonus. This is a notion that we return to later in this chapter.

In the seminal work *Thought and Language* (1987/1934,), Vygotsky deliberates three contrasting definitions of the term "inner speech": (1) verbal memory; (2) to speak without sound; and (3) all internal aspects of speech (256).

The first definition describes inner speech as a memory-based representation of external speech in the same way that the memory of a dog is a representation of that object. The second definition refers to inner speech as the same process by which external speech is produced, but with an obstruction existing that restricts the external voice. Definition three asserts that the process of inner speech is continuously active irrespective of whether the individual is producing external speech. Vygotsky observes that this definition incorporates the two others and, in doing so, labels speech retrieved from memory, language that precedes and guides external speech, and internal dialogue/monologue all as forms of inner speech. One of the most easily comprehensible explanations of inner speech (relating to Vygotsky's work) is that of inner speech or "self-talk" (see Williams, Bowler, and Jarrold 2012). According to Vygotsky, inner speech has its origin in behavior-regulating dialogue between parent and child. Then, in later development, children learn to execute this alone, self-regulating their behavior by way of conversation with themselves. The final step to inner speech is the internalization of the dialogue between children and themselves. This becomes what is arguably an extremely common habit among both children and adults in which we regularly hold either internal monologues or dialogues that support our judgments and decision making.

Geva and colleagues (2011) review various academic texts that appoint inner speech as crucial to reading and thinking, language acquisition and comprehension, and consciousness and reflective thought. According to them, inner speech is also beneficial for memory function. It has been suggested that when an audience chews popcorn in a movie theater they become less receptive to advertising, as the physical action disturbs the inner speech processes that help commit to memory the information presented on the screen (npr.org 2013).

The concept of inner speech and the various observable functionalities with which it is associated supports the assertion that endosonic events are beneficial but does not settle the question of whether internal instigations of sound generate genuine auditory experiences. Neuroscience studies may provide us with an answer by way of assessing neural activation of the auditory cortex during inner speech. Several studies (see Numminen and Curio1999) have revealed the existence of distinct activity within this region of the brain during inner speech, suggesting that the comparable neural responses to external and inner speech are indicative of a similar perceptual experience—specifically, that we do indeed experience inner speech within an auditory modality rather than a textual or graphical one.

With regard to the neural characteristics of inner speech, Scott (2013) asserts that it is corollary discharge (the absence of which we discussed in chapter 5 as a potential explanation of auditory hallucinations) that we experience as inner speech. The theory here is that, during external speech, corollary discharge produces a parallel reproduction that attenuates our auditory reception to the sound waves produced by the external speech. This enables us to not be distracted by our own speaking voice; as Scott (2013) proposes, this process permits the auditory system to remain receptive to the soundscape of the environment. Neuroscience research has provided empirical evidence in support of the presence of corollary discharge routines within the auditory system and it has been described as a component of a feed-forward mechanism that prepares the sensory cortices for stimuli (Ford and Mathalon 2004). This would explain our ability to talk "on autopilot" or simultaneously cogitate what we are going to say next while we are already in the process of speaking.

Designated by Baddeley and Hitch (1974) as part of their *working memory* framework, the *phonological store* (also described as the inner ear) refers to a short-term memory function in which linguistic information is held in a sonic representation (speech-based/spoken word). Within this model, textual information is processed into an auditory format before it is banked within the phonological store. At the point of storage, language information is now an auditory entity rather than visual or textual and (in accordance with Baddeley and Hitch's model) the rehearsal of the information (essentially listening to the information by way of the inner ear) enables the information to progress through to the long-term memory. One example of this process includes memorization of a telephone number via the phonological rehearsal of pitch variation, rhythmic constitution, and articulation. While not a common practice today, during the 1980s it was most common to answer a phone by speaking (in some ways almost singing) the number with a bespoke inflection of pitch and rhythm. Another example can be observed in the process of learning the words from a dramatic script through the rehearsal of associated melodic structures and phrasing characteristics. Several short books written for younger children, such as the Dr. Seuss series, have also embraced this approach, utilizing repetition, rhythm, and rhyme as a core feature of their writing.

Our key assertion here is that the phonological store concept implies that inner speech, although habitually related to language, exists within the mind as sound. This sound is such that we can describe it using acoustic-related terminology and sensuous, experiential, and affective connotations. For us then, there is less distinction to be made between language that is spoken to produce acoustic waveforms and language that is internalized because both produce highly comparable sound perceptions.

Drawing many similarities to the phonological aspects of inner speech, subvocalization (also known as silent speech) refers to the subconscious motor activity that occurs during speech and also during linguistic processing. Research has asserted that subvocalization possesses notable value in terms of comprehension ability during reading (Slowiaczek and Clifton 1980). Reisberg and colleagues (1989) conducted an interesting experiment in which the verbal transformation effect (a linguistic curiosity that occurs when the continuous repetition of particular words or phrases produces a sound-stream from which multiple linguistic perceptions arise—for example, "fly" becomes "life," "ripe" becomes "pry" and "go, man!" becomes "mango!") was shown to be dependent on subvocalization *if* the words were imagined. Participants were able to transform the imagined words with ease but could not do so if subvocalization was blocked (again by chewing—candy this time). This revealed connections between subvocalization and perceptual processing of language.

Creative design has explored the potential of the verbal transformation effect as can be observed in Steve Reich's 1966 composition *Come Out*, which demonstrates the effects of looping and transforming a short sample of speech on the narrative meaning of the words. Limited or atypical subvocalization has been nominated as a potential causal factor in stuttering conditions (Bosshardt 1990) and short-term memory problems (Cole and Young 1975). However, normal subvocalization has itself been argued to have some undesirable consequences, particularly with reference to its supposed negative effects on reading speed (see Aaronson and Ferres 1986).

Subvocalization has recently been proposed as a potential conduit between the body and the brain and also as an opportunity to connect psychology to physiology. Parnin (2011) draws on psychophysiology, employing electromyography to record muscle activity in the larynx. Parnin's application exploited subvocalization to measure the subjective sense of difficulty for participants undertaking a programming task. His results were promising and encouraging in that it may ultimately be possible to access an individual's inner speech without the person ever speaking externally. Unfortunately, a precise and accurate revelation of our thoughts and feelings is not yet a reality, mainly because of the limitations of the hardware in terms of accuracy and also the reliability of the underlying theory. Progress in these areas is ongoing and both technology and theoretical understanding is steadily improving, encouraging us that soon, subvocalization could potentially facilitate advances in speech-generative devices and could even introduce a rudimentary form of telepathy (see also Pasley et al. 2012). Subvocalization is a concept that provides a plentiful source of research with which we can more confidently propose that sound exists in the mind.

Incorporating both inner speech and subvocalization theory, aural imagery refers to the mental processes by which sounds can be organized, analyzed, and interpreted without the presence of a sound wave. It has been posited that aural imagery has, much like visual imagery, dimensional characteristics that include pitch, time (Halpern 1988), loudness (Farah and Smith 1983), and tempo (Levitin and Cook 1996). One of the central research interests relevant to aural imagery is the neurological question of whether the brain processes that are activated during imagery are comparable to those activated during exposure to sensory stimulation, essentially asking if our neural response to the originator of an emergent sound perception is constant, irrespective of whether said stimuli is endosonus or exosonus. Farah (1988) observed comparable deficits between visual imagery and perception skills in patients who had sustained damage to specific regions of the brain. More recently, researchers have begun to examine imagery with particular focus on the auditory system. Halpern (1988) discovered that when asked to compare the pitches that corresponded to two words within a recognized song, participants would respond slower the greater the number of beats placed between the two words. This suggested that the participants were creating a horizontal perception of physical distance between two points despite being asked to compare a vertical property of the notes. Aural imagery has also been asserted to function in anticipation of external stimuli in circumstances such as musical performance, in which a musician utilizes anticipatory imagery to facilitate interpersonal coordination within an ensemble (Keller 2012). This arguably relates to the feed-forward mechanism observed in studies of inner speech.

Neuroscience research has acknowledged the existence of aural imagery and testified to the value of studying it (see Halpern and Zatorre 1999). Neurological studies, utilizing positron emission tomography and functional magnetic resonance imaging have revealed that a particular configuration of neural activity (specifically in the right frontal lobe, right thalamus, and supplementary motor area [the latter of which is located on the midline between hemispheres anterior to the primary motor cortex and typically associated with coordination and stabilization events]) is exclusively associated with aural imagery. One additional point of interest here is the observation that during aural imagery, activity within the visual cortex is greatly attenuated.

The phenomena documented here have been brought together here for the purpose of highlighting further examples of imaginary sounds that originate from within the brain and have no direct association to sound waves within the immediate temporal and spatial environment. This is not to suggest that their origin was purely internal. For example, we might ask you to imagine the sound of a glass pane shattering. Were you to oblige, the sound created within your imagination would have no direct connection to any sound wave within the immediate environment (presuming a window was not actually being shattered at that precise moment). However, it would have indirect connection to the immediate exosonic soundscape—most notably our voice as we ask you to imagine the sound. But also, it cannot be refuted that the exact acoustic makeup of the sound you imagine is susceptible to influence from the environment (see our discussion in chapter 3 on embodied cognition). For example, a loud soundscape might result in the imagined sound being of greater intensity so that it can be perceived clearly among the competing sound waves. Another indirect connection relates to time rather than space, the obvious example of this being previous sound waves, the impressions of which (formed from the emergent perception), now stored within the long-term memory, you have experienced in the past and that enable you to create the imagined sound. Such past-sounds might be of high relevance (e.g., glass shattering) or have acoustic or semantic associations (e.g., bursting steam vent, splintering wood). Irrespective of the specifics, we assert that neural activity engaged during auditory imagining retrieves sound-related information from memory and sensory input from the immediate environment and that these elements interact to produce the final product (in this case an internally generated sound of glass shattering).

Such connections between the immediate acoustic environment, auditory memory, and an imagined sound cannot be easily dismissed. However, what these connections do not do is reveal a direct pathway between an immediate sound wave and an imagined sound. The two remain clearly distinct entities (to perceive sound from the imagination is not the same as perceiving sound from sensory experience) that, nevertheless, cannot be fully separated from one another. An acoustic sound wave cannot be realized as an emergent perception without influence from the imagination. Likewise, sounds formed primarily from the imagination cannot escape the effects of the immediate

acoustic environment (unless the listener is placed within sensory deprivation) or past auditory sensations recalled from the memory. These ideas are
discussed in the following section that moves further away from automated
psychological processes and explores creativity and the practical applications
of auditory imagination.

Imagining Sound for Creative Purpose

> The distance between insanity and genius is measured only by success.
> (Elliot Carver, *Tomorrow Never Dies*, 1997)

Much like the Carver quotation, the line of distinction separating creativity
and madness has also long been a rather indistinct one. In support of this
statement, hallucination has been shown to share a common space with creativity and imagination. Imagination can be readily associated with hallucination by way of the concepts *quarantining* and *contagion* (Gendler 2011). The
former refers to an individual's capacity to maintain within the mind a contextual perimeter around the imaginary material. In doing so, the individual creates a clear barrier between reality and imagination and it is when this barrier
becomes porous and the distinctions between the two worlds blur that hallucinatory and delusional perceptions are expected to occur. Contagion occurs
when failure to quarantine imagination has an observable impact on behavior.
An example of this would be the little boy (and before you ask, *yes* we are
referring to one of our own personal experiences) who had recently watched
the motion picture *Jaws*. This caused him to imagine a great white lurking in
the depths of his hotel swimming pool and, consequently, he refused to enter
the water despite the fact that, on visual examination, there was clearly no shark
in the pool. In this boy's defense he had also recently watched *Thunderball*
and there was always the possibility that some nefarious villain was poised to
release the shark into the pool through a secret hatch.

This section of the chapter investigates contemporary attitudes toward
creative sound design and considers the nature of imagined sound within
the creative context. Here, we enquire as to how artificial sounds are generated within the mind and examine the difference between internalized and
externalized sound design processes. As we discuss in greater detail, internal
design refers to the concept of idea generation by way of mental processing.
For example, to imagine a fully conceived and easily describable sound that
does not exist in the external environment (natural or artificial) without any
cognitive offloading (utilizing the physical environment to manipulate existing

sound ideas as a means to create something new, see Wilson [2002]) would be considered "internal." Conversely, exploiting elements of the physical environment to systematically transpose existing sonic material into something unique (pure uniqueness being something that we have already questioned earlier within this chapter) would be best described as external. Ultimately, we ask whether a sound whose existence is entirely enclosed within the imagination (purely internal) can actually occur and also if sound that is imaginary can legitimately be described as sound. If we are to accept that sound can be imagined, exactly what do we mean by this? To what extent can an imagined sound be considered "imaginary" and is it possible to differentiate sounds by degrees of imagination?

Relating to the notion of imagination and creativity, Simpson (1922) asserts that creativity can be best thought of as descriptive of an imagination that is exhibiting frequency of spontaneity and initiative of deviation. Within this understanding, creative thought would denote regular and consistent production of concepts (output) that deviated significantly from the entities of external stimuli and retrieved memories (inputs), all in the absence of a systematic method of transposition. For example, a creative sound designer might be engaged in generating a range of audio files that represent an alien species. According to Simpson's criteria, the output audio must clearly deviate from potential comparisons (uniqueness) while simultaneously fulfilling the connotative requirements of the sound (as experienced by the audience). Furthermore, the designer must be able to produce the output sounds effectively with much haste and not employ an externally observable method for creation. Explanations for such ability have in the past referenced the soul or a similar concept. However, our examination of several contemporary approaches to creative sound design that follows suggests a less romantic interpretation that questions the capacity of human creativity to live up to Simpson's ideal.

Craig Berkey (2011) reveals his philosophy of sound design for cinema to be a hybrid of conscious strategy and intuitive inspiration. The former he relates to several techniques that include what could best be described as "randomization effects," in which various audio files sounds are arbitrarily positioned along the timeline of the film rather than purposefully synchronized to events. The result is then auditioned with the hope that an unexpected combinatory effect between the audio files and the visual material will cause the emergence of "good" sound (i.e., the sonic aggregate that includes, but is not limited to, visual and auditory elements from the film creates a sound that fits). This is also a good example of the cognitive offloading that we discuss later in the chapter (see also chapter 3). Seemingly arbitrary experimentation features prominently in Berkey's design approach and, due to the heavy reliance on the external environment to organize the sound, is certainly more closely related to external than internal imagination. More internal processes are mentioned, however, such as imbibing the visual material with a focus on more abstract entities that include tone, affect, and aesthetic before then replaying the content internally (via the imagination) and developing sound design ideas along the way. Such activity cannot feasibly be described as fully internal, however, as the strategy of disregarding preconceived sound design preferences and utilizing the visual material is itself a preconceived idea (and, of course, the visual material is part of the external environment). Nonetheless, it would still be inappropriate not to distinguish between Berkey's (more external) experimental and (more internal) inspirational design approaches. Once again, we find that binary differentiation is overly simplistic and that we must conceive internal and external sound design processes not in black and white but in shades of gray.

Many sounds within science fiction and fantasy genre films cannot be sourced directly from nature and must be constructed with a greater degree of artificiality. An interview with *Jurassic Park* sound designer Gary Rydstrom (Buchanan 2013) revealed that the almighty roar of the tyrannosaurus rex began rather humbly as the cry of an infant elephant and that the communication exchanges between velociraptors are, in fact, copulating tortoises. Relating these design approaches to Currie and Ravenscroft (2002), both appear to utilize creative imagination because existing components (ideas, objects, movements, etc.) are being transposed to create something new. These examples reveal an indirect connection between the inputs (the sound waves [typically from audio files] as utilized by the designer as part of the creative process) and the final output (the produced audio recording) because, before it was created, the output sound did not exist (at least not within the personal existence of the designer). For example, the infant elephant was not in actual fact a roaring tyrannosaurus but an infant elephant. For Rydstrom, however, enough acoustic similarity between the elephant sound wave and his imagined tyrannosaurus must have been auditioned for him to then employ the elephant sample as the foundation of his design. What is unclear from the factual information we have access to is whether Rydstrom's conception of the tyrannosaur was actually an imagined sound or rather a collection of semantically associated information (a conception of its physical parameters, the emotional and circumstantial context, etc.). It is possible that the elephant sound resonated, not with an imagined sound, but with Rydstrom's overall concept of the tyrannosaur.

In the mid-1970s, Ben Burtt, a young projectionist and graduate student, noticed that the harmonization of two simultaneously running film projectors produced a rather distinctive timbre and a dramatic beat effect as their frequencies moved in and out of unison. At the time, Burtt had been commissioned to develop sound effects for an upcoming cinematic project and, hoping to recreate and record a more intense variation of this sound, he began experimenting in his studio. One day, Burtt left his equipment active while maneuvering a microphone across the studio. As the microphone passed the cathode tube of an active but silent television set, the sound that followed was exactly what Burtt was looking for; he had discovered (sonically of course) the lightsaber. Examining Burtt's lightsaber discovery, the details of the process suggest even more compellingly that the imagining and internal analysis of sound did not preface the final output sound but rather it was created by chance as various objects within the environment were allowed to interact. However, the accidental creation of the cathode tube-against-microphone sound could not have been connected with the concept of the lightsaber without imagination (and a predisposition to pay attention to sound). A question remains, however, as to the specific nature of the imagined concept against which the sound wave was evaluated.

Another element of design worth considering is the notion that associations between the sound and its creative function work both ways. Sound designer Randy Thom began his career alongside Ben Burtt in designing sound effects for *Star Wars Episode V: The Empire Strikes Back* and has enjoyed a successful career, most distinguished in his work for computer-generated animation pictures. In a short article, Thom (1999) insists that the most effective sound effects come not from simply finding the right sound as accompaniment for established visuals, but from a more ecological relationship where the other elements of film (visual design, plot, characterization, blocking, etc.) are open to change in response to the sound. Using this approach, the creative team would be as likely to construct an object or scene to fit a compelling sound as they would the reverse; as the title of Thom's article states, such an approach is "designing a movie for sound." While neither Rydstrom nor Burtt explicitly comments on this, it is worth considering that the sonic properties of the lightsaber (and the Tyrannosaur equally so) influenced the visual and kinesthetic properties of the overall design. Were this to be true, however, it would be providing additional support against directly employing imagined sound as an approach to creative sound design.

Scrutinizing the creative process of sound design for motion pictures from subjective descriptions sourced from the designers themselves reveals significant consistency between reports, most notably relating to focus on the external environment and *not* internal cognitive, imaginative, or perceptual processes. The elements of the external environment that include technology (equipment used, digital signal processing, surround sound, etc.), interpersonal relationships, and visual material/concepts repeatedly appear across various interviews. This suggests that sound designers, as a general rule, do not consider their craft from an internal perspective and, instead, regularly employ technological, social, and technique-based cognitive offloading. Further examples of this include utilizing relative size information from visual material to inform the frequency characteristics of the monster in *The Thing*; recording a hummingbird from the natural environment then experimenting with digital signal processing via a combination of trial-and-error, interpersonal, and established editing techniques in *Cowboys and Aliens*; and reusing spell-casting sounds that have become generic with the series in *Harry Potter and the Deathly Hallows: Part 2*. This does not disprove the proposal that part of the design process employs imagined sound; it merely shows that when qualitatively describing their craft, designers do not regularly consider that particular aspect of the overall process—an aspect that is potentially hidden within the subconscious and difficult for designers to observe while they are simultaneously engaged in their creative tasks. Establishing the facts with regard to auditory imagination within the creative process, we suggest that neuroimaging has significant potential to reveal the neural processes that occur during the course of a creative sound task. Improvements in hardware portability, affordability (namely, functional magnetic resonance imagers), reliability, and accuracy (electroencephalograms) could enable us to observe the points within the creative process that engage aural imagery and that generate, combine, and morph sounds by way of the imagination.

Examining the creative process of computer game sound design from a more philosophical perspective is a difficult task. This is primarily because the production pipeline is predominantly technical and that the role of the sound designer often involves the recycling of pre-existing sound FX from third-party sources that can include sample libraries, previous game titles, or films (see Collins 2008). Several design professionals have revealed snippets of their imaginative process with relevance to generating sound for the fantastic (science fiction, horror, and fantasy genres). For game sound designer Rob Bridgett (2013), interpersonal interactions during the development process between the various individuals within the team (and teams within the department) account for at least one third of the creative output. For Bridgett, then, creative imagination is a shared process that takes existing ideas and bounces them between individuals, each of whom makes small adaptations before passing the idea onward.

Tomoya Kishi (2013) acknowledges the impact of audience expectation on the creative process, specifically the limitations this imposes when the end-users have been saturated in contemporary Hollywood-style sound aesthetics (hyper-real and subjective audio processing techniques that accentuate impact or increase consistency with overarching thematic content [see Milicevic 2013]) and consequently demand a comparable output in games. For Kishi, then, re-creative imagination is an essential component of the creative process, as understanding the audience's expectations and demands is paramount to producing a successful product.

In *Game Sound* (2008), Karen Collins provides an overview of the contemporary production pipeline in audio design for games (incorporating sound effects, dialogue, and music). Her account references the business hierarchy, financial restraints, and technical limitations. Furthermore, the development process is described as rigorously structured with numerous examples of cognitive offloading, including design documents written as part of pre-planning; minutes taken to record meetings between various teams within the development process; and storyboards, concept art, and temporary scores of pre-existing music and effects. While Collins also notes that sound designers will consider the emotional, aesthetic, and thematic content, these elements are also described as significantly standardized processes in which pre-existing games, other relevant media, and established frameworks of design practice are all employed as key components (what some might call quality assurance components) of the creative process. This kind of process, taken to its extreme, relates to the concept of design by committee, in which the restrictions are placed on the creative process with the intention to maximize the output of "safe" creative decisions.

Imagination and Imagery: A Neuroscience Exploration of the Imagination

The foundational premise of functional magnetic resonance imaging (fMRI) is that cerebral blood flow correlates significantly with neural activation. The technology behind fMRI exploits this connection, measuring blood flow throughout the brain. It achieves this by producing a precise pattern of radio waves and magnetic fields that affect oxygen-rich and oxygen-poor hemoglobin molecules in different ways. This enables the scanner to differentiate cerebral regions rich in oxygen from those with comparatively less within a particular time window (typically 5 seconds per measurement of the whole brain), ultimately enabling neuroimaging scientists to observe which regions of the brain are most active at a given time within the typically 5-second window of observation.

With regard to perceptual and imaginative processes, fMRI studies have revealed that perception and imagination of a comparable stimulus present similar topographical patterns of activity (Kosslyn, Ganis, and Thompson 2001), suggesting that the way in which our brains process sensory information (in the auditory, or indeed any other, modality) gathered from physical and external sources is not entirely distinct from how we attend to imaginary percepts, thus narrowing the gap to our thinking between endosonic and exosonic sound. Functional neuroimaging has also supported the assertion that sounds instigated by the imagination can be vivid and evocative by way of the correlations between activity patterns observed from fMRI data and subjective user experience data (Halpern et al. 2004).

Daselaar and colleagues (2010), in an article concerning modality differentiation in the human imagery system by way of fMRI, reveal the existence of common and distinct patterns of activity for specific sensory modalities. Even more interesting, however, is their assertion that a "modality-independent component" (677) of imagery processing could be observed from fMRI data. For Daselaar and colleagues, the structure of the imagery system included a core component that was consistently present during imagination irrespective of whether the individual under observation was imagining sounds, images, actions, or any other modality. This modality-independent component acted as a foundation, upon which the modality (and several other variables) determined the extended neural activation patterns.

Hassabis and colleagues (2007) utilized fMRI to compare between the activation patterns responding to imagination of a fictitious scenario and those responding to plausible futurities. Their results characteristically mirror those of various other neuroimaging studies in that both similarities and differences were found. They concluded that for imaginative functions such as these, a core foundational neural network was present that co-opted peripheral brain regions depending on the specific requirements of the imaginative task.

With reference to auditory processing research, Bunzeck and colleagues (2005) executed an interesting experiment using fMRI to compare neural activity patterns between perception and imagination groups. Specifically, they wanted to compare neural responses to sound that did not fit into the categories of music or speech, what they labeled "complex sound" (1119). In their results, different from equivalent experiments that presented musical or speech forms of auditory stimuli, imagining complex sound dictated a significantly different activation pattern when compared to the results of previous studies that tested music and speech. Specifically, imagining complex sounds revealed activity within the secondary auditory cortex but not the primary (music and speech presented activity in both).

Functional magnetic resonance imaging technology has also been utilized within auditory research beyond studies of imagination. For example, Mutschler and colleagues (2007) used fMRI, electroencephalography, and transcranial magnetic stimulation to observe differences in neural activation patterns between audition of actively familiarized music (rehearsed to perform themselves) and passively familiarized music (simply listened to at various times).

Magnetoencephalography (MEG) dates back to David Cohen (1968) and is, essentially, an observation of the magnetic fields that are induced during synaptic transmission (the process by which action potentials connect multiple neurons to transmit information). The magnetic fields themselves are extremely weak in comparison to those in the natural environment and, consequently, the MEG sensors are housed within a substantial, magnetically shielded casing to attenuate the magnetic noise. MEG technology enables researchers to extract information from the brain at temporal resolutions high enough that they more appropriately reflect the rate of cortical dynamics (Hari, Levänen, and Raij 2000). The most prominent compromise with MEG approaches to neuroimaging is that of spatial resolution, which is considerably lower when compared to fMRI or positron emission tomography (Ullsperger and Debener 2010, 209).

With regard to aural imagery, MEG has been utilized to overcome the low temporal resolution problems associated with fMRI to successfully identify the areas of the brain responsible for initiating auditory imagination (Hoshiyama, Gunji, and Kakigi 2001) and to actually follow the direction of the neural activity during an imagination task (Schürmann et al. 2001). MEG has also enabled researchers to propose that sound has the potential to alter visual perception (Shams et al. 2005). Kuriki, Kanda, and Hirata (2006) examined the auditory evoked field responses (neural latency responses occurring between 30-400ms after onset of an auditory stimulus) with MEG technology to compare the auditory networks of long-term trained musicians with non-musicians. Their results revealed a reliably recurring feature (specifically the P2m response, a fluctuation in MEG readings that occurs between 160–180ms after onset of stimulus) present only in trained musicians, suggesting that our brains can change (via neuroplasticity [see chapter 2 for neuroplasticity in the context of sound wave source localization]) throughout our lifetimes depending on how we attune to sound. MEG has also been used in conjunction with fMRI to enable each approach to negate the limitations of the other; one example of this includes comparison of auditory processing effects in response to localization effects (Romani et al. 2006).

In a remarkable article, Bowyer and colleagues (2006) claim to have discovered an effective treatment for bilateral subjective tinnitus (subjects reported intermittently worse tinnitus in one ear), the foundation of which employs MEG technology. Within their study, two patients were qualitatively assessed to discover the perceived frequency and loudness of their tinnitus. Auditory tones matching the frequency and loudness profiles were then presented to the patients and the neural region that responded to these stimuli was identified by way of MEG. Following this, neuro-stimulation (a low-voltage electrical charge applied to a particular brain region) was employed as a means of blocking the tinnitus sensation. This was shown to have both immediate and long-term benefits.

Finally, positron emission tomography (PET) utilizes radionuclides that emit positrons and gamma rays that act as tracers. The radionuclides react to active neurons and the PET scanner is capable of detecting the gamma radiation emitted during this reaction to infer the presence of neuronal activation. Consequently, PET measurements are different from fMRI measurements in that the former measures dynamic cerebral blood flow while the latter reveals the oxygenation levels of particular neural regions. In a chapter in the *Handbook of Functional Neuroimaging of Cognition* (Cabeza and Kingstone 2001), Buckner and Logan evaluate the effectiveness of both fMRI and PET as approaches to functional neuroimaging. Like fMRI, PET is shown to be limited with regard to temporal resolution (PET is typically able to produce a snapshot of neural activity every 10–90 seconds) but strong in terms of spatial resolution in addition to being exceptionally resistant to erroneous variables arising from the surrounding environment.

PET technology has been employed to identify regions of the brain associated with representational imagery, such as the imagining of hand grasping movements (Grafton et al. 1996). Through the use of PET technology, Djordjevic and colleagues (2005) discovered that imagination overlaps with perception within the olfactory modality, revealing that actual and imagined experiences of smell produce comparable but, again, non-identical patterns of neural activity. Ruby and Decety (2004) made use of PET systems to differentiate first-person (understanding of one's own emotional state) and third-person (empathetic understanding) social emotions by way of neuroimaging data. PET has also provided data to compare auditory activation patterns in response to dynamically changing sound localization (Griffiths, Bench, and Frackowiak 1994) and revealed different neural responses to quantifiable acoustic parameters such as pitch and lateralization (Tzourio et al. 1997). Research utilizing PET systems relevant to imagining sound are comparatively rare but certainly exist. In an experiment similar to that of Halpern's (1988, discussed earlier in this chapter), Zatorre and colleagues (1996) utilized PET methodologies to compare the auditory cortex during exosonus (sounds associated with an immediate external and material acoustic event) and endosonus (in this case, imagination) perceptions, their results revealing much similarity in terms of neural activity patterns between the two groups.

Functional neuroimaging research examining activity relevant to aural imagery is primarily focused on language and music (Bunzeck et al. 2005). Of the research that has been conducted, the evidence gathered supports claims that neural structures within the auditory cortex system are the primary sites activated during imagination of sound (see Goldenberg et al. 1991). This means that in terms of perceptual processing, the brain deals with imagined sound in much the same way it does with sounds based on external sound wave stimuli.

Examining neural activity in relation to mental imagery is fraught with methodological challenges, specifically those that question the presumed associations between the independent variables (what is being imagined) and the dependent variables (cerebral blood flow, oxygenation levels, magnetic fields, etc.). Zatorre and Halpern (2005) assert that correlating neuroimaging with behavioral data is an appropriate solution to this problem. Their investigation demonstrated the validity of this assertion by asking participants to imagine the first four notes of Beethoven's Fifth Symphony and to then identify the note with the lowest pitch, thereby correlating the neuroimaging and overt response data to confirm that the former relates to imagining of pitch.

In a recent article, Dietrich (2008) asserts, in no uncertain terms, that the connection between actual action and imagined action (in this case relating to motor imagery as a proxy for physical movement in sport) is tenuous at best. Consequently, and for Dietrich, any conclusions made from neuroimaging experimentation that substitutes imagined action (or indeed perception) for actual action are untrustworthy. Dietrich's criticisms are expanded within the article to attack the assumption that is being made across much of neuroscience research—that the patterns of activity between actual and imagined action/perception are notably comparable. Dietrich goes so far as to describe such connections as extreme generalizations, perpetrated by over-eager researchers. It is not entirely clear to what extent Dietrich's questioning refers solely to motor activation and associated imagery, and how much can be equally applied to auditory perception. Ultimately the literature, overall, does appear inconclusive. There are certainly comparisons to be observed but inconsistencies between research results do unfortunately limit the power we have to associate imagination and perception with absolute confidence. We must therefore be careful not to allow our own imaginations to run away with us, if you'll forgive the terrible pun.

Bearing Dietrich's argument in mind, even providing concrete and detailed identification of the auditory cortex, within which all auditory stimuli (includ-ing imaginary) are supposedly (partially) processed, is not an exact science. The regions within which sound is processed are susceptible to interrelating cognitive process and other systems (such as the visual and motor systems, memory, attention, and cross-modal effects) that, in contributing to the sonic aggregate, form the sound perception. The auditory cortex has also revealed itself to be susceptible to influence from other sensory modalities (Schroeder and Foxe 2005), suggesting that although the brain can be separated into dis-crete processing regions, these modalities are not isolated systems and inter-connectivity exists between them. Zatorre (2007) considers these difficulties and states that it is not only possible to observe activation in the auditory cortical region during a complete absence of sound wave input, but also that various regions, not typically associated with auditory processing, can be seen activating in response to an auditory stimulus. Further recent research can likewise be cited that has witnessed activation within the auditory cortex in the complete absence of sound waves (Hunter et al. 2006, Voisin et al. 2006). In a short review of auditory focused neuroimaging studies, King (2006) notes that patterns of activation between auditory perception and imagination are com-parable but not identical. Referencing Kraemer and colleagues (2005), King also states that the auditory imagination is neurologically similar to sensory response during subconscious activation. This was exemplified in an experi-ment in which individuals, listening to a piece of well-known popular music that had been overlaid with brief moments of silence, would subconsciously fill in the blanks, using their imagination and memory recall to maintain lis-tening coherence during the periods of silence (Kraemer et al. 2005).

Wu and colleagues (2006) contributed to this research with their tempo-ral assessment of imaginary sound, measuring the event-related potentials during acoustic imagery of animal sounds. Their results revealed significant distinction within particular regions of the event-related potential waveform between actual sensation and imagination groups, suggesting that there are noteworthy variances in the temporal characteristics between sounds that are primarily formed from external stimuli and sounds that are self-generated. Referring back to the research concerning internal/external distinction and corollary discharge theory, these differences in neural processing between perception and imagination certainly can be construed as supportive of our interactions within the world.

With reference to our thesis we posit that the inconclusiveness of the neuroscience research in its current stage of progress does in fact support our perceptual framework of sound. As we have stated previously within this book, the exosonus and endosonus are discrete classifications by which elements of the sonic aggregate are grouped. However, because no sonic aggregate can be entirely exosonic in its constitution (and there is the possibility that endosonic-only sound is, in fact, driven by external stimuli such as suggestion), it stands to reason that the various measures of neurological activity would reveal both consistencies and differences. Every emergent perception of sound evokes environmental and imaginative processes in varying ratios, which accounts for overlapping of exosonic-related and endosonic-related neural structures and activation patterns that present themselves when sound is actualized.

Concluding Remarks

Many of the studies mentioned in this chapter distinguish between imagined and perceived sound, which in some regard contradicts our framework in which such a thing as imagined sound does not exist, but rather sound-related imagination exists as part of the endosonus, which is itself part of the sonic aggregate. We do not want to suggest that sound can be an imagined entity as that reinforces traditional perspectives that present imagined sound as a counterpart to *real*, physical sound. Because no sound can be entirely imaginary it is arguably more appropriate to describe aural imagery as another piece of the endosonus. Within our framework, all elements of the sonic aggregate, irrespective of being endosonic or exosonic, are perceived. However, there remains a consistency with regard to acknowledging that sound can exist within the mind as an imaginary based entity. It should be mentioned, though, that there is still a uniqueness within our framework in that *all* sound exists within the mind as opposed to stating that sound can exist in either form. With regard to the components of the sonic aggregate, we do acknowledge a fundamental difference between the endosonus and the exosonus.

Our assertion is that *all* sound is formed as a perception and exists within the mind but not all sound is generated by the same type of precursor. For us, several classifications of sound-origin can most certainly coexist. A sound wave is not a sound but may be a component in the formation of sound as a perception in the brain. Equally, any information stored within the memory is not to be considered sound until it is recalled and subject to the same perceptual processes. This would account for both the similarities and differences observed in neuroimaging research between imagined sound and sound perceived in the presence of a sound wave. It is the patterns of neural activity themselves that are the closest reflection we can currently observe of sound as a perceptual entity.

Within a comprehensive ecological framework of sound, we must account for differences between components of the exosonic (e.g., sound waves) and those of the endosonic (e.g., retrieved memory) as these elements are fundamentally different in terms of their origin and character. It should also be restated here that, in alignment with the embodiment theory of our acoustic framework (see chapter 3), no emergent perception of sound can result from a purely exosonic sonic aggregate and we acknowledge that, even where we state that sound can emerge from a purely endosonic aggregate, there will have been prior, related, external stimulus. We cannot shut out our imaginations or our memories any more than we can close our ears and disconnect our senses. For us, then, determining a sound as "primarily" exosonic or endosonic is established by the frequency and significance of observable elements within the sonic aggregate that are classified as exosonic or endosonic.

Chapters 5 and 6 together have examined the nature of imagined sound, in both its pathological and creative forms. Our central assertion raised is that both auditory hallucinations and aural imagery produce sound by way of an emergent perception arising from the sonic aggregate. As such, what we identify as sound accounts comprehensively for such imaginary (endosonic) origins alongside those primarily resulting from environmental (exosonic) sources. This framework accounts for the intense sensuousness and emotion-evoking potential of imagination-based sound and also provides an explanation for everyday hallucinatory experiences while accounting for the lack of neural tomography distinction in patterns of auditory processing between sounds that are imagined and sounds that are sensed. The discussions of these and other preceding chapters are consolidated next, in a detailed account of the most central element of our framework of sound, sonic virtuality.

7 SONIC VIRTUALITY

Empty space is a boiling, bubbling brew of virtual particles that pop
in and out of existence in a time scale so short that you can't even
measure them.

—LAWRENCE M. KRAUSS

Introduction

There is perhaps no other term in our modern consciousness that
has such widespread usage and importance, and yet is subject to
such varying interpretations and understandings and, indeed,
radically polarized meanings, as "the virtual." One might, in fact,
refer to a virtual war, a long-standing and simmering proxy con-
flict, generally conducted on the level of low-key insurgency and
encroachment with the occasional flash point, were it not for the
risk of inflaming the debate through the term itself being subject to
misunderstanding about its intended meaning. Although our conception of sonic virtuality belongs firmly in the one camp, before
we begin to express that conception fully we must first clear the
way by describing briefly the two opposing views of virtuality and
the virtual. That they are opposed and polarizing should be in no
doubt as the one in extremis conception of the virtual is that it is
the antithesis of reality whereas, in the other conception, the virtual
forms part of the substance of reality. In this second conception,
the virtual is real but it is a transitional process with immaterial and
nonsensuous properties as opposed to the actual, also real, which is
a set of material and sensuous properties contained within a form
and which are objective and measurable.

We deal first with the common approach to, and application of,
the term that has grown out of its association to the prefix *pseudo-*.
In particular, such usage is connected in everyday thinking to computers and the Internet. Rheingold (1993) may have been the first

to ascribe the term "virtual" to the Internet in describing the imaginary spaces and virtual communities that the networking technology made possible, but he has since retracted the latter idea; that is, virtual communities are in fact real communities (2000). The phrase "virtual reality" gained currency through the 1980s along with the increasingly widespread use of computing, but the concept of simulating reality (initially, and still in the main, using the visual modality) or ideas of the existence of other realities than our own have long been a staple of fiction and myth (see, for example, Bittarello 2014). Devised in 1968, by Sutherland and Sproull (Sutherland 1968), the Sword of Damocles is commonly accepted as the first virtual reality system. Common to these approaches is the concept that what is formed by virtual communities or created by virtual reality is not itself real, in the sense of our everyday reality, but that it is opposed to reality and therefore is something other than what is real.

This difference between virtuality and reality is noted by Cornwell and Cornwell (2006) in a report that critically describes as doxa (that is, uncritically accepted and widespread beliefs inside a community) the descriptions of Internet activities as virtual (4) and proclaims the death of virtuality while, at the same time, ignoring the opposing, and still very much alive, view of virtuality that we deal with later in the chapter. There is the "assumption of difference between real space (offline) and virtual space (online)" (9) in descriptions of various Internet communities such as social, academic, and business groupings. An example of the uncritical use of this sense of the virtual may be found in Gibson and Gibbs (2006) who provide us with four characteristics of virtuality in an article that discusses the concept of innovation in the context of *virtual teams*. They see virtuality as having geographic dispersion, electronic dependence, structural dynamism, and national diversity. Here the assumption is that "virtual" implies networking through the Internet: the communication, management, and innovation that are electronically mediated through the use of virtual tools that are not available in reality.

One also finds within these doxa other descriptions of virtuality such as the use of the descriptive terms "virtual world" and "virtual environment." Such worlds are typically represented by the computer-generated environments of computer games and the term "virtual world" is widely used in both common parlance and in academic writing dealing with the subject. In both usages, the term is shorthand for the environments and possibilities generated by the game software and that are manifested, in the case of environments, through visual and auditive means and, in the case of possibilities, opportunities for engaging with and affecting those environments through a variety of usually manual tools enabling an interactive human-computer interface. Within particular academic fields, use of the term is not necessarily problematic as it has the common understanding that we paraphrase with the description given earlier. We ourselves have used the term in previous writings about sound and computer games (e.g., Garner and Grimshaw 2014), as have many others (e.g., Collins, Kapralos, and Tessler 2014), and it appears in a similar manner in writings about computer-generated environments other than those used as games (e.g., Lichty 2014 who writes about visual art in environments such as *Second Life*) and in writings about concepts of presence (e.g., Riva and Waterworth 2014 discussing virtual reality environments) to name just a few fields where the term is commonly used. In all these cases, the virtuality of virtual worlds is used as shorthand to indicate that what is presented allows for different objects, perceptions, experiences, and possibilities to what is available in reality. Regardless of some gray areas of overlap, a virtual world is other than real.

And this brings us to the second application of the term "virtual." To some, the use of the term as outlined above is anathema. Thus, Massumi (1998) bemoans

> the poverty of prevailing conceptions of the virtual, in its popular compound with "reality," [that has] become all too apparent. "Virtual reality" has a short conceptual half-life, tending rapidly to degrade into a synonym for "artificial" or "simulation," used with tiresome predictability as antonyms for "reality". . . a creature of the press, a death warrant on its usefulness as a conceptual tool. (16)

Following the work of Deluze and Guattari, who themselves developed that of Bergson, Massumi states that when correctly understood and used, the virtual is a mode of the real, an abstract mode that stands in opposition to the actual (rather than the real) and that is "implicated in the emergence of new potentials" (16). In Deleuze and Guattari's conception, the reality of the virtual is that of change, the event, and so, Massumi continues, virtuality is opposed to actuality because, as an abstract mode of reality, it "is not contained in any actual form assumed by things or states of things. It runs in the transitions from one form to another" (17).

In *The Actual and the Virtual*, Deleuze (2002) argues that all individual actuals, sensuous and material properties contained within a form, are surrounded by clouds of virtuality, each unit of which self-renews by way of generating associative virtuals that expand the virtual cloud. Virtuality is described as fundamentally uncertain and indeterminate due to its capacity to form, evolve, and disappear within time periods infinitely shorter than those we can perceive. For Deleuze, the virtual retains a power over the actual by way of their mutual inextricability.

As an example, within this model of virtuality, the Necker Cube in Figure 7.1 has limited actual characteristics; it is a cube, a two-dimensional vector graphic, an arrangement of ink printed on the page (or pixels displayed on some type of monitor should you be reading this as a digital text). Its virtual characteristics, however, are much greater in number. Whether the composite squares are perceived as a whole or as components creates a variable; the order in which each square is perceived, the attention to individual lines, the way in which each line is followed by the eye, and the almost infinitesimal variations in timing as the eye darts from one element of the image to the next reveals the much greater virtual cloud surrounding the actual image. What is most interesting about this image is that as you observe it, you realize how impossible it is to observe it separately from the virtual cloud. To look on the image without interacting with the virtual, and consequently acknowledging its existence, is to not look on it at all (and to avert your eyes from the image is still an interaction with the virtual as the concepts and associations of the image form a part of your decision to not look).

This, then, is the conception of virtuality we base our work on. It is the reason we have been careful throughout this book to refer to game worlds rather than virtual worlds when discussing our past work—although we have stayed true to the original terminology (virtual world, virtual environment, virtual reality, and so on) where the context, such as the discussion of others' work or the widespread use of such terminology in a particular field, dictates that we do so. Before we delve deeper into sonic virtuality, we need to discuss

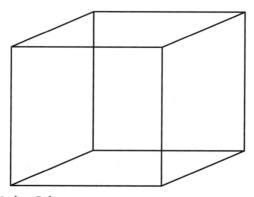

FIGURE 7.1 A Necker Cube.

a recent work of Massumi's that develops Deleuzian virtuality further because it has provided much of the inspiration for the thinking that we set out here.

Massumi uses the visual modality to exemplify his conception of virtuality and others have used the same modality for similar purposes. Deleuze often used cinematic imagery as his exemplar and Berthier (1985) uses the example of the image in a mirror to develop the concept of the virtual in a slightly different direction (that while the virtual object may not itself be real, our perception of it and our relationship to it are very real). Here, we apply Massumi's explanation of the virtuality of the Kanizsa Triangle to sound rather than image. Virtuality has been used to explain sound before (e.g., Grimshaw and Garner [2014], Garner and Grimshaw [2014], and Knakkergaard [2014]), but these authors refer to the acoustic ecologies of game worlds and the impossible acoustic spaces of some recorded music productions and their writings are not attempts to use virtuality to explain the conception of sound as perception that we provide here. Given the implication of time in the virtual, it is somewhat surprising that sound waves, whose existence would be nothing without time, have not received more attention in the literature of the virtual; any student of perception or the media will recognize that the visual modality has long been the dominant modality in any discussion of perception.

Of Pac-men and Virtuality

In a recent work, Massumi (2014) addresses the virtuality inherent in the Kanizsa Triangle (Figure 7.2), an image in which the triangle that emerges is often described as an illusion. Massumi, though, is insistent that this is not an illusion as an illusion is a suggestion and, in this case, the triangle cannot

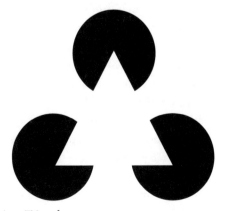

FIGURE 7.2 A Kanizsa Triangle.

not be seen. Rather, Massumi explains that emergence through the processes of the virtual. In his analysis, he assembles the components of actuality and virtuality, describing how their particular spatio-temporal relationship forms the potential from which the triangle emerges. It is this process of the actu-alization of virtuality that enables us to achieve the perception of the triangle.

Massumi identifies the two sets of components forming the basis for the perception of the triangle as actual and virtual. The first and smaller set com-prises components that are material and sensuous and, in this set, Massumi places the three cut-out circles that he refers to as pac-men. These sensuous elements, sensuous in the sense that they are actual (in their design and print-ing) and can be sensed, are placed on the page in a particular spatial disposi-tion.[1] As they are separated from each other by the intervening white of the page (another sensuous component), they are "countable one by one... an aggregate of singles" (58). Each pac-man can be counted and observed singly (accounted for) yet they also come together in their spatio-temporal relation-ship. They exist in the same space and can be perceived in the same instant of time. This aggregate of singles is what Massumi refers to as a *disjunctive plurality*.

Conversely, the triangle is a *singularity* as it cannot be counted one by one and it can only be seen as one entity in an emergent act of perception. Nonsensuous itself, the triangle pops out at us (to use Massumi's term) from the conjunction of the first material and sensuous set of components (the pac-men) with a second set of components. This second set is immaterial and nonsensuous, yet it is as real as the actual components of the first set. These nonsensuous components are generally biological, and developed and refined through evolution, or are cognitive. Thus, there are innate habits (such as our propensity to isolate and recognize forms such as a triangle) and there are acquired habits (such as the habits of counting and grouping) (63), but we might also add cognitive aspects that are either shared to some extent or individual (such as memory and experience—past resonances—and expecta-tion and anticipation—futurities—that form part of the constantly shifting and growing cloud of virtuality surrounding the actuality of the image). We expand on Massumi's description by stating that these nonsensuous com-ponents too are a disjunct plurality in that they can be counted, or at least accounted for, one by one but that they act as one under the right conditions. It is the spatio-temporal conjunction of these two sets of components, the mate-rial and sensuous and the immaterial and nonsensuous, in which multiple potentials arise. Massumi introduces the term "tension" (61) to describe the immediate and simultaneous contrast between the two sets and the pressure that leads to the emergence of the triangle. What we witness as the emergent triangle under the right spatio-temporal conditions is the actualization of the virtual that is allied to the potential inherent in our prehension of the image on the page.

A single pac-man on the page would not accomplish this as it is not a part of an aggregate of singles, a disjunctive plurality, that, under the right spatio-temporal conditions, leads to the perceptual emergence of the triangle. It may well form other potentials in its relationship to the page or the printed text but the spatio-temporal conditions are lacking that would lead to the actualization of the virtual.

Whitehead's terms "sensuous" and "nonsensuous" are utilized by Massumi to explain the perceptual immediacy and simultaneity of the "actual elements conditioning [the triangle's] appearance" (58) and the effect of the virtual (the actualization of the virtual inherent in the potential—the appearance of the triangle). The terms sensuous and nonsensuous come from Whitehead's concept of prehension (for example, Whitehead 1967; 1978), which is an uncognitive apprehension of experience of the world from which abstract knowledge is distilled and thus, ultimately, conscious cognition and awareness become possible. Prehension is the uncognitive, pre-epistemic grasping of the sensuous (that which can be sensed with our sensory apparatus) when combined with the nonsensuous (the mode of the perception of our past that includes uncognitive memory and experience). The actualization of an occasion is the process of prehension of the past in the form of sensuous and nonsensuous elements that are combined in a perceptual immediacy and simultaneity to form the present occasion. This, now actual occasion, then forms part of the uncognitive substrate from which future prehension arises.

As will become clear, we expand on this bipolar distinction of sensuous/ nonsensuous by also including consciously cognitive elements as components of the sonic aggregate. This is because we wish to account for all sound perception including that in which cognition is used to imaginatively and consciously create sound as perception such as in aural imagery. It seems to us too that such higher-level cognition also plays a role in sound perception when that perception is stimulated by the presence of sound waves. *Pace* Whitehead and Massumi, we conceptually group such cognitive components with the immaterial because they are just that, immaterial and nonsensuous, because cognition within neuroscience can be conscious or unconscious, and because reason and knowledge have their part to play in making, for example, a conscious assessment of the provenance of sound waves (little Claire and Alexander have different cognitive routes to assessing the provenance of mysterious sound waves emanating from the stairs). Since Whitehead wrote (his work on prehension and the concept of the nonsensuous and the uncognitive was first published in the 1920s), findings from neuroscience show the tightly interwoven, multi-directional effects of cognition, perception, and sensation across all sensory modalities.

The Sonic Aggregate

Fundamental to our definition of sound, that *sound is an emergent perception arising primarily in the auditory cortex and that is formed through spatio-temporal processes in an embodied system,* is the conception of the sonic aggregate. It forms the basis for the exposition of sonic virtuality that follows and is a development of Deleuzian conceptions of the virtual and, in particular, is a transposition to the sonic domain and development of Massumi's use of Deleuzian virtuality to explain image as an emergent perception. We go further than Massumi in suggesting that our explanation functions for all sound and not just that sound that has previously been passed off as imaginary, hallucinatory, or illusory in the same way that the Kanizsa Triangle is often described as an optical illusion.

We use the term "sonic aggregate" to describe all the components that together create the potential for the perception of sound to emerge. While the definition of sound is intended to encapsulate experiences of sound that are not accounted for by other definitions, the sonic aggregate is intended to function as a conceptual tool kit for the analysis of sound and the design of sound. Using it, one should be able to identify all components that form the perception of sound and, conversely, one can use it to design sound for a particular purpose and context. As with Massumi's explanation of image perception, we divide components of the sonic aggregate into two groups: those components that are exosonic (material and sensuous) and those that are endosonic (immaterial and nonsensuous).

The Exosonus

In the first group of the sonic aggregate, the exosonus, we place all those components that have materiality and that can either be sensed directly with our sensory apparatus or that have a sensuous effect on the hearing sensations we experience. Our hearing apparatus is important here as it allows us to sense sound waves but it is not the only means through which we sense sound waves. For example, Riddoch (2012), in his definition of non-cochlear sound, provides the example of infrasonic sound that can be detected by the skin (12–13) while the profoundly deaf percussionist Evelyn Glennie (1993) maintains that hearing is "a specialized form of touch."

As we have stressed throughout this book, sound waves are not themselves sound but, as part of the sonic aggregate—and in conjunction with other components of that aggregate—they can lead to sound perception. In their materiality, they can be described through physical and objective means such as frequency and amplitude as well as other descriptions of complex waves such as sharpness and phase. They can be measured and assessed through these means and they have physical, material impact on the mechanisms of our ears. They can thus be sensed and so can be defined as sensuous. In both their propagation and their reception by the ears, sound waves are formed and shaped in ways that impart an individual sensation that is the first of the processes leading to the perception of a sound that is unique for each of us.

A sound wave that may be described in its physical dimensions as having certain and precise characteristics at the sound wave source is shaped into one of many potential components of the sonic aggregate by the time our hearing apparatus starts its transformation of it from acoustical energy to electrical energy. This happens in a number of ways, and these too form part of the sonic aggregate; and because these ways can be sensed, or the effects they have on the sound wave can be sensed, they are exosonic components. The first of these is the medium the sound wave travels through. Typically, for humans and many other creatures, this is air. Because air is a material medium with density, viscosity, elasticity, humidity, level of pollution, and temperature, it transforms the sound waves that propagate in it through geometric and absorbing processes. In the main, this manifests itself as decreasing amplitude of the sound wave with increasing distance from the sound wave source but there are also frequency effects. In the case of amplitude, the decrease results from a number of factors that include the geometric spread of the sound wave through the medium; dispersion of the energy present at source over a wider volume means that at any point away from the sound wave source, the intensity of the sound wave is less than at source and decreases with increased distance. Air, being a viscous and elastic medium, has a direct role in the absorption of acoustical energy as the sound wave moves away from its source and high frequencies are absorbed to a greater extent than low frequencies. The humidity of the air and its temperature and level of pollution also affect the absorption of acoustical energy (for example, temperature and wind gradients refract sound waves) although, depending on the context and purpose of measurement, differences in absorption at various frequencies are usually not viewed as significant when one is close to the sound wave source.

Perhaps more important in the effect it has on the sensation of a sound wave is the presence of other materials and objects in the space in which that sound wave propagates. There is no naturally occurring space that comprises only the medium carrying the sound wave, particularly where a listener is required to be present to sense that sound wave. Even in what is known acoustically as an open field, the surface on which a listener stands absorbs acoustical energy and reflects acoustical energy, some of it in the direction of the listener, as does the body of the listener itself. In typical listening conditions, such as a living room or a concert hall, there are many surfaces of differing sizes and shapes comprising different materials each of which absorb and reflect acoustical energy at different levels and to greater or lesser extents depending on the frequencies present in the sound wave.

The cumulative effect, and therefore specific effect on sensation, depends on the location of the listener in the acoustic space. In particular, the location of the listener with respect to the sound wave source and his or her location with respect to surfaces that absorb or reflect sound are important. If the listener or sound wave source moves within that space, the effect on the frequency and amplitude of that sound wave and its consequent composition at the point of sensation can be quite dramatic. Equally, because no two listeners can occupy the same space, each listener will experience the sound wave propagating from the one sound wave source to be different from the way any other listener experiences it depending on his or her relative locations in that acoustic space. This can be very noticeable in urban environments with multiple sound wave sources not intended to work in concert and to present a uniform sound image, but it can also be experienced in concert halls where, despite the best intentions of architects and acoustic engineers, the composite sound wave of an orchestra can be so affected by building design, materials, and placement of objects, such as balconies, that very often listeners in different seating areas will experience the music entirely differently.

We come now to the ear. Chapter 2 dealt with the importance of the ear in localizing the sound wave source. Specifically, it mentioned the role of the two pinnae in localizing the source. The effect works by delaying and filtering the sound waves as they impinge on the pinnae (and there is some prior effect of delay and filtering from the torso and head as well) and because, like fingerprints, no two human pinnae are anatomically alike, this filtering and delaying effect, the head-related transfer function, is unique to each person. Similarly, the ear canal, in its dimensions and direction, is unique to each person. Thus, as the pinna has delay and filtering effects, the ear canal has a unique resonance pattern, typically amplifying signals with frequencies in the approximate range of 2kHz-5kHz (the amount of amplification reduces after birth and the third harmonic within this range—centered approximately on 13kHz—is also amplified but to a lesser extent).

Any sound wave impinging on the ear, after having already undergone transformation at the hands of the external acoustic environment—and such transformation varies for each person in that environment—undergoes further transformation that depends not only on the unique head-related transfer functions of the individual but also on the relative angle of the person's body and head (and thus the folds of the pinnae and entrance to the ear canals) to the direction of travel of the sound wave. This is further complicated by the multiple sound waves and reverberation (that is, dense delays of those sound waves) that are found in the typical acoustic environment. Our point here is that human anatomy shapes, in individual ways, the acoustical energy prior to its transformation to electrical energy within the inner ear.

This is one of the issues bedeviling the recreation of human-like binaural hearing in external acoustic space (as opposed to using the techniques of standard stereo recording and reproduction). While we could record a binaural image with tiny microphones inserted into our ear canals (necessarily entailing some corruption because part of the ear canal would not figure in the recording), anyone else listening to that recording would have the strange sensation of listening with someone else's ears or, at the very least, they would experience a stereo image that did not represent the actuality at point of recording and as experienced by someone else. Attempts to record binaurally using dummy heads with pinnae of average dimensions, or to use averages of multiple individual head-related transfer functions to process recorded audio before reproduction over earphones or headphones, are only partly successful because we resist listening with someone else's ears; as mentioned in chapter 1, such attempts are part of the drive to objectify and standardize subjective experience.

Finally, we wish our model to account also for the effects of cross-modality—that is, the role of other senses in the emergent perception of a sound. In previous chapters, we have discussed the influence that other sensory modalities have on a number of factors to do with sound. A major part of the literature deals with cross-modal effects between sight and hearing. A significantly lesser part has to do with the relationship of sound to smell, taste, and touch. Much of the reason for this, in the Western world at least, has to do with the creative arts and their role in academia. Overwhelmingly, the creative arts, if they are bi-modal, are audiovisual—theater, opera, cinema, and computer games—and, with this, comes academic investigation and analysis. This is not to say that cross-modality between hearing and senses other than sight has little if any importance; merely that there is less investigation into any effect taking place and, consequently, less evidence available.

Cross-modal metaphor has long been used in connection with hearing, either with sound-based metaphors to describe and enhance the depiction of the perception of other senses or with language of other senses to describe sounds. An early example is found in the field of perfumery where Piesse (1857) uses metaphors such as musical harmony, octaves, and keys to describe the combinatory powers of scents (30) while non-sound metaphor is commonly used to describe sound balance, depth, color, intensity, and so forth when recording and producing music (see, for example, Walther-Hansen 2014). In psychology and neuroscience, some evidence has been found for cross-modal effects involving hearing and smell, taste, or touch. For example, work has been conducted on the perceived taste and crunchiness of potato chips when munched to different sounds (Zampini and Spence 2004) and the effects on tactility and comfort of the different sounds fabrics make as they glide across the skin (Cho, Yi, and Cho 2001), and the new field of real virtuality combines the interactional effects of all five classical senses in the pursuit of realism in virtual environments (Chalmers 2014). A recent experiment has suggested a sensory rather than a perceptual basis for this cross-modality: a high proportion of the units in the olfactory tubercle (a multisensory area of the forebrain) of mice is activated in the simultaneous presence of auditory and olfactory stimuli (Wesson and Wilson 2010). This notion of a common neurological basis for interaction between smell and hearing is, as Wesson and Wilson acknowledge, prefigured by Piesse who wrote in his perfumery manual: "Scents, like sounds, appear to influence the olfactory nerve in certain degrees" (30).

The Endosonus

The second group of components in the sonic aggregate comprises those that are immaterial and nonsensuous, the endosonus. The over-riding distinctions between this group and the first group of exosonic components are that the engagement of these components is not primarily sensory and that they maintain a high propensity to be private. They might be initiated by sensation but they can be initiated in other non-sensory ways such as imagination (see chapters 5 and 6). This is not to say that such components are always entirely private to the individual; some components have a degree of sociability in that they can be shared to a lesser or greater extent with others of the population yet still retain a particular character that is attributed to the individual and that comes about through the experience of the exosonic components (not necessarily sound waves) that, as we have seen, have a certain individual-based character themselves. Arising from cognition, the components in this group comprise memory, expectation, belief, and emotion. Necessarily, time, especially in the sense of the past, is intimately bound up with many of these components. From our chapter on embodied cognition (chapter 4), we clearly take the view that perception is not entirely brain-based nor, indeed, entirely body-based, so it will be no surprise to discover that, in this group, emotion also makes an appearance given its close relationship to bodily states and gestures and the interrelationship of the environment and the body.

We have spent a large proportion of this book discussing the cognitive and perceptual aspects of sound—aspects such as memory, expectation, belief, and emotion—and so will not spend further time on them other than to restate our reasons for including them as part of the sonic aggregate. We do spend some time discussing those nonsensuous components that Whitehead might term uncognitive and that have a direct bearing on the time and space that figure so much in the Deluezian theory of the virtual.

Our over-riding reason for including conscious cognition as part of the sonic aggregate has to do with the larger philosophical debate over free will and determinism; we can find instances where both views can be applied to the perception of sound. If we were to adopt the free will view, we would argue that sound can be freely and actively formed in the mind, within the here and now, because, as human beings, we have the capacity of executive function that enables us to choose and control our thoughts, which would include the ability (in circumstances where exosonic components of the sonic aggregate are critically analyzed) to decide how we will attune to those components. For example, while playing a first-person shooter computer game, the player may have the option to focus her auditory attention on either footstep sounds (to support detection of approaching enemies) or on a series of tones emanating from a security keypad (memorizing these tones will enable the player to escape to the next stage). In this scenario, the exosonus of both potential sounds are within the player's perceptual space and also in the immediate present, so both have the potential to be perceived as sound. In the free will view, it is the player's choice that will determine which sonic aggregate is actualized and would thereby attain the status of sound (it is actualized by our conscious decision to attend to it); that which is not chosen would remain potential. An alternative use of free will is the one proposed by Libet (1985) who, noticing significant brain activity up to half a second before actions apparently initiated by the decision's occurrence, suggests that free will is not involved in initiation of intentions but in the selection or not of those intentions after they have arisen.

Determinists on the other hand would renounce free will to assert that all of our auditory experiences are beyond conscious control and as a result, we have no choice in the matter: there is sound that is perceived and sound that is not; there is no option for choosing from among the range of potentialities. Referring back to our computer gameplay example, determinism would argue that the decision to select either the footsteps or the tone sequence is purely illusory and that a complex matrix of causal events means that the choice of which sound is eventually perceived is inevitable. Consequently, because the perceived sound was guaranteed to be so, there was never a possibility for other sounds to be perceived. Referring back to the Kanizsa Triangle, according to Massumi, we cannot not see the triangle and so the process of perceiving it is deterministic; we have no free will in the matter.[2]

We suggest that what occurs when sound is actualized as perception is a combination of non-deterministic and deterministic processes, the pendulum swinging one way or the other depending on the balance between consciously cognitive and uncognitive aspects. This can be illustrated with two examples of the well-known cocktail party effect in combination with two different forms of a priori knowledge in recent memory and long-term memory. In scenario one, in the noisy environment of the cocktail party, the listener, aware that an object of potential affection is somewhere in the room, can direct his attention to her speech, even though he is some distance from her and is himself engaged in another conversation. In scenario two, the listener, engaged in another conversation, finds his attention drawn to the voice of an ex-lover holding forth in another conversation across the room, even though he didn't know she would be at the party. Strictly speaking, this is not an argument for or against determinism as there is no evidence here that either of the scenarios was fated to be, but it is an example of the role free will can take in directing hearing attention. As another example of free will in the creation of aural imagery, we can point to the pro-active use of such imagery by film sound designers that we have extensively discussed in chapter 6. Conversely, Hermann and Ritter (2004) argue from what might be seen as a deterministic point of view when they discuss the "elementary dimensions of meaning [in sound waves], whose deepest roots ultimately can be seen in physics, reflecting very fundamental laws that connect physical and geometrical properties of our environment to sound characteristics in a rather universal manner" (731).

This externally deterministic role for sound waves, in which it might be argued to the full extent that some elementary meanings are inherent in sound waves, is not something that we necessarily agree with. Our view is that we ourselves create meaning in the world and that any "very fundamental laws" to be found in the universe are merely projections of pareidolia, the urge to create order from chaos (for a suggestion that pareidolia has a part in the formation of phantom sounds, see Lunn and Hunt 2013). But what is of interest is the role that the environment plays in shaping sound waves and also, importantly, the role that the environment plays in shaping our perception of sound in addition to the ways in which we make use of the environment for that shaping.

This brings us back to embodied cognition, which we investigated in some detail in chapter 4. Here, we wish to flag up the importance of implicit memory and its connection to sonic virtuality. According to Wilson (2002), implicit memory is automated action; formed through habituation, it is a type of off-line processing that is decoupled from physical inputs such as sensations. There is a bridge here to Whitehead's conception of uncognition and the nonsensuous. Such implicit memory forms part of the sonic aggregate, forming, with other components, the virtual cloud from which one occasion of actualization takes place that is the emergent perception of sound (see Figure 7.3). Garbarini and Adenzato (2004) touch on this actualization when describing what they term virtual activation: "[Mental] representation does not consist in a duplication of reality, but in the virtual activation of perceptual and motor procedures" (106). This virtual activation forms part of a

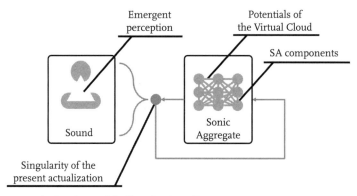

FIGURE 7.3 A simple model of sonic virtuality.

representational system for the perceptual recognition of external objects by evoking simulations or approximations of autonomic and somatic processes (i.e., those processes taking place in the involuntary and voluntary nervous systems) in order to embody input stimuli. There is no cortical processing; it is immediate embodiment.[3]

Spatio-Temporality

We now deal with the spatio-temporal nature of sonic virtuality. In doing so, we also account for the manner in which the two components of the sonic aggregate, the exosonic and the endosonic, are virtually combined to emerge as the act of perception of sound. Two points should be noted. First, in this emergence, while the endosonus is necessary to that emergence, the exosonus is not; certainly not in the present act of emergence although the exosonus is likely to have played a past role in the formation of components of the endosonus. Sound has meaning; elements that are sonically material and sensuous but are not conjoined to a set of immaterial and nonsensuous components are not exosonic and so give rise to no emergent perception and thus no meaning. A sound wave is inherently meaningless and is only perceived as sound/meaning when it is part of a sonic aggregate that has an endosonus. Conversely, the sonic aggregate may comprise only endosonic components in which case it has the potential to give rise to the emergent perception that is aural imagery. Second, this emergence can take place either under the conditions of free will or as a matter of determinism, and the former can take the form of selection or abnegation of singularities.

In chapter 1, we asserted that at the moment that in-utero babies develop initial functionality in their auditory processing system, they do not perceive sounds, they merely sense sound waves. It is teaching, learning, and experience (the development of the endosonus) that ultimately leads to the ability to perceive sounds. At an early stage, then, the exosonus (primarily, but not exclusively, comprised of sound waves) is necessary to the formation of sound perceptions but, as the endosonus expands and the capacity to imagine develops alongside, sound can be perceived through the endosonus alone. Supportive of this notion is the view that those born profoundly deaf have no conception of sound (see Goycoolea, Iniguez, and Perez 1995; Westfall et al. 2014); lacking the ability to sense the exosonus from birth, there has been no opportunity to learn to learn the act of sound perception.

By meaning, we intend that a sound refers, denotatively or connotatively, to something other than itself and this is at heart a self-reflexive process as what is fundamentally meant is one or more of the components of the sonic aggregate. It is also a process of expansion whereby each unit of the virtual cloud surrounding the sonic aggregate self-renews by generating new associative virtuals, thereby growing the virtual cloud. This is most clearly seen in our everyday listening in which sounds are referenced by either the event that set a sound wave in motion or the source object from whence the sound wave originated. For example, we can refer to a sound as an explosion (an event) or a car (a vibrating object) and this typically generates other associative meanings. The car, for instance, is itself a shorthand reference for an event, as in, for example, a car driving along a road, but it might be nuanced and enhanced with other meanings deriving from perceptions of the car's size, model, speed, or direction of travel, which themselves lead to other meanings, such as, *I must be careful crossing the road* or *that might be my taxi arriving*. All such meanings form part of the virtual cloud buzzing around the sensation of the sound wave and the actualization of any one of an infinitely combinatorial virtuality is thus made available for future experience.

These meanings arise from the spatio-temporality that relates the components of the sonic aggregate into the potentiality from which the emergent perception arises as an actualization of the virtual. This is a spatio-temporality that is the basis of the accounting for the disjunct plurality of the sonic aggregate and the emergence of the singularity that are dimensions of "the same occasion of experience" (Massumi 2014, 59). Where Massumi refers to the emergent singularity of the triangle as "the visible being of a relation" (59), we can state that the singularity of sound is the sonic being of a relation of components within the sonic aggregate.

There is a potential problem here. Visually, the perception of images in a spatio-temporal relationship, as the pac-men on the page are, is immediate. The pac-men are actual and separate on the page, being the countable one by one dimension of the occasion, but the accounting for them as a disjunct plurality is immediate as forced by the emergence of the triangle (the counts-as-one dimension of the occasion). Were the pac-men to shift slightly in their relation to each other, there would be no such accounting as there would be no emergent triangle to bind them in perceptual unity and immediacy. We can grasp the relationship of the three pac-men in the one perceptual occasion, the same perceptual occasion that forces the pop-out of the triangle. Looking at sonic virtuality rather than visual virtuality, were the sonic aggregate to include a sound wave as part of its exosonus, then we need to explain how we grasp the entirety of the sound wave, with its temporal implication as it unfolds over time, as one sensuous entity that then forms part of the disjunct plurality in its present immediacy.

The answer lies in a feat of perceptual legerdemain. We cannot and do not grasp the sound wave in its entirety before we arrive at the perception of sound, but we grasp it in its parts. (This conception bears similarity to Noë's [2004] statement paraphrasing Dennett: "Consciousness is *really* discontinuous. It *appears to us* to be continuous" [54].) This can be demonstrated very simply by the example of a violinist before us playing a single sustained note. Theoretically, and as long as the violinist has the energy to sustain it, the sound wave of the note can continue forever. Yet, we are not required to sit listening through that eternity in order to perceive the violin's sound wave and other components of a violin sound. Such perception is grasped in the immediacy of the actualization of the sonic aggregate's virtuality, emerging from the formation of the disjunct plurality from the image of the violinist and violin, the act of the bowing, perhaps even the puff of virgin resin exploding into the air under the force of the vibration of bow and string, and the peculiar qualities of the sound wave as it is first sensed by our hearing. Even without the presence of the sound wave, we create the futurity that is our expectation, projecting our perception of past remembrances of violin sounds and violin-like situations into a prehension of the future that itself forces the components of this sonic aggregate into the spatio-temporal relationship that, with the addition of the sound wave, results in the singularity of the emergent sound.

Underlying this expectation is the aural imagery that itself is the perception of a violin sound; our auditory cortex is primed and warmed up, ready to play its part in slotting the sound wave as exosonic component into the sonic aggregate. The legerdemain in this feat is the simultaneous projection into the future, the expectation that gives rises to the aural imagery that is the sound of the violin, with the assemblage in the present of the immediate past, the violinist, bow poised, and the recollection of the distant past in the form of remembered sound and context. Were the sound wave to be unviolin-like, a cat's meow, absurdity and a perceptual tactical retreat and regrouping occurs because the addition of the unexpected destroys the prehensive spatio-temporal relationship actualized in the aural imagery. The violin sound wave merely confirms what was already there, adding the dimension of materiality to the immateriality of the aural image.

What if the violinist were not physically present? What if the sound wave were schizophonic, to use Schafer's term, projecting into the air without the baggage of original context? There are two possible present contexts here that determine the nature of the emergent sound. In the first, there is a listener with previous experience, and therefore knowledge, of violin sounds and, in the second, a listener without such knowledge and for whom the sound wave is a novel experience. Certainly in the first case, but also in the second, prior experience and knowledge form part of the endosonus. While, in the first case, such endosonic components may well lead to the correct emergence of the sound as a violin, the result in the second case may be more or less ambiguous due to the presence of endosonic components with more or less indexicality to violins and their sounds. Perhaps such experience and knowledge as there are, are enough to lead to the emergence of a musical sound or perhaps the sound recedes further into ambiguity as the perception of some sort of scraping sound the origin of whose sound wave is unknown.

The process of perceiving a previously unknown and unexperienced sound that is instigated by a sound wave demonstrates further the legerdemain of perception that is at the root of sonic virtuality. As the sound wave propagates over linear time, the listener perceives the sonic aggregate in perceptual packets. These are perceived in terms of energy differences that occur within perceptible units of time. The human ear can differentiate two pitches separated by approximately 3.5Hz when in the 1kHz–2kHz range. Therefore, in perceiving that there is a difference between one tone at 1,500Hz (a waveform period of approximately 666μsecs) and another at 1,504Hz (a period of approximately 664μsecs), the frequency resolution of the ear is in the range of 2μsecs. Likewise, when localizing the sound wave source, interaural time differences of down to about 10μsecs can be perceptually registered. This resolution operates at the level of the uncognitive but, consciously cognitively, we tend to operate on larger scales and thus, for example, we have the concept of the amplitude envelope in which there is acknowledgment of the sound wave's attack (possibly decay and possibly sustain) and release phases as macro-segments of the sound wave. Whatever the size of the perceptual packet, each prior-received packet forms part of the sonic aggregate, increasing the size and potentiality of the virtual cloud. Each just-received packet is perceptually grouped in the present with the prior packets (not to mention the non-sound wave components of the sonic aggregate); tension increases in the sonic aggregate until the futurity that the process of actualization is projected toward emerges, actualized as the sound that is perception in the present occasion of experience.

There is some evidence from neuroscience for this sonic, but temporally stretched, pointillism. McDermott, Schemitsch, and Simoncelli (2013), for example, provide evidence from a variety of experiments that tested the storage of representations of audio stimuli of differing statistical properties and the ability to discriminate among audio textures. Their conclusion is that, in some cases, the brain stores snapshots of audio stimuli and these are averaged over time until such point that the texture of the stimulus is grasped.

Concluding Remarks

In arguing in *Action in Perception* that the detail of experience is not represented in consciousness but is accessible to it, Noë (2004) contends that the content of perception or, as he also phrases it, the content of experience, is virtual (215): "Qualities are available in experience as possibilities, as potentialities, but not as completed givens. Experience is a dynamic process of navigating the pathways of these possibilities" (217). As is typical with much of the literature on perception, Noë concentrates on vision[4] and, in this case, somewhat glosses over the finer details of virtuality, surprisingly so given his statement that "perceptual experience is virtual" (215).

In this book and chapter, we have attempted to redress the balance by concentrating on the perception of sound and by exploring in a little more detail the use-value of viewing such an emergent process as a matter of actualization of the virtual. The main benefit, we feel, in such a conception of sonic virtuality is in the possibilities of the potential inherent in the sonic aggregate. Sound is not a monolithic, material object subject to objectification and scientific measurement. Its properties and qualities are subjective and, while some components of the exosonus and the endosonus may have a basis in shared and social experience, it is instead subject to individual shaping in its emergence as a perception. Each sound is unique in its formation, unique in its qualities, and unique to the unique individual who perceives it. Thus, sonic virtuality is how we sonically experience our selves.

In the final chapter, we look at practical applications of sonic virtuality as expressed through our definition of sound and our concept of the sonic aggregate. We start the chapter by recapitulating the key points and assertions made throughout the book and by summing up the ideas in a diagrammatic model of sonic virtuality. In the second section, two case studies are presented, an analytical one from the point of audition of perceivers of sound and the second from a sound designer's perspective when planning and designing the audio files for a typical first-person shooter computer game. We close the book by speculating on one future implication of our definition of sound and the concepts arising from it.

8 USING SONIC VIRTUALITY

The only difference between reality and fiction is that fiction needs to be credible.

—MARK TWAIN

Introduction

Throughout this book, we have argued and provided evidence for a new definition of sound that is perceptual—*sound is an emergent perception arising primarily in the auditory cortex and that is formed through spatio-temporal processes in an embodied system*—and have underpinned that definition with the concept of the sonic aggregate. The purpose of this definition is to fully encapsulate all our experiences and understandings of sound within the one definition. In particular, it aims to account for sound not accounted for in other definitions and to explain sonic anomalies not satisfactorily explained by empirical research in the neurosciences. In order to do this, we have shifted the locus and domain of sound from its typical position in the environment—a physical phenomenon, external and separate from our bodies, as expressed in the standard view that sound is a sound wave—to a position that is perceptually based and fully within an embodied system. This shift in focus is a move away from the analysis and design of sound within a one-size-fits-all conceptualization to an understanding that sound is an individual experience that is capable of perceptually emerging in very different forms in two individuals exposed to the same external stimuli. This privatization of sound (Grimshaw 2015) allows for different approaches to sound analysis and design as we demonstrate later in this chapter.

In practical terms, one of the logical conclusions of this thinking is that neither is sound a sound wave nor does sound require a sound wave for the perception to arise. We hold to no absolutes or exclusivity of definitions and so we do not deny that the acoustic definition of sound is perfectly serviceable in particular contexts (as are other definitions), only that acoustics and psychoacoustics, at heart, pertain to sound waves, not sound. However, we do not feel that it is usable in many other contexts, especially those contexts made newly available by recent advances in technology and neuroscience research. In order to be able to work within and explore these contexts, we need new ways to conceptualize and think about sound and it is for this reason that we have developed the conception of sound presented in this book.

We devised the concept of the sonic aggregate to encompass a range of components, sonic or otherwise, that forms the potential to emerge as sound perception. These components may be material and sensuous, the exosonus, or immaterial and nonsensuous, the endosonus. Exosonic components can be sound waves, physical space, the ears, or any other element that is physical and can be sensed or which acts on sensation and such components have the ability to effect, in part, and in conjunction with the endosonus, our perception of sound. The endosonus comprises a range of the mainly cognitive elements memory, expectation, belief, and emotion. The exosonus and endosonus components may have a shared social and cultural dimension or discourse to them (particularly the endosonus) but there is also a strong individual flavor to the sonic aggregate. The aggregate thus conceived accounts for a number of observed phenomena including a shared experience of sound, the personalization of sonic meaning, and the effects of cross-modality. It is, especially, a major part of our contention that the sounds of aural imagery are perceptually similar to sounds perceived in the presence of sound waves and thus should be treated as sounds themselves. Sounds in which components of the sonic aggregate are primarily exosonic and include sound waves are auditioned whereas a sonic aggregate that does not include sound waves and which is primarily, if not exclusively, endosonic forms sounds that emerge under conditions of aural imagery.

To explain how the sonic aggregate forms a perception of sound, we turned to theories of virtuality. The sonic aggregate is to be thought of as a complex of potentialities comprising a virtual cloud, any point of which may lead to the actualization that is sound. The multiple possibilities arise from the natures and interrelationships, of which there are many, of the components of the sonic aggregate; one possibility emerges as the perception of sound. This perception involves a process of the continual recomposing of the sonic aggregate, as the perception itself feeds back, and continual emergence of sound in a present that is composed of fragments of the past and expectations of the future. Perceptual packets of emergent sound, at intervals too small to be cognized, are the basis for the illusory continuity of sound perception.

Combining our definition of sound as emergent perception, our concept of the sonic aggregate, and a number of theories and empirical evidence from neuroscience, embodied cognition, acoustic ecology, belief and epistemology, and studies of imagination, we have arrived at various assertions other than those recapitulated earlier. These include the following:

- Sound is located in the mind, where mind is an embodied system comprising brain, body, and environment. As a hypothesis, sound as emergent perception originates in the secondary auditory cortex. This thinking derives from the assertion that imagined sound is sound and this itself derives from a study of the evidence from auditory neuroscience that shows similar activity in the secondary auditory cortex in conditions of both aural imagery and audition. The significant difference is that the perception of sound, in the case of aural imagery, is driven by a top-down cognitive process whereas the perception of sound in the presence of sound waves is a bottom-up sensory process.
- Formed from the sonic aggregate, sound always contains its provenance. Thus, while sound waves may be acousmatic in that their originating event may be hidden from view or disguised through technological reproduction, sound is never acousmatic. This leads to the logical conclusion that the concept of reduced listening remains a theoretical concept that, in practice, is never achieved. Equally, sound waves are inherently meaningless; sound as emergent perception is meaningful and this meaning includes the source of the sound. Meaning, a property of sound, is learned and derives from experience (which is a part of memory and so is part of the sonic aggregate).
- The endosonus is a prerequisite for sound to emerge; the exosonus is not. Thus, sound waves are not sound; if present, they are merely part of the exosonus. Although we assert that the endosonus is all that is required for sound to be perceived in the case of aural imagery, components of the endosonus are, in their origins, derived from external stimuli at some point in the past.
- We have the ability to cognitively offload the location of sound onto the environment. This process, derived from theories of Embodied Cognition, can occur automatically or can be a conscious act and this provides the sonic basis for locating our selves in the environment and navigating through it.

- Our memory, expectation, belief, and emotion systems, as part of the endosonus, have a significant role in determining any emergent perception of sound. Similarly, emergent perception can affect our epistemic perspective and emotional responses.

The thinking expressed here is encapsulated in Figure 8.1 that shows the sonic aggregate and its components combined with the concept of sonic virtuality. Sound is located within the embodied mind, which comprises brain, body, and environment. Components of the exosonus and endosonus are listed and form the basis of the emergent perception of sound while the sound itself feeds back to the endosonus in a process of continual perceptual emergence. The actualization of that perception as sound is classified in one of two forms: aural imagery, which is the perception of sound under conditions of imagination; and audition, which is the perception of sound in the presence of sound waves.

The concept we are intending to elucidate with Figure 8.1 has a classical precedent, one that dates back to Platonism. In the *Republic* (see Jowett 1941), Plato writes a dialogue in which his mentor, Socrates, describes the Allegory of the Cave. The essential premise of the cave positions several individuals, labeled "prisoners," facing a wall from which they cannot turn away. Projected

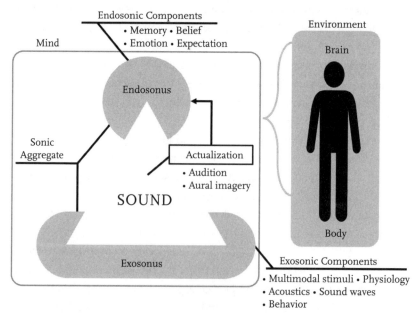

FIGURE 8.1 The Sonic Aggregate as the basis for Sonic Virtuality.

onto the wall are shadows, formed by the light of a fire, of various objects that cannot be observed directly by the prisoners. As the prisoners continue to view the wall of the cave, they begin to attribute names and meanings to the shadows, eventually coming to perceive them as reality. The Allegory of the Cave is typically understood as a metaphor for perception, asserting that what we directly interact with is our perception of the objects and events that make up reality, not the objects themselves. The underlying assertion of the allegory states that the actions of the prisoners reflect how everyday people attune to the world; not by direct observation of reality, but by the experience of its reflection.

The Allegory of the Cave resonates with our thesis of emergent perception with regard to a shared assertion that direct observation of the physical environment is impossible and we can only experience the world as a function of perception that creates an ongoing and inextricable connection between object and its many associations. The cave references the perception of the reflection to assert that the object cannot be separated from its meaning once that meaning has been ascribed. In relation to our model, the exosonus is most comparable to the objects that cast the shadow while the endosonus reflects with the ascribed meaning that is attached to the shadows, which are themselves related to the emergent perception.

We develop this notion to posit a more complex and embodied set of connections in addition to meaning, many of which are absolute and constant. For example, consider an individual who is receiving sound waves generated by the depressing of a single piano key. The Allegory of the Cave would lead us to assert that should the listener have an already established concept of "piano sound," then that concept will consistently influence his or her experience. The listener cannot experience the sonic physical characteristics of the note in its purity because the perception is always adding material to the experience. Our thesis of emergent perception takes things further to propose that the sound wave is not only transformed by way of an established semantic connection but also by way of the surrounding acoustic environment: the presence (or even absence) of any additional stimulus (object, color, temperature, etc.), the physiology of the listener, the intricate unique structures of the listener's neural network, and the listener's memories (and unique memory retrieval characteristics) all form the sonic aggregate—a complex matrix of innumerable points and connections between each point that, by way of the virtuality of the emergent perception, bring forth an actual experience. For Plato, the shadows that represented experience were of a linear formation as the objects, positioned between the wall and the fire, created the reflection.

For us, the shadows of the emergent perception arise when the immeasurable number of objects and meanings that form the virtual cloud are positioned in a precise, and unrepeatable, spatio-temporal arrangement.

We close the chapter and the book by exploring the usefulness of our definition and its utility both in current contexts of analysis and potential design and in future, more speculative contexts that might arise. Throughout, our motivation arises from our interest in and research into computer game sound, particularly the three-dimensional game worlds of the first-person perspective game. The chapter's tone becomes unashamedly speculative but such speculation does have solid ground beneath it. Speculation, too, serves the purpose of inspiration; inspiration to examine and develop the possibilities provided by our conception of sonic virtuality and the possibilities promised by existing technology and the technology to come. It is only through envisioning the future that that future can be made actual.

As stated in the Introduction, our work to date with sound and computer games has been directed toward the goal of further integration of the player with the game technology and the game world. Specifically, our objective is to implement a game engine as an empathy engine capable of responding to the player's emotional state through the use of the real-time processing of audio samples or the synthesis of sound waves that themselves further elicit emotion. In this way we aim to enhance the immersive capabilities of computer game technology so that the player feels more present in the game world. With modern first-person perspective game engines, it is a relatively simple matter to interface the game audio engine with commercial-grade biofeedback devices. Thus the audio processing capabilities of the CryEngine, for example, can be used to manipulate audio samples during gameplay as psychophysiological data change, (such data provided by the likes of the Emotiv EPOC headset). This has been done (e.g., Garner 2013) and similar use of biofeedback has long been used in the service of music composition and performance. For example, the composer Alvin Lucier designed a series of musical performances in the 1960s in which electroencephalography was used to drive loudspeakers (audification of the brainwave signals) or the output of which was mapped to controls on synthesizers (sonification of the brainwave signals), and similar musical work continues to the present day (see Ortiz 2000 for an overview).

However, this work is directed toward music and, very often, musical performance in a concert hall context. The area we work in is different in that the focus is sound and the context is the immersive virtual world, whether virtual reality or computer game worlds. In particular, it is the context and the emotion we concentrate on that marks the difference. However, while we concentrate on fear, and while we concentrate on computer games, we think that our definition of sound and the models we present in this book can be used for other emotions and other sound-related fields too. Importantly, for us, we do not view our speculations as mere crystal ball-gazing; we view speculation instead as a means to spur development of systems we would like to use and to play with by leading to the hypotheses initiating the experimentation that itself might provide results that can be made practicable.

Applying Sonic Virtuality

We have maintained that any new definition of sound, and the concepts and ideas arising from it, should have a practical use-value. In this section, we provide two case studies to demonstrate the practical use-value of sonic virtuality. The first provides the opportunity to demonstrate the use of the concept of the sonic aggregate applied to the analysis of an everyday acoustic ecology. The second uses that concept to demonstrate its future practicality when applied to the design of acoustic ecologies typically found within computer game worlds.

Case Study 1: Analysis

Claire and Alexander are enjoying a day on the beach with their parents. The sun is shining, the sand is warm, the wind is a tickling breeze, and the water beckons brilliant blue as the waves gently sigh their last on the white sands. A number of sounds are perceived: the gentle, rhythmic lapping of the waves; seagulls flapping overhead, rancorously squawking as they pass; the children's mother popping the lids off plastic boxes as she prepares lunch; the occasional slightly repressed burp from their father lying in the sun, swigging from a beer bottle; other children playing and shouting to each other farther down the beach; and the frequent buzzing passage of a high-powered motorboat across the horizon. Alexander hungrily watches the sandwiches and cupcakes as they are shared out on the paper plates and his agile mind is set in motion. While mother has shut her eyes and placed a mask of resigned exasperation on her face at the eruption of another burp, Alexander pinches a few grains of sand between thumb and forefinger and sprinkles them on the top of the cupcakes, cunningly disguising them among the hundreds and thousands decorating the icing. He watches Claire reach for a cupcake and pleasurably anticipates the vicariously spine-tingling crunch of sand between delicate molars as his beloved sister opens her mouth. This brings to mind the painful sound of such crunching when, the last time they had been at the seaside, he had made the mistake of picking up and popping back into his mouth a bright red, boiled sweet that had just flown from his mouth into the sand because Claire had decided to bounce a beachball off the back of his head. Claire has a different perception as her teeth bite down on the cupcake. As the sand is ground to powder, causing her teeth to stand on edge, a sharp pain in her left mandibular first molar causes her to perceive the whining sound of a dental drill, auditioned during her recent visit to the dentist, coming closer and closer to her tightly clamped mouth as that monster spouts his lies to her: *You won't feel a thing my dear.*

The sounds in this everyday scenario may be analyzed through our model of sonic virtuality. In particular, we can use the concept of the sonic aggregate to pick out the components of that aggregate and to assess them in ways that emphasize the private universe of sound we perceive within our minds. We may group these sounds, at a first pass, into two: those that have an exosonic component and so are auditioned; and those that are purely endosonic and so are imagined. In this case, the auditioned sounds include the sounds of waves, seagulls, children playing, lunch being prepared, the father's burps and beer swigging, and the distant motorboat.

We must not make the mistake, though, of assuming such sounds are monolithic in their meaning and implication, such meaning being the same to each perceiver in this scenario. It may be, for example, that while the father takes a secret pleasure in his burping, relaxing in an all too short-lived and infrequent freedom as his beer-distended stomach soaks up the warmth of the sun, the mother takes a different meaning from the sound, leading her to wonder whom she has married and why. Equally, were we to treat sound as a sound wave, and thus describe the sound of the motorboat in terms of frequency and amplitude, the only differences we could ascribe to the sound that the driver of the boat hears and that sound heard by the mother would be those caused by the exosonic component of the acoustic space (changes in frequency spectra and intensity). Viewing sound as perception, though, allows us to take account of the exhilaration and joy the sound represents for the driver and the annoyance and frustration felt by the mother at having her peaceful day at the seaside ruined by boys and their toys. We must also not forget that the driver locates his self at the source of the sound wave and does not move in relation to it while the mother locates the sound as moving somewhere in the distance. In everyday listening terms, one might label the sound "the power" or "my boat" while the other might simply term the sound "that bloody selfish idiot." Thus sounds are fundamentally unique and subjective in their experiences even when the primary component, the sound wave, is exosonic.

These auditioned sounds allow for a localization of self within space. As we have seen with the example of the sound of the motorboat, the perception of sound enables each perceiver to be located either at the source of the sound wave or to locate the sound away from herself. The mother locates the sound on the periphery of her sonic environment, on the auditory horizon, threatening invasion into her sonic sanctum. Paying too close attention to it would shift the location of the sound closer.

The sonic aggregates for these auditioned sounds may be analyzed in terms of the type of exosonic or endosonic components making up the aggregates and the balance between the two sets. Exosonically, we can begin with the sound wave that is a product of the event that sets it in motion and the source features of the vibrating object (material, dimensions, shape, and so on). The physiology of the perceiver and the acoustics of the environment affect the composition and quality of the sound wave that is sensed as does behavior (such as blocking the ears or turning away from the sound wave source) and the effect is different for each person; different physiologies and different spatial dispositions of the body in relation to the source each provide different sensations leading to different perceptions of sound.

Cross-modality plays a role in the exosonus. In this scenario, it is the view of the sea, the warmth of the sand, the scent of salt in the air, and the sugary sweetness of the cupcakes that add to the contextualization that is part of the emergence of sound.

Those sounds we class as imagined are the two examples of aural imagery: that of the crunching of sand between the teeth; and that of the dentist's drill. Alexander imagines the crunching of sand both from his past experience and in anticipation of his sister's displeasure. Here there are elements of memory (the past experience), expectation and belief (this is the sound his sister will perceive), and emotion (the pleasure he gains thinking of Claire's discomfort). The dental drill, strictly speaking, has exosonic components in that the crunching of sand between teeth is the external stimulus (and possibly the distant buzzing of the motorboat plays a role too), but we can view it as aural imagery because the sound itself is imagined. Here again are elements of memory (a recent visit to the dentist), expectation (that a visit will be necessary once again and thus that sound will be re-experienced), belief (it will hurt), and emotion (driven by not only the present experience, but also that to come).

Each sonic aggregate, therefore, provides a different set of potentials for each perceiver. Some of these potentials may be based on primarily shared social understandings and experiences, such as the recognition of what sounds seagulls make as they fly overhead. Others are primarily personal and, in these, the balance is toward the endosonus. Thus, with these sonic aggregates and their potentials, there are highly individual and often unique memories, expectations, beliefs, and emotions to draw on that become more private if combined with exosonic components that themselves depend on physiology, behavior, cross-modality, and physical relation to acoustic space. Thus, within our scenario, each perceiver bears his or her own sonic aggregates, scintillating with private virtual clouds of potentiality, and this explains the different actualizations of sound that emerge, whether these have some common social basis or are intensely private.

Case Study 2: Design

When designing audio files (that is, sound FX rather than music) for a typical first-person perspective computer game—we shall assume this is a first-person shooter with elements of the survival horror genre—a typical process might briefly be described as follows:

- Ensure that the setting and plot (and any narrative) are clearly understood. In this case, let us assume that the setting is mid-15th-century Transylvania under constant threat from the Prince of Wallachia, Vlad III, and within the wider context of Ottoman expansion in the Balkans. Our hero is Hermann of Thuringia, the Grandmaster of the Teutonic Knights, determined to restore his order's once pre-eminent position in the area by defeating both Vlad and the Ottomans and establishing once and for all the independence of Transylvania. This will be achieved once the Ottoman Sultan has been beheaded and Vlad, suffering the punishment usually reserved for *his* enemies, has been impaled (naturally Hermann himself must avoid this fate if the game is to be won). To aid in this endeavor, Hermann has the aid of a dwindling band of knights, whose loyalty is suspect, and a ragtag peasant army to be used as cannon fodder. Ranged against him are the secretive sect of Assassins, the fanatical Ottoman Janissaries, and a small army of Vlad's undead, werewolves, and seductive, vampire virgins.
- Additionally, the audio possibilities afforded by the game engine must be understood. Let us assume this is a typical first-person perspective game

engine of 2014 that uses audio samples, that can mix multiple samples on the fly (so there is no need to be overly concerned with how many samples can be played back simultaneously), and that can process audio samples with reverberation, filtering, and dynamics during gameplay.

• After having read up on contemporary weaponry and history and after having watched several epic films detailing the clashes of the period, we produce an audio design document. This lists a number of audio assets, cross-referencing them with particular locations, events, and characters in the game world. These might include, but not be limited to, a selection of voices for various characters; other vocal utterances, such as grunts, screams, yells, and battle cries; a range of footsteps, horse hoof sounds, and cartwheel rumblings on a variety of surfaces; atmospheric sounds, such as wind through castle towers, the deceptively peaceful twittering of birds in a meadow, and the howl of wolves in a dark wood; and, of course, the all-important sounds of warfare.

• Next begins the fun part—the creation and recording of the audio files. Some of these tasks are relatively straightforward; many weapons' sound waves can be recorded by working with historical re-enactment societies and museums, for example, and the sounds of cannons can be recreated (with some tweaks for modern Hollywood-influenced audiences) by mixing and processing several artillery recordings available in libraries of sound FX. The sound of the act of impaling someone proves a little problematic but is eventually solved by carrying out the act itself on the carcass of a freshly slaughtered pig.

• Finally begins the process of placing the audio files in the game's level editor and, for event- and character-related sounds, working with the programmers and character editors to ensure such audio files are correctly triggered. At the same time, the audio processing capabilities of the game engine are used to set, for example, the reverberation characteristics of various locations and materials within the game world.

Bar a few details, such as testing, this, substantially, is the process of audio design for a modern first-person shooter. In chapter 6, we distinguished between audio design and sound design—the former being a technical-creative process centered on the creation and manipulation of audio files and the latter being an imaginative-creative process centered on the emergent perception of sound. What we just described is the method of audio design where the end result is the creation of audio files leading to a sound that has a functional purpose. That is, each audio file, and the sound it results in, is assumed to have a socially and culturally universal function and meaning. While there is some sound design taking place—for example, the use of aural imagery in the imagining of the sound of the act of human impaling, which, we hope, the audio designer has never actually heard—most of the other audio files have the specific purpose of providing an auditory analogue of the events, characters, and places depicted on the screen.

It would be fair to say that we hope the whole is greater than the sum of its parts; that emotion, for instance, rather than being designed into the soundscape from the start, magically arises from the combination of sounds, images, and actions. If the induction of an emotion such as fear (and related emotions such as concern, apprehension, suspense, surprise, shock, and terror) is to be a part of the design process, then we suggest that the approach of sound design that we present later would be better suited. As we have developed our ideas to account also for the sonic paradigms enabled by coming embodied and psychophysiological technologies, there is an assumption in our example that biofeedback will be routinely integrated into computer games within a few years.[1]

Our theoretical framework is intended to fundamentally alter the creative process of sound design with regard to how the designers position themselves in it. Within the archetypal audio design process, the designer's primary direction when generating a foley recording (that is, a recording of a sound effect) is most frequently to make the sound "realistic." When the player sees the act of impaling or, as a character in the game, experiences it, the foley audio must match his or her expectations. Of course, such expectations are unlikely to be established by witnessing such an act directly. They could instead be based on the audience's prior experience of related foley recordings, auditioned in previously played games. They could potentially be based on connected experiences that have semantic association to the act of impaling—be it the skewering of a steak on the barbecue or that memory, buried in their childhood, that their schoolyard pals used to make with their mouths when acting out "that Father Brennan scene" from *The Omen*. The problem here is that these expectations are individual and bespoke, both for the audience and the designer; therefore there is always the potential for a mismatch of realism, in which the personal expectations of the audience and the designer are significantly different.

The practical application of our model becomes apparent in circumstances where designers do not consider themselves or their own perceptual biases within the creative process. For example, if our audio designer uses the sound of a pig being skewered as the foley audio to accompany the graphical depiction of an impaling action, he is arguably making an assumption that the foley audio and (what he would term) the actual sound will be characteristically comparable because there is sufficient semantic connection between the two (both deal with the dramatic invasion of flesh with a sharp implement). This thought process is then validated by the designer as he auditions the recording, benchmarking it against his own expectations. While this is a relatively logical deduction there is a rather wide margin for error. The expectations of the designer are not self-evaluated or considered but, instead, uncritically accepted. For him, the recording *feels* right and so he is confident in its implementation. Furthermore, he doesn't appraise the individual expectations of the audience, leaving a great deal of uncertainty regarding whether for them a recording of a pig being skewered will generate the desired cross-modal continuity between sound, graphics, and context.

Many more senior audio designers would argue that such a mistake is that of a novice and that with experience, new designers develop and hone these skills as they become more adept at understanding the audience. However, there are two notable problems with this perspective. The first is that building up such experience takes a significant investment in time for the designer and an equally significant investment in forgiveness for the audience as they are subjected to the mismatch. The second issue is a more inherent problem when designing audio material based on prior audio design experience, that of homogenization. If we define foley audio within a computer game (or any other medium) as "good" based on its ability to match expectations, we form an ecological process of homogeneity that is built around expectation—specifically that of perceived realism.

Going back to our impaling recording, built on a semantic-based deduction by our designer, the recording is without question not that of a person being impaled but it is nonetheless accepted by the audience (by way of suspension of disbelief). Within that context, the sound was "good." Now, within our perceptual model of sound, a new component is established within the sonic aggregates of both the audience and the designer. The audience has received an expectation update based on their acceptance of match between the impaled pig recording and the synchronized visual depiction. The designer also receives an expectation update; for him, the result of his observation is that the recording has been successfully representative (*this recording worked; I shall use it again the next time I need to represent an impaling*). The result is that from now on, when our audience observes a fictional impaling, they expect to hear the skewering of a pig. Thus, when our (or another) designer is required to design an audio file for impaling, out comes the skewer. Repetition of this process is reinforcing as expectation becomes convention and, even though it is unlikely to be the most ideal recording (surpassing all potential others), our audio designer becomes cautious of straying from such an established pathway. This has particular ramifications with regard to the potential for creative freedom and begins to trap us within a cycle of "realism" that, in fact, is completely artificial.

This design story uses our theory of sound to critique certain practices within contemporary sound design but we assert that our ideas also have significant potential as a positive driver for the creative design process. Within our model, sound exists in the embodied mind and therefore sound design must be responsive to all of the mind's primary components: the brain, the body, and the environment. While it is important to note that we do not consider most of the following points to be positioned solely within one element of the mind, we describe them as such to more clearly define our creative approach.

Acknowledging the brain would require consideration of the memory, the cognition, and the emotion of the audience. Memory might incorporate expectation but, we assert, would also relate to the experience of dynamic flow, change, and time. This particular area is where many designers fail to impact their audience to the extent they would wish, because they consider their audio material and the receiving audience within a notably small window of time. "Jump scares" fall into this category, in which only the immediate, reflexive emotions and thought processes of the audience are considered, creating experiences that are intense only for a very limited time, leave little lasting impact, and are significantly lacking in emotional depth. Greater consideration of time requires designers to consider their material in its entirety, manipulating each individual element with regard to the one that preceded it and the one that will follow. This could be extended even further to consider time (with regard to audience experience) before and after the audience is presented with the material as a whole. Just as a well-crafted rollercoaster construction considers the design of its queue so that those in line are ideally positioned to hear the screams of those currently riding, so too could a film soundtrack consider the auditory experience of a cinema theater audience before the film has even begun. For example, our impaling sound might be intended to act as a shocking stimulus at the very beginning of the film, but in many theater experiences, the soundscape within the first few moments of a film often includes people talking while devouring their popcorn and a few stragglers still jostling to find their seats. In such a distracting sonic environment, the impact of our impaling sound would be completely lost.

Incorporating the body into the creative process could take many forms, several of which relate to the interrelations between physiology and affect. Incorporating elements of human physiology into real-time content generation/processing is already an established area of study and much of our own prior research (see the Introduction for a summary) has considered the potential of biometrics and interpretive frameworks to collect physiological data from which to then infer affective state and adjust content in response. This has particular application with regard to computer game sound and the potential for interactivity, with the possibility for the game engine architecture to automatically construct an understanding of the player's emotions to inform a sonic response that is bespoke for the individual. If the game engine were to sense that sudden stimuli were causing severe anxiety spikes it could attenuate the intensity of our impaling sound so as to save our poor player from a cardiac arrest. Conversely, such a system could monitor heart rate and electro-dermal activity (both via a simple sensor integrated into the game controller) to establish the player's base reading and activity range in order to find the fear "sweet-spot" that appears just after the slow-building peak of suspense-driven anxiety: the player is psychophysiologically primed for the horrific revelation of a sudden impaling but has just begun to doubt that such an event is inevitable and, as a result, has lowered her guard.

When we discussed time earlier, we also addressed several elements that could be positioned in our third component of the mind, the environment. However, the elements we position for consideration within the environment are comparatively more fixed (at least typically so over short periods of time). This could include the material, scale, and spatial and architectural characteristics of the acoustic space. With regard again to computer games (but equally applicable to home cinema and other media), design considerations within this area could include audio optimization for architectural spaces in which the act of playing is common, such as emphasizing reverberation in sounds that are intended to have such a quality to compensate for the lack of acoustic reflection a typical den or bedroom affords.

Thinking beyond the sound wave, and attempting to design sound rather than audio, requires the designer to consider the environment within which the audio is to be placed. One relevant and noteworthy approach to *sound* design is consideration of cross-modal effects. As a technique this relates to Thom's (1999, see chapter 6) notion of "designing a movie for sound," in which the audio is fixed and the designer manipulates the other elements of the film to shape the sound. Returning to our impaling sound and accompanying pig skewering foley audio, the commonplace perspective assumes that the sound can only be altered by manipulating the audio. This can potentially be extremely limiting as it discounts all other options for changing the sound (as it is emergently perceived by the player) such as adjusting the graphics, pacing, or context. As the re-recording of the audio is likely to be a time-consuming endeavor, such a limitation of perspective could prove highly inefficient in plausible scenarios in which a minor graphical tweak could adjust the overall experience to create a much more effective sound.

This approach centralizes its focus on the sonic aggregate, within which all of the elements listed are components. We assert that design based on the sonic aggregate encourages the creative expansion of the possibilities afforded by design by way of viewing the perception of sound as unique, with no two sounds ever being alike. This perspective moves design away from homogenizing processes and fixed audience demands to encourage more willing reception to greater variety and to new experiences that are dramatically different to the extent that they are felt as such.

If we take our approach further, we can begin to talk about the personalization of computer game sound (and, indeed, the personalization of sound in other media). Given the role that individual disposition plays in the sonic aggregate, a player's shared cultural and unique psychological composition, we might indeed say that computer game sound design *should* be personalized if it is to function properly. There is little point in designing an audio sample designed to evoke terror if the player's experience, and therefore expectations founded on knowledge of the game genre conventions, renders the player blasé when confronted by that sound wave. Three things are required to enable such personalized sound design: first, the player-game interface, the biofeedback hardware and software, must be capable of recognizing various emotions; second, the game engine must be able to track and store those emotions as they change over multiple games and in response to audio stimuli; third, game sound design must develop beyond the direct manipulation of sound wave parameters to a system that allows audio to be designed according to emotional parameters.

If there is one thing we have discovered in our empirical work, it is that it is very difficult to infer emotions from psychophysiological data. This is difficult enough with clinical devices, such as +60 channel electroencephalography in sterile experimental conditions, but it is currently impossible with cheaper and less precise consumer equipment, especially when allied to the messiness and ad hoc nature of the typical gaming environment. We are at the stage where the best we can do is to track arousal levels without the all-too-invasive procedures needed to assess emotion that would disturb the sheer enjoyment of gameplay. Nevertheless, this is a stage further than we were several years ago and we believe that the system we envision will come to pass.

Once this happens, we envisage a system that can accurately track phasic psychophysiology that is tied to specific sound events. These events take place in a context and so the system needs to note the elements of this context and the emotion triggered. The context may be momentary or it may be a chain of situations and will include factors such as narrative/plot, lighting, non-player character and other player activity, single or multi-player configurations, and so on. Furthermore, the system must be able to note changes in psychophysiology that occur with increasing habituation of the player to context and specific events in the game, sound or otherwise. In other words, the system must be able to learn and thus be able to produce a sound wave that is better suited to a particular affect once the initial effect of the original audio sample has been lost through repeat playing of the game.

To produce this new sound wave, whether through manipulation of pre-existing audio samples or through sound synthesis, the system should be able to carry out its task with the knowledge of which audio parameters in a specific context (as per the emotional profiling detailed earlier) will result in the desired emotional effect. This requires the development of a meta-language for sound design that uses emotion terminology. For example, rather than shape an audio sample according to standard parameters such as amplitude envelope and reverberation, the sound designer, who, in any case, is increasingly akin to a computer programmer, specifies a sonic emotional contour over the particular section of gameplay. Then, behind the scenes, and as the player plays, the game engine translates this personalized contour into appropriate audio by manipulating sound wave parameters.

Concluding Remarks

If sound is within us, a logical question to ask is, *can sound be extracted from us?* Or, more precisely, can sound, particularly aural imagery, be decomposed into its sonic aggregate components and a sound wave synthesized from those components for others to audition? If our hypothesis is correct, that the emergent perception of sound originates in the secondary auditory cortex, and if we can neurologically examine and gather components of the sonic aggregate that form this perception, can these data be decoded to create a sound wave?[2]

This is not as far-fetched as it might seem. For a number of years now, such neural decoding has been taking place in the study of vision: the extraction of images from brain activity. For example, Nishimoto and colleagues

(2011) have reformulated moving images from an individual's brain activity (gathered using functional magnetic resonance imaging) during the viewing of a film. The resulting images, though low resolution, are recognizable in color (somewhat), shape, and movement from the original.[3] As far as we know, there has been no similar work on sound. Thompson, Casey, and Torresani (2013) have recently presented a model for audio stimulus reconstruction but this is for music retrieval and is theoretical. There have been successful experiments in decoding speech from neurological activity (again, while the listener is subjected to the stimulus) but this is entirely different from what we propose. Such work does not reconstruct the sound of speech but the words, which are then made audible through text-to-voice synthesis, and it makes use of statistical techniques and prediction based on the rules of linguistics rather than dealing with sound and the parameters of sound waves.

The system we speculate on would be able, ultimately, to construct a digital representation of a sound wave whose parameters derive from the sonic aggregate. Parameters such as reverberation, location in three-dimensional space, timbre, duration, amplitude and frequency envelopes, and so forth are part of the memory and imagining of sound and are used to recall or imagine sounds. The vision and speech work described earlier is conducted during reception of the sensory stimuli (movie or speech) and there is some speculation in the literature that similar techniques can be used to construct movies and speech from memories and imaginings. Being able to do this with sound opens up a number of possibilities.

One of these is the possibility of simply thinking a sound when one wishes to design audio files. Thus, a designer would think a sound with a particular character and the resultant neural activity would be decoded into digital audio and stored in a digital audio workstation for manipulation, reuse, and, ultimately, public audibility. Once the sound is publicly available, then other scenarios can be imagined; we briefly discuss two.

If sound can be extracted from one person, then it should be possible to place it into another person. This requires that the neurological data gathered from one person are used to excite the neurons of another. Brain stimulation is becoming widely studied, if not yet widely used; for example, the use of functional electrical stimulation can translate motor control signals in the brain directly into muscles in paralyzed limbs thereby moving them (see, for example, Ethier et al. 2012). In the auditory field, work proceeds on stimulating the auditory cortex in pursuit of a treatment for tinnitus (see Zhang 2013 for a review). Some time in the future, we imagine it will be possible to directly transfer sound from one person to another.[4]

In a similar vein, cinemas and clubs and concert halls with amplified music may become acoustically silent; rather than sound waves, wired or wireless neural activation may be sent to the audience to form the sounds within their minds. This can also occur with headphones and earphones being replaced by neural activity transmitters.[5] In the field of sound design, where sounds can be thought into digital audio workstations and undergo manipulation as audio files, those audio files can be reconverted to sound through neural manipulation. What sound will emerge, given the perceiver's unique endosonus, remains to be heard.

NOTES

INTRODUCTION

1. At the time, the prevailing notion of immersion in game studies was one that somewhat conflated the term with presence and these experiments follow that convention.

CHAPTER 1

1. Although, as any musician will know, sounds below approximately 20hz can still be detected by the human ear and are thus cochlear sounds; but rather than being continuous (if, for example, a musical tone), they are perceived as a rhythm or pulse.
2. Carl Stumpf's *Tonpsychologie* (1883/1890) is an earlier example but is strongly psychological in its focus and deals in the main with music.
3. One must always be careful in appealing to common sense and the practices of language. Despite centuries of often heretical scientific discourse attempting to prove the opposite, it is a still common statement to make, and a common-sense one, that the stars move across the night sky or that the sun crosses the sky from east to west.

CHAPTER 2

1. Although, given the recent disappointing experience one of us had at a brand new concert hall, one could be forgiven for thinking otherwise.
2. It seems somewhat perverse to use such auditory perception as an argument against both the aspatial theories, particularly as Casati and Dokic argue that each theory is independent of the other.
3. For a more comprehensive treatment of the subject, we can recommend a number of textbooks including, as an introduction, *Acoustics and Psychoacoustics* by

Howard and Angus (1996) and *Auditory Neuroscience* by Schnupp, Nelkin, and King (2011).

4. Humans also have a propensity to regularly change the physicality of the outer auditory system through the use of, for example, hats, earmuffs, or earlobe plugs and this affects our sound localization.
5. In recording studios, engineers treat sound as a commodity to be moved at will, being able to pan sound signals between loudspeakers, and quite freely talk of positioning, for example, "the sound on the left."
6. And here is another distinction between sound and sound wave. The latter is by definition moving but the former, while it can move, can also be in a static location.
7. For a fuller discussion, see chapter 5 in Schnupp, Nelkin, and King (2011).
8. Sound has ephemerality; to be heard is to be known.
9. This relates to the Platonic Allegory of the Cave, in which we (as observers) cannot turn to face the world in its truly objective form; we can only witness its reflections.

CHAPTER 3

1. This was personally observed at the IHCI conference in Prague 2013—a presenter played an example sound asking what the audience thought it was and received answers including popcorn popping and a Geiger counter (the sought for answer).

CHAPTER 4

1. This powerful argument is routinely used to persuade by the scientific community, particularly the medical community. How many times do we hear a physician or medical researcher stating on the air: "Ten years ago we used to think X. Now we know Y." Although the motivation behind such statements may well be political, these spokesmen are not necessarily lying. However, the chances are that, in another ten years, someone else will blithely state: "Ten years ago we used to think Y. Now we know Z."

CHAPTER 5

1. "Not otherwise specified" is itself a little problematic and, as something of a baroque obfuscation, somewhat undermines the legitimacy of such psychiatric diagnoses. Nevertheless, it is arguably a term that inspires more confidence in the patient than "your guess is as good as ours."
2. In the same way that misunderstanding too can lead to significant benefit. In the 1860s, Alexander Graham Bell read Hermann von Helmholtz's *On the*

Sensations of Tone as a Physiological Basis for the Theory of Music in the German original. However, his poor knowledge of the German language led him to mistakenly believe that von Helmholtz was claiming that vowel sounds could be transmitted electronically over wire whereas von Helmholtz had, in fact, demonstrated that sounding electro-magnetized tuning forks within his resonators could produce vowel sounds. This imprecision in translation, and the resulting technological breakthrough as he attempted to actualize his mistaken understanding of von Helmholtz's work, led Bell to later state: "If I had been able to read German, I might never have begun my experiments in electricity [that led to the invention of the telephone]" (quoted in Picker 2003, 100). One should always maintain a healthy skepticism of the overly fanatical application of precise, tunnel-vision-inducing methodologies.

3. Haydn was said to have probably suffered from an otic lesion, causing hearing loss, pulsatile tinnitus, hyperacusis, and musical hallucinations (Hughes, R. 1978. *Haydn*. London: J. M. Dent.). Schumann is also associated with auditory hallucinations, alongside syphilitic hallucinosis, lucid dreams/hypnagogic states, and auditory verbal hallucinations. It has been said that "he claimed to have written some of his best works at the urging of innervoices" (http://hallucinations.enacademic.com/1687/Schumann,_Robert).

CHAPTER 7

1. In an endnote to his article, Massumi acknowledges that the black ink of the pac-men represents an absorption of light on the page but argues that the pac-men are sensuous because they are "objectively plottable."

2. That we cannot not see the triangle turns out not to be true, or at least rarely not to be true. When one of us showed, quite unscientifically, the Kanizsa Triangle to an acquaintance and asked what she could see (to which the immediate retort was *what am I meant to see?*), the triangle did not appear in the response. It was only when the diagram was described as a Kanizsa Triangle and the apices of the triangle pointed out that it was perceived. This effect could be argued from either free will (a refusal to give as an answer something that was not printed on the page followed by an acceptance of the possibility of seeing the pac-men in a relationship, as a plurality) or determinism (she really could not see the triangle—perhaps different brain processes—but the perception was achieved with the inclusion of further information and now she really cannot *not* see the triangle every time she is presented with it).

3. While we agree with the sentiment and find in it common ground with our conception of sound as perception, it should be noted that the authors' usage of the word "virtual" functions as a convenient catch-all for simulation and emulation rather than being rooted in any thorough conception of virtuality.

4. Noë's book, purportedly dealing with perception in general and almost 300 pages in length, devotes just over one page to sound.

CHAPTER 8

1. Several start-up games companies were marketing such games in 2014 (e.g., http://www.nevermindgame.com/ and http://crooked-tree-studios.myshopify.com/collections/all) and some larger companies already use biofeedback for play testing, with plans to develop biofeedback games in the future (e.g., http://www.gdcvault.com/play/1014734/Biofeedback-in-Gameplay-How-Valve).
2. This raises other questions such as, would a second person perceiving sound in the presence of that sound wave perceive the same sound as that decoded from the originating perceiver? The answer to this is no, according to our theory.
3. There might be more accuracy in decoding the images if vision too were subject to the same conceptualization as what we provide for sound—that is, that there is a *visual* aggregate and so other areas of the brain contributing to that aggregate should be assessed and their neurological activity collated and decoded together with visual cortex neural data.
4. Brain-to-brain communication, although elaborately mediated via electronics and working with relatively simple motor cognition, is now possible (see, for example, http://homes.cs.washington.edu/~rao/brain2brain/index.html).
5. This will solve the problem of public transport passengers being plagued by another's musical taste.

GLOSSARY

Acoustic community: Truax's term for a soundscape where acoustic information has a widespread role in the inhabitants' lives.

Acoustic ecology: First originating in the work of Schafer and Truax; acoustic ecology examines the relationships that exist between sounds and living beings within the natural environment.

Acousmatic sound: The deliberate obfuscation of the sound wave's cause or of the original event of a recording. Typically used in the description of musique concrète or sounds in cinema and computer games where the sound object or event is off-screen.

Actualization: The outcome of the process of virtuality in which potentials from the *virtual cloud* give rise to an emergent perception. Sound exists as a personal experience of actualization.

Alief: A process within cognition that exerts direct control over behavioral response; essentially the particular component of cognition that is for action. Alief is most commonly revealed in circumstances when there is a discordance with belief and the physical behavior mismatches the conscious appraisal of a situation.

Aspatial theory of sound: Asserts that neither sound nor the process of auditory perception is inherently spatial.

Audioanalgesia: Term coined by Schaffer referring to the use of sound to intentionally block out other distractions.

Auditory acuity/blunting: Scenarios in which the listener perceives sound as either louder (acuity) or softer (blunting) than would be expected when considering the decibel level of the associated sound wave.

Auditory cortex: A component of the cerebral cortex primarily concerned with the processing of auditory information. With reference to our thesis, the auditory cortex is the component of the mind from which the emergent perception of sound comes forth.

Auditory stream: Bregman's term; related qualities of an auditory event are perceptually clustered. Grouping into low or high, far or near, allows us to separate simultaneous sounds and provides the basis for the comprehension of music, for example.

Aural imagery: Also known as auditory imagery; this is the imagination of sound in the absence of sound waves. For us, this is as much sound as that perceived in the presence of sound waves.

Causal listening (see *modes of listening*): Identifies the source object/event of a sound.

Cognition: Refers to mental information processing and can incorporate functions that include attention, memory, language/communication, and problem solving to name a few.

Cognitive offloading: From theories of *Embodied Cognition*, the idea that we can use the environment for the storage of information and the processing of cognitive tasks. This exploitation of the environment reduces the cognitive workload.

Connotative listening (see *modes of listening*): Theory of listening in which auditory perception establishes pre-cognitive semantic associations from the incoming stream of sound waves.

Construal-level theory: Increasingly abstract levels of thought follow increasing psychological distance; the smaller our psychological distance is, the more we are able to focus on the task at hand.

Critical listening (see *modes of listening*): Generating a critical appraisal of sound.

Cross-modality: Important element of the sonic aggregate that accounts for the effects that stimuli of other modalities can have upon the emergent perception.

Disjunct plurality: In the theory of the virtual, a set of spatially separated elements that perceptually counts as one and that contributes to the emergences of the *singularity*.

Distal theory: The theory that sounds are located at or near the objects or events that generated them.

Duplex theory: A theory from psychoacoustics describing the process of localization of sound. It is never clear whether this refers to the sound wave or the source of the sound wave but the theory puts forward two explanations for this localization: *interaural level difference* and *interaural time difference*.

Embodied cognition: An opposition to cognitivism and Cartesian dualism that asserts all mental processes (inclusive of imagination and reasoning) are determined by the physical character of the human body.

Empathic listening (see *modes of listening*): Attaching affective information to a sound from which the perspectives of others can be inferred.

Endosonus: A set of immaterial and nonsensuous components of the *sonic aggregate* that broadly comprise memory, expectation, belief, and emotion.

Everyday listening: Descriptive of Gaver's approach to sound analysis and design that parallels our mundane experience of sound and the language we use to describe it. Thus sound is the object or event that is the source of the sound wave.

Exosonus: A set of material and sensuous components of the *sonic aggregate* that comprise those elements that can be sensed or that act upon the sensing of physical objects.

Functional listening (see *modes of listening*): Attributing function to sound and the associated source object/event.

Gettier problem: The proposal, put forth by Edmund Gettier, that questions *justified true belief* and asserts that it is possible for a statement to be justified, true, and believed but not to count as genuine knowledge, should the justification be based on a false premise, but still be true by chance.

Immersion: Often conflated with the term *presence*; it is what is delivered by immersive technologies and is thus an objective measurement. According to presence theories, presence is proportional to the level of immersion achieved in the technology and this is proportional to level of realism achieved.

Interaural level difference: Part of the *duplex theory* of sound localization; sounds of higher frequency and shorter wavelength are blocked by the head and therefore the intensity of the sound wave at one ear will be lower than at the other where that sound wave source is to one side.

Interaural time difference: Part of the *duplex theory* of sound localization; sounds of lower frequency and longer wavelength are not blocked by the head, therefore the difference in time of arrival of the sound wave at each ear is used to calculate the location of the sound wave source where that sound wave source is to one side.

Justified true belief: Derived from Plato's *Theaetetus*; this account of knowledge proposes that for a statement or proposal to be considered as something that is known it must be simultaneously true and believed to be true, and there must be a logical rationale to justify belief.

Medial theory: A theory in which the location of sounds is best understood as being somewhere in the space between the source object or event and the listener—whether sound moves or not in this theory is ambiguous.

Modes of listening (see *connotative listening, empathic listening, reflexive listening, functional listening, causal listening, reduced listening* and *critical listening*): Various conceptual forms of listening proposed by Tuuri and colleagues.

Navigational listening: Originally referencing computer game sound but equally applicable to everyday experiencing; refers to utilizing positional information of the sound wave source (the audio beacon) within the environment as a means of supporting navigation of the self.

Neuroplasticity: The ability of the brain to adapt its neural pathways and synapses under new conditions, such as a change in the auditory capabilities of one ear.

Non-cochlear sound: Riddoch's term for sound not sensed by the cochlea. He provides three types: synaesthetic, infrasonic, and auditory imagination.

Pareidolia: A psychological phenomenon in which vague or random stimuli are perceived as meaningful; the urge to form order from chaos. An auditory example of this is the *phantom signal effect*.

Perception: The interpretation of sensory information that supports understanding of the environment. With reference to our thesis, sound is a perceptual emergence, generated within the mind.

Perceptual blindness: Sometimes referred to as inattentional blindness, circumstances in which an object or event is not seen because the individual's attention is focused on another task.

Presence: The feeling of being in a space, of embodiment in an environment, and typically used in the field of virtual reality and related areas. It is a subjective response to immersive technologies and is often conflated with the term *immersion*.

Proprioception/Proprioceptive sound: The perception of sound (waves) as originating from within the listener's own body (e.g., hearing one's own heart beat).

Proximal theory: A theory in which sounds are thought to exist where the listener is.

Reduced listening (see *modes of listening*): A mode of listening to sounds for their acoustic properties alone.

Reflexive listening (see *modes of listening*): Immediate, pre-cognitive physiological responses to a sound.

Schizophonia: Schafer's neologism to describe the violence done to natural ecologies by the separation of sound from its original source object or event. It has been enabled only within the last century and a half by audio recording, reproduction, and broadcast technologies.

Sensation: The act of receiving sensory information from the physical environment. Commonplace assertion is that sensation is essential to perception. Our thesis questions this assumption to argue that a perceptual experience does not always require sensation.

Singularity: In the theory of the virtual, the singularity is what emerges from the act of perception of the *disjunct plurality* in combination with nonsensuous elements such as evolutionary and acquired habits.

Sonic aggregate: The set of potentialities from which sound emerges. These are drawn from a mix of *endosonic* and, optionally, *exosonic* components; the sonic aggregate is encompassed in a *virtual cloud* from which sound is actualized as emergent perception.

Sonification: The conversion of non-auditory data to audio by mapping between parameters of the data to parameters of audio.

Spatio-temporality: Refers to the precise arrangement of each component and relationship within the sonic aggregate within both space and time; particular spatio-temporal arrangements lead to the emergent perception of sound.

Standard definition of sound: The definition of sound that is currently widely accepted and that forms the basis for the typical dictionary definition of sound;

sound is a sound wave, a moving pressure wave propagated through a medium such as air, and can be defined and measured objectively mainly in terms of frequency and amplitude.

Subvocalization: Motor activity primarily around the throat and mouth that can occur during speech and linguistic processing and that has been asserted to support comprehension during reading.

Synchresis: Coined by Chion (and labeled as synchrony by Anderson), this term describes the process by which physically disjunct sound waves from loudspeakers in a cinema are perceptually synchronized to the events taking place on the screen. Similar to the psychoacoustic terms the audio-visual proximity effect and the ventriloquism effect.

Thrownness (Geworfenheit): Heidegger's notion that we cannot grasp or understand existence because we are continually caught up in it.

Umwelt: Von Uexkull's early 20th-century theory that our relationship to the environment and much of our cognition is determined by our biological nature and physical form.

Virtual cloud: A Deleuzian term, describing his concept of a dynamic matrix of possibilities that envelops the here and now of existence and through which the future becomes the present as a function of *virtuality*.

Virtuality: The process by which potentials become actualized depending on the precise spatio-temporal arrangement of the innumerable variables that comprise the *virtual cloud*.

Verleugnung (disavowal): Coined by Freud, the term refers to a psychological defense mechanism in which individuals refuse to accept a "truth" in order to protect their own mental well-being.

REFERENCES

Aaronson, D., and S. Ferres. 1986. Reading Strategies for Children and Adults: A Quantitative Model. *Psychological Review* 93 (1): 89–112.

Abrams, R., and M. Taylor. 1978. A Rating Scale for Emotional Blunting. *American Journal of Psychiatry* 135: 226–229.

Abu-Salha, M., and R. S. Dhillon. 1998. Folie á Deux: Two Case Reports. *Jefferson Journal of Psychiatry* 14 (1): 12–18.

Alzheimer's Association. 2014. *Hallucinations, Delusions and Paranoia.* http://www.alz.org/national/documents/topicsheet_hallucinations.pdf. Accessed June 23, 2014.

Amad, A. et al. 2013. The Multimodal Connectivity of the Hippocampal Complex in Auditory and Visual Hallucinations. *Molecular Psychiatry* 19 (2): 184–191.

Anderson, J. D. 1996. *The Reality of Illusion: An Ecological Approach to Cognitive Film Theory.* Carbondale: Southern Illinois University Press.

Anderson, M. L. 2003. Embodied Cognition: A Field Guide. *Artificial Intelligence* 149: 91–130.

Andreasen, N. C. 2004. Scale for the Assessment of Positive Symptoms. *Group* 1 (4).

Asutay, E., D. Västfjäll, A. Tajadura-Jimenez, A. Genell, P. Bergman, and M. Kleiner. 2012. Emoacoustics: A Study of the Psychoacoustical and Psychological Dimensions of Emotional Sound Design. *Journal of the Audio Engineering Society* 60 (1/2): 21–28.

Baddeley, A. D., and G. Hitch. 1974. Working Memory. In *The Psychology of Learning and Motivation: Advances in Research and Theory*, vol. 8, edited by G. H. Bower, 47–89. New York: Academic Press.

Ballas, J. A., and T. Mullins. 1991. Effects of Context on the Identification of Everyday Sounds. *Human Performance* 4 (3): 199–219.

Bar, M. 2004. Visual Objects in Context. *Nature Reviews: Neuroscience* 5 (8): 617–629.

Bar, M., and S. Ullman. 1996. Spatial Context in Recognition. *Perception* 25: 343–352.

Bar-Anan, Y., N. Liberman, Y. Trope, and D. Algom. 2007. Automatic Processing of Psychological Distance: Evidence from a Stroop Task. *Journal of Experimental Psychology* 136: 610–622.

Barot, T. 1999. Songbirds Forget Their Tunes in Cacophony of Road Noise. *Sunday Times*, January 10.

Barthes, R. 1977. The Death of the Author. In *Image, Music, Text: Roland Barthes*, edited and translated by S. Heath. New York: Hill and Wang, 146.

Berkey, C. 2011. *Behind the Art: Craig Berkey.* http://designingsound.org/2011/06/behind-the-art-craig-berkey/. Accessed November 11, 2013.

Berthier, D. 1985. Intentionality and the Virtual. *Intellectica* 2005 (40): 91–108.

Bittarello, M. 2014. Mythologies of Virtuality: "Other Space" and "Shared Dimension" from Ancient Myths to Cyberspace. *The Oxford Handbook of Virtuality*, edited by M. Grimshaw, 86–110. New York: Oxford University Press.

Blakemore, S. J., J. Smith, R. Steel, C. E. Johnstone, and C. D. Frith. 2000. The Perception of Self-Produced Sensory Stimuli in Patients with Auditory Hallucinations and Passivity Experiences: Evidence for a Breakdown in Self-Monitoring. *Psychological Medicine* 30 (5): 1131–1139.

Blascovich, J., and J. Bailenson. 2011. *Infinite Reality.* New York: Harper Collins.

Bosshardt, H. G. 1990. Subvocalization and Reading Rate Differences between Stuttering and Nonstuttering Children and Adults. *Journal of Speech, Language and Hearing Research* 33 (4): 776–785.

Bottomore, S. 1999. The Panicking Audience? Early Cinema and the "Train Effect." *Historical Journal of Film, Radio and Television* 19 (2): 177–216.

Bowyer, S. M., M. Seidman, K. Elisevich, D. De Ridder, K. M. Mason, J. Dria, Q. Jiang, I. Darrat, F. Leong, G. L. Barkley, and N. Tepley. 2006. *MEG Localization of the Suspected Cortical Generators of Tinnitus.* http://www.megimaging.com/tinnitusbiomag2006.pdf. Accessed May 31, 2014.

Bregman, A. S. 1990. *Auditory Scene Analysis: The Perceptual Organization of Sound.* Cambridge (MA): MIT Press.

Breinbjerg, M. 2005. The Aesthetic Experience of Sound—Staging of Auditory Spaces in 3D Computer Games. Paper presented to *Aesthetics of Play*, October 14–15, Bergen, Norway. http://www.aestheticsofplay.org/breinbjerg.php. Accessed June 10, 2014.

Bridgett, R. 2013. *Rob Bridgett and Game Audio Culture.* http://designingsound.org/2013/09/interview-rob-bridgett-and-game-audio-culture/. Accessed November 7, 2013.

Britton, R. 1998. *Belief and Imagination: Explorations in Psychoanalysis.* London: Routledge.

Bronkhorst, A. W. 1995. Localization of Real and Virtual Sound Sources. *Journal of the Acoustical Society of America* 98(5): 2542–2553.

Brown, E., and P. Cairns. 2004. A Grounded Investigation of Game Immersion. Paper presented to *Human Factors in Computing Systems*, April 24–29, Vienna, Austria.

Buchanan, K. 2013. *You'll Never Guess How the Dinosaur Sounds in Jurassic Park Were Made.* http://www.vulture.com/2013/04/how-the-dino-sounds-in-jurassic-park-were-made.html. Accessed October 20, 2013.

Buchsbaum, B. R., S. Lemire-Rodger, C. Fang, and H. Abdi. 2012. The Neural Basis of Vivid Memory Is Patterned on Perception. *Journal of Cognitive Neuroscience* 24 (9): 1867–83.

Buckner, R., and J. Logan. 2001. Functional Neuroimaging Methods: PET and fMRI. In *Handbook of Functional Neuroimaging of Cognition,* edited by R. Cabeza and A. Kingstone, 27–48. Cambridge (MA): MIT Press.

Bunzeck, N., T. Wuestenberg, K. Lutz, H. J. Heinze, and L. Jancke. 2005. Scanning Silence: Mental Imagery of Complex Sounds. *Neuroimage* 26 (4): 1119–1127.

Burns, S. A. 2014. *Gettier Examples, Evolutionary Pragmatism: A Discourse on Modern Philosophy for the 21st Century.* http://www3.sympatico.ca/saburns/pg0306b.htm. Accessed July 7, 2014.

Cabello, A., and M. T. Cunha. 2013. State-independent Contextuality with Identical Particles. *Physical Review A* 87 (2): 022126.

Calleja, G. 2014. Immersion in Virtual Worlds. In *The Oxford Handbook of Virtuality,* edited by M. Grimshaw, 222–236. New York: Oxford University Press.

Casati, R., and J. Dokic. 2005/2010. Sounds. *Stanford Encyclopedia of Philosophy.* http://plato.stanford.edu/entries/sounds/. Accessed June 4, 2014.

Casati, R., and J. Dokic. 2009. Some Varieties of Spatial Hearing. In *Sounds and Perception,* edited by M. Nudds and C. O'Callaghan, 97–110. Oxford: Oxford University Press.

Casey, E. (1939) 2000. *Imagining: A Phenomenological Study.* Bloomington: Indiana University Press.

Chadwick, P., and M. Birchwood. 1994. The Omnipotence of Voices. A Cognitive Approach to Auditory Hallucinations. *British Journal of Psychiatry* 164 (2): 190–201.

Chakravarty, A. 2008. Exploding Head Syndrome: Report of Two New Cases. *Cephalalgia* 28 (4): 399–400.

Chalmers, A. 2014. Level of Realism: Feel, Smell, and Taste in Virtual Environments. *The Oxford Handbook of Virtuality,* edited by M. Grimshaw, 602–614. New York: Oxford University Press.

Chaney, W. 2007. *Dynamic Mind.* Las Vegas: Houghton-Brace, 33–35.

Chion, M. 1994. *Audio-Vision: Sound on Screen,* translated by C. Gorbman. New York: Columbia University Press.

Cho, J., E. Yi, and G. Cho. 2001. Physiological Responses Evoked by Fabric Sounds and Related Mechanical and Acoustical Properties. *Textile Research Journal* 71 (12): 1068–1073.

Christianson, S. Å. 1992. Emotional Stress and Eyewitness Memory: A Critical Review. *Psychological Bulletin* 112 (2): 284–309.

Clarke, A. 1997. *Being There: Putting Brain, Body, and World Together Again.* Cambridge (MA): MIT Press.

Cohen, A. 2013. *Parenting Made Easy: The Middle Years*. Australia: Xlibris.

Cohen, A., S.-L. Tan, R. Kendall, and S. D. Lipscomb (eds.). 2013. *Psychology of Music in Multimedia*. New York: Oxford University Press.

Cohen D. 1968. Magnetoencephalography: Evidence of Magnetic Fields Produced by Alpha Rhythm Currents. *Science* 161: 784–786.

Cole, R. A., and M. Young. 1975. Effect of Subvocalization on Memory for Speech Sounds. *Journal of Experimental Psychology: Human Learning and Memory* 1 (6): 772–779.

Collins, K. 2006. *Introduction to the Participatory and Non-Linear Aspects of Video Games Audio*. http://www.gamessound.com. Accessed July 31, 2013.

Collins, K. 2008. *Game Sound*. Cambridge (MA): MIT Press.

Collins, K., B. Kapralos, and H. Tessler (eds.). 2014. *The Oxford Handbook of Interactive Audio*. New York: Oxford University Press.

Cope, T. E., and D. M. Baguley. 2009. Is Musical Hallucination an Otological Phenomenon? A Review of the Literature. *Clinical Otolaryngology* 34 (5): 423–430.

Cornwell, W. R., and J. R. Cornwell. 2006. *The Death of Virtuality: A Proposal for the Resolution of an Internet Research Conundrum*. Center for Internet Research.

Critchley, S. 2009. *Being and Time, Part 4: Thrown into This World*. http://www.theguardian.com/commentisfree/belief/2009/jun/29/religion-philosophy. Accessed June 10, 2014.

Cromer, J. A., J. E. Roy, and E. K. Miller. 2010. Representation of Multiple Independent Categories in the Primate Prefrontal Cortex. *Neuron* 66 (5): 796–807.

Currie, G., and I. Ravenscroft. 2002. *Recreative Minds: Imagination in Philosophy and Psychology*. Oxford: Oxford University Press.

Cusack, R., and R. P. Carlyon. 2004. Auditory Perceptual Organization Inside and Outside the Laboratory. In *Ecological Psychoacoustics*, edited by J. Neuhoff. Waltham (MA): Elsevier Academic Press.

Dancy, J. 1985. *Introduction to Contemporary Epistemology*. Oxford: Blackwell.

Daselaar, S., Y. Porat, W. Huijbers, and C. M. A. Pennartz. 2010. Modality-Specific and Modality-Independent Components of the Human Imagery System. *Neuroimage* 52 (2): 677–685.

David, A. S. 2004. The Cognitive Neuropsychiatry of Auditory Verbal Hallucinations: An Overview. *Cognitive Neuropsychiatry* 9: 107–123.

Deleuze, G. 2002. The Actual and the Virtual. *Dialogues II* (revised edition), translated by E. R. Albert, 148–152. New York: Columbia University Press.

De Silva, L. C., T. Miyasato, and R. Nakats. 1998. Use of Multimodal Information in Facial Emotion Recognition. *IEICE TRANSACTIONS on Information and Systems* E81-D1: 105–114.

Dhomont, F. 1995. Acousmatic Update. *Contact!* 8 (2). http://cec.sonus.ca/contact/contact82Dhom.html. Accessed February 5, 2014.

Dick, P. K. 1985. *I Hope I Shall Arrive Soon*. New York: Doubleday.

Dietrich, A. 2008. Imaging the Imagination: The Trouble with Motor Imagery. *Methods* 45 (4): 319–324.

Djordjevic, J., R. J. Zatorre, M. Petrides, J. A. Boyle, and M. Jones-Gotman. 2005. Functional Neuroimaging of Odor Imagery. *Neuroimage* 24 (3): 791–801.

Dreyfus, H. L. 1991. *Being in the World, a Commentary on Heidegger's "Being and Time," Division I.* Cambridge (MA): MIT Press.

Dror, I. E., and S. Harnad. 2008. Offloading Cognition onto Cognitive Technology. In *Cognition Distributed: How Cognitive Technology Extends Our Minds*, edited by I. Dror and S. Harnad, 1–23. Amsterdam: John Benjamins.

Duckworth, K. L., J. A. Bargh, M. Garcia, and S. Chaiken. 2002. The Automatic Evaluation of Novel Stimuli. *Psychological Science* 13: 513–519.

Ekman, I. 2009. Modelling the Emotional Listener: Making Psychological Processes Audible. In *Proceedings of Audio Mostly 2009*, September 2–3, Glasgow, Scotland.

Ekman, I., and R. Kajastila. 2009. Localisation Cues Affect Emotional Judgements – Results from a User Study on Scary Sound. In *Proceedings of AES 35th Conference on Audio for Games*, London, UK.

Esquirol, É. 1838. Baillière, Jean-Baptiste (and sons), ed. Des maladies mentales considérées sous les rapports médical, hygiénique et médico-légal, Volume 1 [Mental illness as considered in medical, hygienic, and medico-legal reports, Volume 1] (in French). Paris: Chez J.-B. Baillière.

Ethier, C., E. R. Oby, M. J. Bauman, and L. E. Miller. 2012. Restoration of Grasp Following Paralysis through Brain-controlled Stimulation of Muscles. *Nature* 485: 368–371.

Ermi, L., and F. Mäyrä. 2005. Fundamental Components of the Gameplay Experience: Analysing Immersion. Paper presented to *Changing Views—Worlds in Play*, June 16–20, Toronto, Canada.

Evers S. 2006. Musical Hallucinations. *Current Psychiatry Reports* 8: 205–210.

Falloon, I. R., and R. E. Talbot. 1981. Persistent Auditory Hallucinations: Coping Mechanisms and Implications for Management. *Psychological Medicine* 11 (2): 329–339.

Farah, M. J. 1988. Is Visual Imagery Really Visual? Overlooked Evidence from Neuropsychology. *Psychology Review* 95: 307–317.

Farah, M. J., and A. F. Smith. 1983. Perceptional Interference and Facilitation with Auditory Imagery. *Perceptual Psychophysiology* 33: 475–478.

Farnell, A. 2011. Behaviour, Structure and Causality in Procedural Audio. In *Game Sound Technology and Player Interaction: Concepts and Developments*, edited by M. Grimshaw, 313–339. Hershey (PA): IGI.

Ferri, A. J. 2007. *Willing Suspension of Disbelief: Poetic Faith in Film.* Lanham (MD): Lexington Books.

Fischer, C. E., A. Marchie, and M. Norris. 2004, Musical and Auditory Hallucinations: A Spectrum. *Psychiatry and Clinical Neuroscience* 58 (96): 96–98.

Fischer, R. 1971. A Cartography of the Ecstatic and Meditative States *Science* 174 (4012): 897–904.

Ford, J. M., and D. H. Mathalon. 2004. Electrophysiological Evidence of Corollary Discharge Dysfunction in Schizophrenia during Talking and Thinking. *Journal of Psychiatric Research* 38 (1): 37–46.

Fox, R. G. 1997. On Thrownness. Paper presented to *After Postmodernism Conference 1997*. http://www.focusing.org/apm_papers/fox.html. Accessed June 10, 2014.

Franceschi, P. 2004. *On the Plausibility of Psychotic Hallucinations*. http://cogprints. org/3856/1/On_the_Plausibility_of_Psychotic_Hallucinations.htm.   Accessed June 6, 2014.

Freitas, A. L., P. Salovey, and N. Liberman. 2001. Abstract and Concrete Self-Evaluative Goals. *Journal of Personality and Social Psychology* 80: 410–412.

Fricchione G. L., L. Carbone, and W. I. Bennett. 1995. Psychotic Disorder Caused by a General Medical Condition, with Delusions: Secondary "Organic" Delusional Syndromes. *Psychiatric Clinics of North America,* 18 (2): 363–378.

Ganguly, G., M. B. Mridha, A. Khan, and R. A. Rison. 2013. Exploding Head Syndrome: A Case Report. *Case Reports in Neurology* 5 (1): 14–17.

Garbarini, F., and M. Adenzato. 2004. At the Root of Embodied Cognition: Cognitive Science Meets Neurophysiology. *Brain and Cognition* 56 (1): 100–106.

Garner, T. A. 2013. *Game Sound from Behind the Sofa: An Exploration into the Fear Potential of Sound and Psychophysiological Approaches to Audio-Centric, Adaptive Gameplay*. PhD thesis, University of Aalborg, Denmark.

Garner, T., M. Grimshaw, and D. Abdel Nabi. 2010. A Preliminary Experiment to Assess the Fear Value of Preselected Sound Parameters in a Survival Horror Game. In *Proceedings of Audio Mostly 2010*, September 14–16, Piteå, Sweden.

Garner, T., and M. Grimshaw. 2011. A Climate of Fear: Considerations for Designing an Acoustic Ecology for Fear. In *Proceedings of Audio Mostly 2011*, September 7–9, Coimbra, Portugal.

Garner, T., and M. Grimshaw. 2013. The Physiology of Fear and Sound: Working with Biometrics toward Automated Emotion Recognition in Adaptive Gaming Systems. In *IADIS International Journal on WWW/Internet* 11 (2). http://www. iadisportal.org/ijwi/papers/2013112106.pdf. Accessed June 2, 2014.

Garner, T., and M. Grimshaw. 2014. Sonic Virtuality: Understanding Audio in a Virtual World. *The Oxford Handbook of Virtuality*, edited by M. Grimshaw, 364–377. New York: Oxford University Press.

Gaver, W. W. 1993a. What in the World Do We Hear? An Ecological Approach to Auditory Perception. *Ecological Psychology* 5 (1): 1–29.

Gaver, W. W. 1993b. How Do We Hear in the World? Explorations in Ecological Acoustics. *Ecological Psychology* 5 (4): 285–313.

Gavrilescu, M. et al. 2010. Reduced Connectivity of the Auditory Cortex in Patients with Auditory Hallucinations: A Resting State Functional Magnetic Resonance Imaging Study. *Psychological Medicine* 40 (7): 1149–1158.

Gendler, T. S. 2008a. Alief in Action (and Reaction). *Mind and Language* 23 (5): 552–585.

Gendler, T. S. 2008b. Alief and Belief. *Journal of Philosophy* 105 (10): 634–663.

Gendler, T. S. 2010. *Intuition, Imagination, and Philosophical Methodology.* Oxford: Oxford University Press.

Gendler, T. S. 2011. Imagination. *The Stanford Encyclopaedia of Philosophy.* http://plato.stanford.edu/entries/imagination/. Accessed November 3, 2013.

Gettier, E. L. 1963. Is Justified True Belief Knowledge? *Analysis* 23: 121–123.

Geva, S., P. S. Jones, J. T. Crinion, C. J. Price, J. C. Baron, and E. A: Warburton. 2011. The Neural Correlates of Inner Speech Defined by Voxel-based Lesion-Symptom Mapping. *Brain* 134 (10): 3071–3082.

Gibson, C. B., and J. L. Gibbs. 2006. Unpacking the Concept of Virtuality: The Effects of Geographic Dispersion, Electronic Dependence, Dynamic Structure, and National Diversity on Team Innovation. *Administrative Science Quarterly* 51: 451–495.

Gibson, J. J. 1966. *The Senses Considered as Perceptual Systems.* Boston: Houghton Mifflin.

Gibson, J. J. 1979. *The Ecological Approach to Visual Perception.* Hillsdale (NJ): Lawrence Erlbaum.

Glennie, E. 1993. *Hearing Essay.* http://www.evelyn.co.uk/Resources/Essays/Hearing%20Essay.pdf. Accessed April 28, 2014.

Goldenberg, G., I. Podreka, M. Steiner, P. Franzen, and L. Deecke. 1991. Contributions of Occipital and Temporal Brain Regions to Visual and Acoustic Imagery—A SPECT Study. *Neuropsychologia* 29 (7): 695–702.

Goldstein, S., J. Taylor, R. Tumulka, and N. Zanghi. 2005. Are All Particles Identical? *Journal of Physics A: Mathematical and General* 38 (7): 1567.

Goycoolea, M., R. Iniguez, and M. Perez. 1995. Diseases of the Ear: Acquired Diseases. In *Textbook of the Ear, Nose and Throat,* edited by C. de Souza, M. Goycoolea, and C. Ruah. Hyderabad, Andhra Pradesh, India: Orient Longman.

Grafton, S. T., M. A. Arbib, L. Fadiga, and G. Rizzolatti. 1996. Localization of Grasp Representations in Humans by Positron Emission Tomography. *Experimental Brain Research* 112 (1): 103–111.

Grandey, A. A. 2000. Emotion Regulation in the Workplace: A New Way to Conceptualize Emotional Labor. *Journal of Occupational Health Psychology* 5 (1): 95–110.

Griffiths, T. D., C. J. Bench, and R. S. J. Frackowiak. 1994. Human Cortical Areas Selectively Activated by Apparent Sound Movement. *Current Biology* 4 (10): 892–895.

Grimshaw, M. 2007. The Resonating Spaces of First-Person Shooter Games. In *Proceedings of the 5th International Conference on Game Design and Technology,* November 14–15, Liverpool, UK.

Grimshaw, M. 2008a. *The Acoustic Ecology of the First-Person Shooter*. Saarbrücken: VDM Verlag.

Grimshaw, M. 2008b. Autopoiesis and Sonic Immersion: Modelling Sound-Based Player Relationships as a Self-Organizing System. Paper presented to *The Sixth Annual International Conference in Computer Game Design and Technology*, November 12–13, Liverpool, UK.

Grimshaw, M. 2012. Sound and Player Immersion in Digital Games. In *The Oxford Handbook of Sound Studies*, edited by T. Pinch and K. Bijsterveld, 347–366. New York: Oxford University Press.

Grimshaw, M. (2015). The Privatization of Sound Space. In *The Routledge Companion to Sounding Art*, edited by V. Meelberg, M. Cobussen, and B. Truax. London: Routledge.

Grimshaw, M., and G. Schott. 2008. A Conceptual Framework for the Analysis of First-Person Shooter Audio and Its Potential Use for Game Engines. *International Journal of Computer Games Technology* 2008. http://www.hindawi.com/journals/ijcgt/2008/720280/. Accessed June 10, 2014.

Grimshaw, M., C. A. Lindley, and L. Nacke. 2008. Sound and Immersion in the First-Person Shooter: Mixed Measurement of the Player's Sonic Experience. In *Proceedings of Audio Mostly 2008*, October 22–23, Piteå, Sweden.

Grimshaw, M., and T. Garner. 2014. Embodied Virtual Acoustic Ecologies of Computer Games. *The Oxford Handbook of Interactive Audio*, edited by K. E. Collins, B. Kapralos, and H. Tessler, 181–195. New York: Oxford University Press.

Haddock, G., J. McCarron, N. Tarrier, and E. B. Faragher. 1999. Scales to Measure Dimensions of Hallucinations and Delusions: The Psychotic Symptom Rating Scales (PSYRATS). *Psychological Medicine* 29 (4): 879–889.

Haqqi, S., and N. Ali. 2012. Folie a Deux: A Case Report. *F1000Research*, 1.

Halpern, A. R. 1988. Mental Scanning in Auditory Imagery for Tunes. *Journal of Experimental Psychology* 14: 434–443.

Halpern, A. R., and R. J. Zatorre. 1999. When That Tune Runs through Your Head: A PET Investigation of Auditory Imagery for Familiar Melodies. *Cerebral Cortex* 9 (7): 697–704.

Halpern, A. R., R. J. Zatorre, M. Bouffard, and J. A. Johnson. 2004. Behavioral and Neural Correlates of Perceived and Imagined Musical Timbre. *Neuropsychologia* 42 (9): 1281–1292.

Hari, R., S. Levänen, and T. Raij. 2000. Timing of Human Cortical Functions during Cognition: Role of MEG. *Trends in Cognitive Sciences* 4 (12): 455–462.

Hassabis, D., D. Kumaran, and E. A. Maguire. 2007. Using Imagination to Understand the Neural Basis of Episodic Memory. *Journal of Neuroscience* 27 (52): 14365–14374.

Hausser-Hauw, C., and J. Bancaud. 1987. Gustatory Hallucinations in Epileptic Seizures Electrophysiological, Clinical and Anatomical Correlates. *Brain* 110 (2): 339–359.

Havas, D. A., A. M. Glenberg, and M. Rinck. 2007. Emotion Simulation during Language Comprehension, *Psychonomic Bulletin and Review* 14 (3): 436–441.

Heidegger, M. 1962. *Being and Time*, translated by John Macquarrie and Edward Robinson. San Francisco: Harper and Row.

Hepper, P. G., and B. S. Shahidullah. 1994. The Development of Fetal Hearing. *Fetal and Maternal Medicine Review* 6 (3): 167–179.

Herculano-Houzel, S., and R. Lent. 2005. Isotropic Fractionator: A Simple, Rapid Method for the Quantification of Total Cell and Neuron Numbers in the Brain. *Journal of Neuroscience* 25 (10): 2518–2521.

Hermann, T., and H. Ritter. 2004. Sound and Meaning in Auditory Data Display. *Proceedings of the IEEE* 92 (4): 730–741.

Hermesh H. 2004. Musical Hallucinations: Prevalence in Psychotic and Nonpsychotic Outpatients. *Journal of Clinical Psychiatry* 65: 191–197.

Hoffman, R. E. 1986. Verbal Hallucinations and Language Production Processes in Schizophrenia. *Behavioural and Brain Sciences* 9: 503–548.

Hoffman, R. E., N. N. Boutros, S. Hu, and R. M. Berman, 2000. Transcranial Magnetic Stimulation and Auditory Hallucinations in Schizophrenia. *Lancet*, 355: 1073–1075.

Hofman, P. M., J. G. A. Van Riswick, and A. J. Van Opstal. 1998. Relearning Sound Localization with New Ears. *Nature Neuroscience* 1 (5): 417–421.

Holdaway, D. 1979. *The Foundations of Literacy*, vol. 138. Sydney: Ashton Scholastic.

Hoshiyama, M., A. Gunji, and R. Kakigi. 2001. Hearing the Sound of Silence: A Magnetoencephalographic Study. *NeuroReport* 12 (6): 1097–1102.

Hota, A. K. 1998. *Talent and Creativity*. New Delhi: Sarup and Sons.

Howard, D. M., and J. Angus. 1996. *Acoustics and Psychoacoustics*. Oxford: Focal Press.

Hughes, H. C., T. M. Darcey, H. I. Barkan, P. D. Williamson, D. W. Roberts, and C. H. Aslin. 2001. Responses of Human Auditory Association Cortex to the Omission of an Expected Acoustic Event. *NeuroImage* 13: 1073–1089.

Hunter, M. D., S. B. Eickhoff, T. R. W. Miller, T. F. D. Farrow, I. D. Wilkinson, and P. W. R. Woodruff. 2006. Neural Activity in Speech-Sensitive Auditory Cortex during Silence. In *Proceedings of the National Academy of Sciences* 103: 189–194.

Ihde, D. 2007. *Listening and Voice: Phenomenologies of Sound* (2nd edition). Albany: State University of New York Press.

IJsselsteijn, W. A., J. Freeman, and H. De Ridder. 2001. Presence: Where Are We? *Cyberpsychology and Behavior* 4 (2): 179–182.

Jack, C. R. et al. 2008. The Alzheimer's Disease Neuroimaging Initiative (ADNI): MRI Methods. *Journal of Magnetic Resonance Imaging* 27 (4): 685–691.

Janata, P., J. L. Birk, J. D. Van Horn, M. Leman, B. Tillmann, and J. J. Bharucha. 2002. The Cortical Topography of Tonal Structures Underlying Western Music. *Science* 298 (5601): 2167–2170.

Johns, L. C., S. Rossell, C. Frith, F. Ahmad, D. Hemsley, E. Kuipers, and P. K. McGuire. 2001. Verbal Self-Monitoring and Auditory Verbal Hallucinations in Patients with Schizophrenia. *Psychological Medicine* 31 (4): 705–715.

Johnston, W. A., V. J. Dark, and L. L. Jacoby. 1985. Perceptual Fluency and Recognition Judgments. *Journal of Experimental Psychology: Learning, Memory, and Cognition* 11: 3–11.

Jowett, B. (ed.). 1941. *Plato's The Republic.* New York: The Modern Library.

Juslin, P. N., and J. A. Sloboda. (eds.). 2002. *Music and Emotion: Theory and Research.* Oxford: Oxford University Press.

Kacelnik, O., F. R. Nodal, K. H. Parsons, and A. J. King. 2006. Training-Induced Plasticity of Auditory Localization in Adult Mammals. *PLoS Biology* 4 (4): 0627–0638.

Kahan, T. L., and S. LaBerge. 1994. Lucid Dreaming as Metacognition: Implications for Cognitive Science. *Consciousness and Cognition* 3: 246–264.

Kant, I. 1781. *Critique of Pure Reason,* New York: St. Martin's.

Keller, P. E. 2012. Mental Imagery in Music Performance: Underlying Mechanisms and Potential Benefits. *Annals of the New York Academy of Sciences* 1252 (1): 206–213.

Kim-Cohen, S. 2009. *In the Blink of an Ear: Toward a Non-Cochlear Sound Art.* London: Continuum.

King, A. J. 2006. Auditory Neuroscience: Activating the Cortex without Sound. *Current Biology* 16 (11): R410–R411.

Kirsh, D., and P. Maglio. 1994. On Distinguishing Epistemic from Pragmatic Action. *Cognitive Science* 18 (4): 513–549.

Kishi, T. 2013. Capcom Audio Director Tomoya Kishi. http://designingsound.org/2013/02/capcom-audio-director-tomoya-kishi-interview/. Accessed November 4, 2013.

Klein, J., V. Damm, and A. Giebeler. 1983. An Outline of a Theory of Imagination. *Zeitschrift für allgemeine Wissenschaftstheorie* 14 (1): 15–23.

Kleinjung, T., P. Eichhammer, B. Langguth, P. Jacob, J. Marienhagen, G. Hajak, S. R. Wolf, and J. Strutz. 2005. Long-Term Effects of Repetitive Transcranial Magnetic Stimulation (rTMS) in Patients with Chronic Tinnitus. *Otolaryngology Head and Neck Surgery* 132 (4): 566–569.

Knakkergaard, M. 2014. The Music That's Not There. *The Oxford Handbook of Virtuality,* edited by M. Grimshaw, 444–462. New York: Oxford University Press.

Knuuttila, S. 2004. *Emotions in Ancient and Medieval Philosophy.* Oxford: Oxford University Press.

Kosslyn, S. M., G. Ganis, and W. L. Thompson. 2001. Neural Foundations of Imagery. *Nature Reviews Neuroscience* 2 (9): 635–642.

Kraemer, D. J., C. N. Macrae, A. E. Green, and W. M. Kelley. 2005. Musical Imagery: Sound of Silence Activates Auditory Cortex. *Nature* 434 (158). http://www.nature.com/nature/journal/v434/n7030/full/434158a.html. Accessed May 31, 2014.

Krause, B. L. 1993. The Niche Hypothesis: A Hidden Symphony of Animal Sounds, the Origins of Musical Expression and the Health of Habitats. *Explorers Journal* Winter 1993: 156–160.

Kromand, D. 2008. Sound and the Diegesis in Survival Horror Games. In *Proceedings of Audio Mostly 2008,* October 22–23, Piteå, Sweden.

Kuriki, S., S. Kanda, and Y. Hirata. 2006. Effects of Musical Experience on Different Components of MEG Responses Elicited by Sequential Piano-Tones and Chords. *Journal of Neuroscience* 26 (15): 4046–4053.

LaBerge, S., and D. J. DeGracia. 1999. Varieties of Lucid Dreaming Experience. In *Individual Differences in Conscious Experience,* edited by R. G. Kunzendorf and B. Wallace. Philadelphia: John Benjamins.

LaBerge, S. and L. Levitan. 1998. Does the Subjective Experience of Pain Require Neuronal Activity below the Level of the Brain? A Study of Pain in Lucid Dreams. *17th annual meeting of the American Pain Association*, San Diego, California.

Langguth, B. 2011. A Review of Tinnitus Symptoms beyond 'Ringing in the Ears': A Call to Action. *Current Medical Research and Opinion* 27: 1635–1643.

Langguth, B., P. M. Kreuzer, T. Kleinjung, and D. De Ridder. 2013. Tinnitus: Causes and Clinical Management. *Lancet Neurology* 12 (9): 920–930.

Lasegue C., and J. Falret. 1877. La Folie à Deux. *Annales Médico-psychologiques.* 18: 321–355.

Laureys, S., and G. Tononi. 2009. *The Neurology of Consciousness: Cognitive Neuroscience and Neuropathology.* Oxford: Elsevier Academic.

Levitin, D. J., and P. R. Cook. 1996. Memory for Musical Tempo: Additional Evidence That Auditory Memory Is Absolute. *Attention, Perception, and Psychophysics* 58 (6): 927–935.

Lewandowski, K. E., J. DePaola, G. B. Camsari, B. M. Cohen, and D. Ongur. 2009. Tactile, Olfactory, and Gustatory Hallucinations in Psychotic Disorders: A Descriptive Study. *Annals Academy of Medicine Singapore* 38 (5): 383–385.

Lerner, J. S., D. A. Small, and G. Loewenstein. 2004. Heart Strings and Purse Strings: Carryover Effects of Emotions on Economic Decisions. *Psychological Science* 15: 337–341.

Lewis, M. L., R. Weber, and N. D. Bowman. 2008. They May Be Pixels, but They're My Pixels: Developing a Metric of Character Attachment in Role-Playing Video Games. *CyberPsychology and Behavior* 11 (4): 515–518.

Liberman, N., and Y. Trope. 2008. The Psychology of Transcending the Here and Now. *Science* 322: 1201–1205.

Liberman, N., and Y. Trope. 2010. Construal-Level Theory of Psychological Distance. *Psychological Review* 117 (2): 440–463.

Libet, B. 1985. Unconscious Cerebral Initiative and the Role of Conscious Will in Voluntary Action. *Behavioral and Brain Sciences* 8 (4): 529–539.

Lichty, P. 2014. The Translation of Art in Virtual Worlds. *The Oxford Handbook of Virtuality*, edited by M. Grimshaw, 444–462. New York: Oxford University Press.

Liebal, K., T. Behne, M. Carpenter, and M. Tomasello. 2009. Infants Use Shared Experience to Interpret Pointing Gestures. *Developmental Science* 12 (2): 264–271.

Lincoln, T. M. 2007. Relevant Dimensions of Delusions: Continuing the Continuum versus Category Debate. *Schizophrenia Research* 93 (1): 211–220.

Locke, J. 1722. *Works*, vol. 1. London: Taylor.

Loukopoulos, L. D., K. Dismukes, and I. Barshi. 2009. *The Multitasking Myth: Handling Complexity in Real-World Operations.* Farnham (UK): Ashgate.

Lunn, P., and A. Hunt. 2013. Phantom Signals: Erroneous Perception Observed during the Audification of Radio Astronomy Data. Paper presented to the *International Conference on Auditory Display*, July 6–10, Łódź, Poland.

Luther, R., and B. Roy. 2013. Folie a Deux-Case Presentation and Discussion. *European Psychiatry* 28: 1.

Mandelbaum, E. 2012. Against Alief. *Philosophical Studies* 165: 197–211.

Mason, O. J., and F. Brady. 2009. The Psychotomimetic Effects of Short-term Sensory Deprivation. *Journal of Nervous and Mental Disease* 197 (10): 783–785.

Massumi, B. 1998. Sensing the Virtual, Building the Insensible. *Hypersurface Architecture* 68 (5/6): 16–24.

Massumi, B. 2005. Fear —The Spectrum Said. *Positions* 13 (1): 31–48.

Massumi, B. 2014. Envisioning the Virtual. In *The Oxford Handbook of Virtuality*, edited by M. Grimshaw, 55–70. New York: Oxford University Press.

McDermott, J. H., M. Schemitsch, and E. P. Simoncelli. 2013. Summary Statistics in Auditory Perception. *Nature Neuroscience* 16 (14): 493–498.

McKay, C. M., D. M. Headlam, and D. L. Copolov. 2000. Central Auditory Processing in Patients with Auditory Hallucinations. *American Journal of Psychiatry* 157: 759–766.

McMahan, A. 2003. Immersion, Engagement, and Presence: A New Method for Analyzing 3-D Video Games. In *The Video Game Theory Reader*, edited by M. J. P. Wolf and B. Perron, 67–87. New York: Routledge.

Meibos, A. 1998. *Kant and A Priori Synthetic Judgments.* http://qirien.icecavern.net/punkus/school/kant.htm. Accessed May 31, 2014.

Merleau-Ponty, M. 1945/2013. *Phenomenology of Perception.* New York: Routledge.

Milicevic, M. 2013. Altered States of Consciousness in Narrative Cinema: Subjective Film Sound. *International Journal of Social, Management, Economics and Business Engineering* 7 (12): 1975–1979.

Mitchell, R. W. 2013. The Comparative Study of Education. In *The Oxford Handbook of the Development of Imagination*, edited by M. Taylor, 468–485. New York: Oxford University Press.

Morrison, A. P., and G. Haddock. 1997. Cognitive Factors in Source Monitoring and Auditory Hallucinations. *Psychological Medicine* 27: 669–679.

Most, S. B. 2010. What's "Inattentional" about Inattentional Blindness? *Consciousness and Cognition* 19 (4): 1107–1109.

Muchnik, C., M. Hildesheimer, and M. Rubinstein. 1980. Effect of Emotional Stress on Hearing. *Archives of Oto-Rhino-Laryngology* 228 (4): 295–298.

Murphy, P., M. A. Peters, and S. Marginson. 2010. *Imagination: Three Models of Imagination in the Age of the Knowledge Economy.* New York: Peter Lang.

Mutschler, I., A. Schulze-Bonhage, V. Glauche, E. Demandt, O. Speck, and T. Ball. 2007. A Rapid Sound-action Association Effect in Human Insular Cortex. *PloS One* 2 (2): e259.

Nacke, L., and M. Grimshaw. 2011. Player-Game Interaction through Affective Sound. In *Game Sound Technology and Player Interaction: Concepts and Developments,* edited by M. Grimshaw, 264–285. Hershey (PA): IGI.

Nacke, L., M. Grimshaw, and C. A. Lindley. 2010. More than a Feeling: Measurement of Sonic User Experience and Psychophysiology in a First-Person Shooter Game. *Interacting with Computers* 22: 336–343.

Nishikawa, N., Makino, S., and Rutkowski, T. M. (2013, October). Spatial Auditory BCI Paradigm Based on Real and Virtual Sound Image Generation. In *Signal and Information Processing Association Annual Summit and Conference (APSIPA), 2013 Asia-Pacific,* 1–5. IEEE.

Nishimoto, S., A. T. Vu, T. Naselaris, Y. Benjamini, B. Yu, and J. L. Gallant. 2011. Reconstructing Visual Experiences from Brain Activity Evoked by Natural Movies. *Current Biology* 21: 1641–1646.

Noë, A. 2004. *Action in Perception.* Cambridge (MA): MIT Press.

npr.org. 2013. *Research: "Inner Speech" Can Be Disturbed by Chewing.* http://www.npr.org/2013/10/14/233790764/the-last-word-in-business. Accessed October 28, 2013.

Norena, A., C. Micheyl, S. Chery-Croze, and L. Collet. 2002. Psychoacoustic Characterization of the Tinnitus Spectrum: Implications for the Underlying Mechanisms of Tinnitus. *Audiol Neurootol* 2002 (7): 358–369.

Nudds, M. 2009. Sounds and Space. In *Sounds and Perception,* edited by M. Nudds and C. O'Callaghan, 69–96. Oxford: Oxford University Press.

Nudds, M., and C. O'Callaghan (eds.). 2009. *Sounds and Perception.* Oxford: Oxford University Press.

Numminen, J., and G. Curio. 1999. Differential Effects of Overt, Covert and Replayed Speech on Vowel-Evoked Responses of the Human Auditory Cortex. *Neuroscience Letters* 272 (1): 29–32.

O'Callaghan, C. 2007. *Sounds.* Oxford: Oxford University Press.

O'Callaghan, C. 2009. Sounds and Events. In *Sounds and Perception,* edited by M. Nudds and C. O'Callaghan, 26–49. Oxford: Oxford University Press.

O'Farrell, L., S. Lewis, A. McKenzie, and L. Jones. (2010). Charles Bonnet Syndrome: A Review of the Literature. *Journal of Visual Impairment and Blindness* 104: 261–274.

Ortiz, M. 2012. A Brief History of Biosignal-Driven Art: From Biofeedback to Biophysical Performance. *econtact* 14 (2). http://cec.sonus.ca/econtact/14_2/ortiz_biofeedback.html. Accessed April 20, 2014.

O'Shaughnessy, C. 2009. The Location of a Perceived Sound. In *Sounds and Perception*, edited by M. Nudds and C. O'Callaghan, 111–125. Oxford: Oxford University Press.

Öhman, A. 2010. Fear and Anxiety: Overlaps and Dissociations. In *Handbook of Emotions* (3rd edition), edited by M. Lewis, J. M. Haviland-Jones, and L. Feldman Barrett. New York: Guilford Press.

Pagliarini, L., and H. H. Lund. 2014. ALife for Real and Virtual Audio-Video Performances. *Journal of Robotics, Networking and Artificial Life* 1 (1): 34–39.

Parker J. R., and J. Heerema. 2008. Audio Interaction in Computer Mediated Games. *International Journal of Computer Games Technology*. http://www.hindawi.com/journals/ijcgt/2008/178923/. Accessed June 10, 2014.

Patel, A. D., J. R. Iversen, M. R. Bregman, and I. Schulz. 2009. Studying Synchronization to a Musical Beat in Nonhuman Animals. *The Neurosciences and Music III—Disorders and Plasticity: Annals of the New York Academy of Sciences* 1169: 459–469.

Parnin, C. 2011. Subvocalization-Toward Hearing the Inner Thoughts of Developers. In *2011 IEEE 19th International Conference on Program Comprehension (ICPC)*, 197–200. IEEE.

Pasley, B. N., S. V. David, N. Mesgarani, A. Flinker, S. A. Shamma, N. E. Crone, R. T. Knight, and E. F. Chang. 2012. Reconstructing Speech from Human Auditory Cortex. *PLoS Biology* 10. http://www.plosbiology.org/article/info%3Adoi%2F10.1371%2Fjournal.pbio.1001251. Accessed May 31, 2014.

Pasnau, R. 1999. What Is Sound? *The Philosophical Quarterly* 49 (196): 309–324.

Pasnau, R. 2007. The Event of Color. *Philosophical Studies* 142: 353–369.

Pearce, J. M. 1989. Clinical Features of the Exploding Head Syndrome. *Journal of Neurology, Neurosurgery and Psychiatry* 1989 (52): 907–910.

Phelps, E. A. 2006. Emotion and Cognition: Insights from Studies of the Human Amygdala. *Annual Review of Psychology* 57: 27–53.

Piaget, J. 1967. *The Child's Conception of the World*, translated by J. and A. Tomlinson. London: Routledge and Kegan Paul.

Picker, J. M. 2003. *Victorian Soundscapes*. New York: Oxford University Press.

Piesse, G. 1857. *The Art of Perfumery and Methods of Obtaining the Odors of Plants*. http://manybooks.net/titles/piesseg16371637816378-8.html. Accessed May 19, 2014.

Plewnia, C., M. Bartels, and C. Gerloff. 2003. Transient Suppression of Tinnitus by Transcranial Magnetic Stimulation. *Annals of Neurology* 53 (2): 263–266.

Pulkki, V., M. Karjalainen, and J. Huopaniemi. 1999. Analyzing Virtual Sound Source Attributes Using a Binaural Auditory Model. *Journal of the Audio Engineering Society* 47 (4): 203–217.

Pylyshyn, Z. W. 2007. *Things and Places: How the Mind Connects with the World.* Cambridge (MA): MIT Press.

Quine, V. W. O. 1953. Two Dogmas of Empiricism. In *From a Logical Point of View.* Cambridge (MA): Harvard University Press.

Redström, J. 1998. *Is Acoustic Ecology about Ecology? Reflections on the International Conference on Acoustic Ecology "Stockholm, Hey Listen!"* http://www.tii.se/play/publications/1998/ecology.pdf. Accessed February 15, 2014.

Reisberg, D., J. D. Smith, D. Baxter, and M. Sonenshine. 1989. "Enacted" Auditory Images Are Ambiguous; "Pure" Auditory Images Are Not. *Quarterly Journal of Experimental Psychology* 41 (3): 619–641.

Rheingold, H. 1993. *The Virtual Community: Homesteading on the Electronic Frontier.* Reading (MA): Addison-Wesley.

Rheingold, H. 2000. *The Virtual Community: Homesteading on the Electronic Frontier* (2nd edition). Cambridge (MA): MIT Press.

Riddoch, M. 2012. On the Non-Cochlearity of the Sounds Themselves. Paper presented to *The International Computer Music Conference,* September 9–14, Ljubljana, Slovenia.

Riva, G., and J. Waterworth. 2014. Being Present in a Virtual World. *The Oxford Handbook of Virtuality,* edited by M. Grimshaw, 205–221. New York: Oxford University Press.

Roberts, L. E., J. J. Eggermont, D. M. Caspary, S. E. Shore, J. R. Melcher, and J. A. Kaltenbach. 2010. Ringing Ears: The Neuroscience of Tinnitus. *Journal of Neuroscience* 2010 (30): 14972–14979.

Rocca, M. A., A. Falini, B. Colombo, G. Scotti, G. Comi, and M. Filippi. 2002. Adaptive Functional Changes in the Cerebral Cortex of Patients with Nondisabling Multiple Sclerosis Correlate with the Extent of Brain Structural Damage. *Annals of Neurology* 51 (3): 330–339.

Rosen, C. 2008. The Myth of Multitasking. *New Atlantis* 20: 105–110.

Ross, C. A., and G. D. Pearlson. 1996. Schizophrenia, the Heteromodal Association Neocortex and Development: Potential for a Neurogenetic Approach. *Trends in Neurosciences* 19 (5): 171–176.

Rovelli, C. 1996. Relational Quantum Mechanics. *International Journal of Theoretical Physics* 35 (8): 1637–1678.

Ruby, P., and J. Decety. 2004. How Would You Feel versus How Do You Think She Would Feel? A Neuroimaging Study of Perspective-Taking with Social Emotions. *Journal of Cognitive Neuroscience* 16 (6): 988–999.

Russell, B. 1912. *The Problems of Philosophy.* New York: Oxford University Press, 1997.

Russell, J. A. 1980. A Circumplex Model of Affect. *Journal of Personality and Social Psychology* 39 (6): 1161–1178.

Sacks, O. 2012. *Hallucinations.* Toronto (ONT): Random House.

Salzarulo, P., and C. Cipolli. 1974. Spontaneously Recalled Verbal Material and Its Linguistic Organization in Relation to Different Stages of Sleep. *Biological Psychology* 2: 47–57.

Sanchez, T. G., S. C. M. Rocha, K. A. B. Knobel, M. A. Kii, R. M. Santos, and C. B. Pereira. 2011. Musical Hallucination Associated with Hearing Loss. *Arquivos de Neuro-psiquiatria* 69 (2B): 395–400.

Schaeffer, P. 1952. *A la Recherche d'une Musique Concrète.* Paris: Editions du Seuil.

Schafer, R. M. (1977) 1994. *The Soundscape: Our Sonic Environment and the Tuning of the World.* Rochester (VT): Destiny Books.

Schmahl, C., and J. D. Bremner. 2006. Neuroimaging in Borderline Personality Disorder. *Journal of Psychiatric Research* 40 (5): 419–427.

Schneiderman, D. 2013. Concept of Original Content Is Pure Fiction. *Chicago Tribune Online.* http://www.chicagotribune.com/chi-plagiarism-perspective,0,5020033. story. Accessed June 27, 2014.

Schnupp, J., I. Nelkin, and A. King. 2001. *Auditory Neuroscience: Making Sense of Sound.* Cambridge (MA): MIT Press.

Schroeder, C., and J. Foxe. 2005. Multisensory Contributions to Low-Level 'Unisensory' Processing. *Current Opinions in Neurobiology* 15: 454–458.

Schürmann, M., T. Raij, N. Fujiki, and R. Hari. 2002. Mind's Ear in a Musician: Where and When in the Brain. *Neuroimage* 16 (2): 434–440.

Schwartz, L. 2006. Fantasy, Realism and the Other in Recent Video Games. *Space and Culture* 9: 313–325.

Scott, M. 2013. Corollary Discharge Provides the Sensory Content of Inner Speech. *Psychological Science* 24 (9): 1824–1830.

Scruton, R. 2009. Sounds as Secondary Objects and Pure Events. In *Sounds and Perception,* edited by M. Nudds and C. O'Callaghan, 50–68. Oxford: Oxford University Press.

Shams, L., S. Iwaki, A. Chawla, and J. Bhattacharya. 2005. Early Modulation of Visual Cortex by Sound: An MEG Study. *Neuroscience Letters* 378 (2): 76–81.

Shiota, M. N., and J. W. Kalat. 2011. *Emotion.* Boston (MA): Wadsworth Publishing.

Simpson, R. M. 1922. Creative Imagination. *American Journal of Psychology* 33: 234–243.

Slater, M. 2003. A Note on Presence Terminology. *Presence Connect* 3 (3). http://publicationslist.org/data/melslater/ref-201/a%20note%20on%20presence%20terminology.pdf. Accessed June 2, 2014.

Slowiaczek, M. L., and C. Clifton Jr. 1980. Subvocalization and Reading for Meaning. *Journal of Verbal Learning and Verbal Behavior* 19 (5): 573–582.

Slattery III, W. H., and J. C. Middlebrooks. 1994. Monaural Sound Localization: Acute versus Chronic Unilateral Impairment. *Hearing Research* 75 (1–2): 38–46.

Solms, M. 1997. *The Neuropsychology of Dreams: A Clinico-Anatomical Study.* Mahwah (NJ): Erlbaum.

Sommer, I. E. C. et al. 2008. Auditory Verbal Hallucinations Predominantly Activate the Right Inferior Frontal Area. *Brain* 131 (12): 3169–3177.

Sommer, M. A., and R. H. Wurtz. 2008. Brain Circuits for the Internal Monitoring of Movements. *Annual Review of Neuroscience* 31: 317–338.

Stein, L. A. 1994. Imagination and Situated Cognition. *Journal of Experimental and Theoretical Artificial Intelligence* 6 (4): 393–407.

Stepper, S., and F. Strack. 1993. Proprioceptive Determinants of Emotional and Nonemotional Feelings. *Journal of Personality and Social Psychology* 64: 211–220.

Sternberg, R. J. 2006. The Nature of Creativity. *Creativity Research Journal* 18 (1): 87–98.

Strawson, P. F. 1964. *Individuals*. London: Routledge.

Sutherland, I. E. 1968. A Head-Mounted Three-Dimensional Display. In *Proceedings of American Federation of Information Processing Societies* 68: 757–764.

Taycan, S. E., I. Capraz, S. Candansayar, and H. B. Belen. 2013. Physical and Neuropsychiatric Symptoms Appear on Pilots during Hypobaric Chamber Training. *European International Journal of Science and Technology* 2 (4): 17–25.

Tierney, S., and J. R. E. Fox. 2010. Living with Anorexic Voices: A Thematic Analysis, *Psychology and Psychotherapy* 83 (3): 243–254.

Teunisse, R. J., F. G. Zitman, J. R. M. Cruysberg, W. H. L. Hoefnagels, and A. L. M. Verbeek.1996. Visual Hallucinations in Psychologically Normal People: Charles Bonnet's Syndrome. *Lancet* 347 (9004): 794–797.

Thom, R. 1999. *Designing a Movie for Sound*. http://filmsound.org/articles/designing_for_sound.htm. Accessed May 27, 2014.

Thompson, E., and F. J. Varela. 2001. Radical Embodiment: Neural Dynamics and Consciousness. *Trends in Cognitive Sciences* 5 (10): 418–425.

Tinwell, A. 2009. The Uncanny as Usability Obstacle. In *Proceedings of the "Online Communities and Social Computing" Workshop*, July 19–24, San Diego (CA).

Truax, B. 1984. *Acoustic Communication*. Norwood (NJ): Ablex.

Tsai, J., E. Bowring, S. Marsella, and M. Tambe. 2011. Empirical Evaluation of Computational Emotional Contagion Models. *Intelligent Virtual Agents* 6895: 384–397.

Tuuri, K., M. Mustonen, and A. Pirhonen. 2007. Same Sound— Different Meanings: A Novel Scheme for Modes of Listening. In *Proceedings of Audio Mostly 2007*, September 27–28, Ilmenau, Germany.

Tzourio, N., F. E. Massioui, F. Crivello, M. Joliot, B. Renault, and B. Mazoyer. 1997. Functional Anatomy of Human Auditory Attention Studied with PET. *Neuroimage* 5 (1): 63–77.

Ullsperger, M., and S. Debener (eds.). 2010. *Simultaneous EEG and FMRI*. New York: Oxford University Press.

van Lutterveld, R., K. M. Diederen, S. Koops, M. J. Begemann, and I. E. Sommer, 2013. The Influence of Stimulus Detection on Activation Patterns during Auditory Hallucinations. *Schizophrenia Research* 145 (1–3): 27–32.

Van den Noort, M., M. Bosch, and K. Hugdahl. 2005. Understanding the Unconscious Brain: Can Humans Process Emotional Information in a Non-Linear Way? Paper presented to *The International Conference on Cognitive Systems*, December 14–15, New Delhi, India.

Vinkhuyzen, A. A., S. van der Sluis, D. Posthuma, and D. I. Boomsma. 2009. The Heritability of Aptitude and Exceptional Talent across Different Domains in Adolescents and Young Adults. *Behavior Genetics* 39 (4): 380–392.

Voisin, J., A. Bidet-Caulet, O. Bertrand, and P. Fonlupt. 2006. Listening in Silence Activates Auditory Areas: A Functional Magnetic Resonance Imaging Study. *Journal of Neuroscience* 26 (1): 273–278.

von Uexkull, J. (1909) 1957. A Stroll through the World of Animals and Men. In *Instinctive Behaviour*, edited by C. Schiller. New York: International Universities Press.

Vygotsky, L. S. (1934) 1987. Thinking and Speech. The Collected Works of Lev Vygotsky, vol. 1. New York: Plenum Press.

Walther-Hansen, M. 2014. The Force Dynamic Structure of the Phonographic Container: How Sound Engineers Conceptualise the "Inside" of the Mix. *Journal of Music and Meaning* 12.

Warnock, M. 1976. *Imagination*. Oakland: University of California Press.

Warren, D. H., R. B. Welch, and T. J. McCarthy. 1981. The Role of Visual-Auditory "Compellingness" in the Ventriloquism Effect: Implications for Transitivity among the Spatial Senses. *Perception and Psychophysics* 30 (6): 557–564.

Waterworth, J. A., and E. L. Waterworth. 2014. Distributed Embodiment: Real Presence in Virtual Bodies. In *The Oxford Handbook of Virtuality*, edited by M. Grimshaw, 589–601. New York: Oxford University Press.

Weerasundera, R. 2013. Musical Hallucinations: A Case Report. *Sri Lanka Journal of Psychiatry* 4 (1): 18–19.

Weiner, B. 1985. An Attributional Theory of Achievement Motivation and Emotion. *Psychological Review* 92 (4): 548–573.

Wenzel, E. M. 1992. Localization in Virtual Acoustic Displays. *Presence* 1 (1): 80–107.

Wesson, D. W., and D. A. Wilson. 2010. Smelling Sounds: Olfactory-Auditory Sensory Convergence in the Olfactory Tubercle. *Journal of Neuroscience* 30 (8): 3013–3021.

Westfall, M., N. Frishberg, M. Hessling, and B. Roy. 2014. *Does Someone Born with a Hearing Loss "Hear" an Inner Voice? Independent Online.* http://www.independent.co.uk/life-style/food-and-drink/features/does-someone-born-with-a-hearing-loss-hear-an-inner-voice-9012669.html. Accessed July 9 2014.

Whitehead, A. N. 1967. *Science and the Modern World*. New York: Free Press.

Whitehead, A. N. 1978. *Process and Reality*. New York: Free Press.

Wightman, F. L., and D. J. Kistler. 1997. Monaural Sound Localization Revisited. *Journal of the Acoustical Society of America* 101 (2): 1050–1063.

Williams, D. M., D. M. Bowler, and C. Jarrold. 2012. Inner Speech Is Used to Mediate Short-Term Memory, but Not Planning, among Intellectually High-Functioning Adults with Autism Spectrum Disorder. *Development and Psychopathology* 24 (1): 225–239.

Wilson, M. 2002. Six Views of Embodied Cognition. *Psychonomic Bulletin and Review* 9 (4): 625–636.

Winnicott, D. (1964) 1992. *The Child, the Family and the Outside World*. Cambridge (MA): Da Capo Press.

World Health Organization. 2010. *International Classification of Diseases*, vol. 10. http://www.who.int/classifications/icd/en/index.html. Accessed June 18, 2014.

Wrightson, K. 2000. An Introduction to Acoustic Ecology. *Soundscape: The Journal of Acoustic Ecology* 1 (1): 10–13.

Wu, J., X. Mai, C. C. Chan, Y. Zheng, and Y. Luo. 2006. Event-Related Potentials during Mental Imagery of Animal Sounds. *Psychophysiology* 43 (6): 592–597.

Zampini, M., and C. Spence. 2004. The Role of Auditory Cues in Modulating the Perceived Crispness and Staleness of Potato Chips. *Journal of Sensory Studies* 19: 347–363.

Zatorre, R. J. 2007. There's More to Auditory Cortex than Meets the Ear. *Hearing Research* 229: 24–30.

Zatorre, R. J., and A. R. Halpern. 2005. Mental Concerts: Musical Imagery and Auditory Cortex. *Neuron* 47 (1): 9–12.s

Zatorre, R. J., A. R. Halpern, D. W. Perry, E. Meyer, and A. C. Evans. 1996. Hearing in the Mind's Ear: A PET Investigation of Musical Imagery and Perception. *Journal of Cognitive Neuroscience* 8 (1): 29–46.

Zhang, J. 2013. Auditory Cortex Stimulation to Suppress Tinnitus: Mechanisms and Strategies. *Hearing Research* 295: 38–57.

INDEX